WICHITA BLUES

Kansas African American Museum, photo by author.

WICHITA BLUES

Music in the African American Community

Patrick Joseph O'Connor

Foreword by Dr. David H. Evans

University Press of Mississippi / Jackson

American Made Music Series

ADVISORY BOARD

The University Press of Mississippi is the scholarly publishing agency of the Mississippi Institutions of Higher Learning: Alcorn State University, Delta State University, Jackson State University, Mississippi State University, Mississippi University for Women, Mississippi Valley State University, University of Mississippi, and University of Southern Mississippi.

www.upress.state.ms.us

The University Press of Mississippi is a member of the Association of University Presses.

Library of Congress Cataloging-in-Publication Data

Names: O'Connor, Patrick Joseph, 1948– author. |
Evans, David, 1944– writer of foreword.
Title: Wichita blues : music in the African American community /
Patrick Joseph O'Connor, Dr. David H. Evans.
Other titles: American made music series.
Description: Jackson : University Press of Mississippi, 2024. | Series:
American made music series | Includes bibliographical references and index.
Identifiers: LCCN 2024013156(print) | LCCN 2024013157 (ebook) | ISBN
9781496853011 (hardback) | ISBN 9781496853004 (trade paperback) | ISBN
9781496852991 (epub) | ISBN 9781496852984 (epub) | ISBN 9781496852977
(pdf) | ISBN 9781496852960 (pdf)
Subjects: LCSH: Blues (Music)—Kansas—Wichita—History and criticism. |
Blues musicians—Kansas—Wichita—Interviews. | African American
musicians—Kansas—Wichita—Interviews.
Classification: LCC ML3521 .O35 2024 (print) | LCC ML3521 (ebook) | DDC
781.64309781/86—dc23/eng/20240509
LC record available at https://lccn.loc.gov/2024013156
LC ebook record available at https://lccn.loc.gov/2024013157

British Library Cataloging-in-Publication Data available

CONTENTS

ACKNOWLEDGMENTS

Dodging gunfire on stage in blues clubs, trading a pig for a Model A, cutting up three candy bars as a meal for six on the road, being surprised by a stripper joining your show, going blind one evening and making your way on foot to the gig later that night, three sisters rescuing a disused Black church and turning it into an African American museum, a teenager working as a musician in a Black carnival that went from Florida to Alaska, taking Tina Turner's place one night when she was too ill to perform, playing in a 1940s tin can band with cymbals made out of chitlin buckets—carried by the power of the blues. These are some of the stories contained in the interviews in this book.

The majority of these interviews and portraits were part of a 1996–97 study conducted at the Kansas African American Museum in Wichita, which was funded in part by the Wichita Community Foundation and the Kansas Humanities Council, an affiliate of the National Endowment for the Humanities. The findings, conclusions, and analysis do not necessarily represent the views of the WCF, the KHC, or the NEH. I give grateful acknowledgment to photographer Arthur Kenyon, the Kansas African American Museum, Executive Director Denise Sherman, Dr. David H. Evans, Wichita's African American community, as well as the blues musicians I interviewed and played with for participation and support in the completion of this book. Earlier excerpts of this work were printed in *Mid-America Folklore*, Spring 1993 (selections from "The Black Experience and the Blues in 1950s Wichita"), *Studies in Popular Culture*, April 1994 ("Cowboy Blues: Early Black Music in the West"), *Wichita Blues: Discovery*, Rowfant Press, 1998 (additional Berry Harris and Harmonica Chuck interviews), and *Overland Review* 32, nos. 1–2, 2005 ("Minstrel and Medicine Shows—Creating a Market for the Blues").

FOREWORD

Over the past few decades there have been a number of published studies that survey the blues artists and blues activity of a region or city. The Mississippi Delta, the Carolina Piedmont, Chicago, Houston, Memphis, New Orleans, and Los Angeles come immediately to mind. These places are familiar blues strongholds that have produced many well-known and influential artists and have had a rich history of recorded documentation and research over a long period. Artists who were born and raised in these locations, or who migrated to them, had an advantage, both in being able to participate in a well-established blues scene and in having opportunities to become more widely known through commercial recordings or through discovery by promoters and researchers.

Blues artists who found themselves in other places were not so fortunate and often had to struggle mightily to make themselves widely known or even to sustain a career. At the extreme end, one might cite the great Mississippi Delta artist Son House, once the mentor of both Robert Johnson and Muddy Waters and himself the "king" of blues in the northern part of the Delta in the late 1930s and early 1940s, who in 1943 took a wartime job in the North working for a railroad company, and wound up in the blues desert (relatively speaking) of Rochester, New York, where he eventually gave up music until his fortuitous rediscovery by researchers some twenty years later. There must have been many other fine artists who suffered similar fates, some who never even had the chance that Son House had to leave a trail of early recordings that prompted his rediscovery and renewed career.

This pattern of historical neglect and limited opportunities for wider recognition is particularly apparent in the Midwest heartland, despite the presence there of African American communities of some size and standing. Kansas City's jazz history has been researched, and there's been a fair amount of research on the blues scene of St. Louis, especially in the pre–World War II era. But what of the blues in places like Oklahoma City, Tulsa, Wichita, Topeka, and Omaha—places that weren't "down south" but also weren't all the way "up north"? Who were the artists who supplied blues music for the Black audiences of these cities, without the benefit of any well-developed commercial recording scene to promote their music or leave behind a body of recorded evidence?

Patrick O'Connor answers this question, at least for the city of Wichita, in the present study. Based on personal interviews with blues artists in the 1990s, he paints a picture of a vibrant Black music scene in the city, of which blues was a significant part. It wasn't a large scene like Chicago or Memphis, but it was big enough to sustain some part-time and even full-time careers. Some artists could specialize in blues, others performed a variety of styles and genres for diverse audiences, while yet others expressed their blues feeling through jazz, gospel, or pop music. This must have been the case in other cities with a Black community of comparable size, and in fact it was actually the case in the better-known blues centers like Chicago and Memphis where we tend to focus only on those artists who were full-time blues specialists.

♪ ♪ ♪

O'Connor lets the Wichita artists tell their own stories. While he groups them into time periods in which they were most active, he doesn't try to force their music into a rigid classification system or "Wichita style." In fact, the artists themselves discuss these issues and mostly conclude that the city's blues are characterized by variety. This, in fact, is exactly what we should expect in a city, as well as its Black community, that has different social and economic strata, people born there and others newly arrived from different parts of the rural and urban South, and of different ages, genders, educational levels, social outlooks, and worldly experiences. It's not a "major" blues scene, but the term "minor" would not do it justice either, and it's big enough for the author to subject the material from his interviews to some solid statistical analysis. There are some patterns that emerge, such as migration to Wichita from further south, especially Oklahoma, but the artists who arrived came variously from urban, rural, and small-town backgrounds, and their music and performance experiences reflect this variety. It is to be hoped that the blues scenes of other cities in the region will be researched just as thoroughly.

DAVID EVANS
The University of Memphis

INTRODUCTION

"Wichita Blues" is the title of a song amateurly recorded of Jay McShann and His Orchestra, with Charlie Parker on alto saxophone, December 2, 1940, at KFBI radio station while the band was in town to play the Trocadero Ballroom.[1] This was the first time Parker was recorded with a group. McShann regularly played Wichita, and Parker also performed in Wichita and small towns in Kansas, according to the following interviews. Seemingly small and isolated, the city actually saw talented territory bands due to being on mainline railroads as well as good highways.

Wichita Blues: Music in the African American Community came about through a desire to look closely at the blues played in the state from the 1930s on. In Wichita, Kansas's largest city, African American numbers increased from 3.5 percent to 11 percent of the population during the twentieth century. Blues held a place in their community and gradually allowed African Americans to play outside the lines drawn by segregation.

The majority of this work has to do migration—inevitably a part of the blues. African Americans came to Kansas in the earliest days of their freedom. Living on Kansas soil was a way to preserve this freedom and take part in the open society of homesteaders and developing towns and cities. A brief history of this early migration will be discussed in chapter one, while chapter two looks at Kansas's largest cities, Topeka and Wichita, and their early treatment of African Americans. During the twentieth century, more African Americans came to the established urban centers, drawn by chance of employment. In both examples, they brought their music with them.

In chapters three through eight, nineteen area African American musicians—the majority of them in their sixties and seventies at the time of interview—give their thoughts and feelings, showing the evolution of the blues from the 1930s to the 1960s and beyond. Some of the items discussed were the use and meaning of poetics of the blues; discovering agents of transferral to younger musicians, white or Black; and identifying regional blues styles and influences traced in their music, acknowledged by them, or put forth by the author.

The primary concern of the interviews is whether Wichita possessed its own style of blues, or if the city simply borrowed styles from the strong regional centers that ringed it: Texas and Chicago. What comes forth is the simple power of the narratives of these performers. This work contains the history of the common folk, those from an oral tradition of music as well as trained musicians who can read notes. As such, the performances fostered one another, forming a blues culture based on the influences to be found in one locale—including recorded music.

In a small setting, what one person does carries more meaning than in the large urban centers. Nineteenth-century Americans came to the Plains to make a difference in their lives in the economic opportunity that the land provided. This opportunity, as well as personal freedom, brought many African Americans to Kansas. When they arrived, most often they found themselves corralled in one part of a town or city. The stories of the place they made for themselves and the music they created are as stirring as those of others who came in wagon trains (and some Blacks did).

Blues musicians who left their native states—primarily Oklahoma, which had a more defined blues culture and style—and came to Kansas brought their stylistic imaginings. Complicating the matter of distinct regional styles, of course, was the emergence of radio and recorded music. But a local tradition could still be built upon area musicians' interpretations of national hits. Muskogee, Guthrie, Oklahoma City, and Tulsa are cited as centers of that state's band vocalists and piano players.[2] Muskogee's blues tradition found a new home in Wichita in the 1950s.

The blues followed the Oklahomans north, both the country blues to remind them of home and the city variety then popular on records. The playing of blues itself can be considered retrogressive, no matter the style, due to the restrictive form of first verse, repeat, third verse. Country blues is often less formalistic than the twelve-bar city blues. To the musician or vocalist, there is a distinct difference between the styles. Many of the African Americans interviewed shunned the "old style" blues, saying it was the type played by their mothers or others in the previous generation.

The blues is a message: the desire for comfort, dignity, understanding—all the things that should be available. The Black men and women had to search for it, however, musically and geographically. Their journey is still being made. The blues is also a natural vent for homesickness. Migrating people carried the music with them and used it to stay the hours of sadness by showing the strength of their new positions. Things would get better; the sun was going to shine in their back door someday, and it was a Kansas sun.

In the southern states there is a tradition of music that is communally encouraged, as shown in the recollections of many of the participants. In Oklahoma, halls were found for rehearsal, instruments were bought by aunts or other relatives, and competitions were held to determine the best entertainer. This is approbation of the highest caliber and directs the energies of youth into creation of good blues. Some of this support also was found in Kansas.

Industry, particularly the aircraft plants in Wichita, had the money, the lure. If just one sister or brother made the trek north, found a job and a place to live, this was a strong call to other siblings. When several family members had settled in Kansas, even though a musician might have found work in California or Chicago, he or she would be tempted to return to be with the majority of his or her family.

Research results are presented in chapter nine, using narrative analysis of scenes in interviews. This applies a systematic sounding of the blues process that may be utilized in regions not associated with major styles. It is a process shown in the following pages and one currently taking place across the United States.

WICHITA BLUES

Chapter One

EARLY AFRICAN AMERICANS IN KANSAS

Cowboys, Soldiers, Settlers, and Minstrels

From its days as a territory, Kansas and African Americans have been inextricably linked. 1854 was a big year for Kansas. The Kansas-Nebraska Act let the territories of Kansas and Nebraska determine whether to allow slavery. This nullified the Missouri Compromise and led to proslavery and abolitionists streaming into Kansas. The stage was set for Bleeding Kansas, with armed factions roaming the countryside, voting with their firearms.

There were degrees of freedom in the offing. The several "Black laws" enacted throughout the West restricted African Americans' actual presence in a territory or state or at the very least the right to vote, hold office, serve on a militia, or marry a Caucasian. At the Free Staters' Topeka convention in 1855, slavery was banned in the territory, but African Americans were barred from voting, holding office, and serving in the militia. This last right was exclusive to "white men and Indian males who would give up their tribal membership."[1]

Many in the territory opposed slavery because they were averse to the presence of African Americans, free or slave. It was thought that the newly freed slaves would take away jobs, working for a fraction of the normal daily wage. The fear of substantial numbers of runaway slaves and free African Americans coming into a locale and competing for arable land was also in evidence.

When Kansas secured statehood in 1861, African Americans were still not allowed to vote and were sent to segregated schools.[2] By the standards of many mid-nineteenth century Kansans, it might be assumed that a step from slavery to second-class citizenship was considered a moderate course. The very fact that Republicans who favored equal rights for African Americans were called Radical Republicans is an indication of the general populace's ideas. Following 1861, Black influence was felt in several arenas of society in Kansas.

COWBOYS (1860s–1990s)

When I was a cowboy,
Out on the western plains,
I made a half a million,
Pullin' on the bridle reins.[3]

This song by folk and blues artist Lead Belly (Huddie Ledbetter) offers a compelling treatment of African American trail riders. Many African Americans took their part in life on the range, from buffalo soldiers, to scouts, to barbers.[4] They were cowboys as well. In the West, "about one cowboy in every six or seven was Mexican; a similar proportion was Black."[5] Other researchers have found that "The typical trail crew of eight usually included two Black cowboys."[6] Durham and Jones found that Mexican cowboys faced more discrimination than Blacks. This could possibly be leftover feeling from the Mexican American War (1846–48) or it could be the beginning of acceptance into American society.

More than five thousand Black cowboys rode north out of Texas during the three decades following the Civil War.[7] In 1868, Abilene was the stopping place for the Texas herds, the first cowtown in the state. The cowboys' revelry caused the city to build a stone jail in 1870. When a Texas outfit, camped on Mud Creek, had a Black cook who hit town and began shooting up the street, the marshal put him in jail, not counting on a trail crew's high estimation of a good cook. The crew came into Abilene and freed him. This would have been a little more difficult the following year, as the marshal then was Wild Bill Hickok.

When the railroad came to Dodge City, southwest of Abilene, the herds on the Western Trail stopped there. There were often problems. When the herd of George Henry Gilland bound for Dodge encountered a Plains thunderstorm, there was a stampede. Gilland and a Black trailhand, Hamm Harris, followed the trail to a corral and a farmer demanding $50 to free the cattle. Calling his bluff in true western style, Hamm Harris opened the gate and Gilland retrieved his stock. It turned out the farmer, who split his time between farming and preaching, had a habit of capturing strays and selling them back in this manner.

The western movies actually had a lot of their facts straight. For instance, a tall Black man named Tex was the first man killed in Dodge City, shot by a stray bullet while standing on the street. This led to the formation of the vigilance committee. As in a Hollywood script,

The committee became a rioting gang of toughs, and their rule ended when a group of them murdered still another Negro. Their victim was a polite, inoffensive, industrious man named Taylor, the servant of the commander of Fort Dodge. . . . The commander took prompt action, and his troopers occupied the town. Dodge City then hired a series of marshals and deputies, including Wyatt Earp and Bat Masterson.[8]

Another colorful if gruesome Dodge City anecdote concerning a cattle-man named Peppard, who reported: "The trail boss had murdered a Negro cook on a drive to Dodge. He took another man, rode down the trail and dug up the body. The Negro had been dead for two weeks and the weather had been warm, so Peppard chopped the head from the body and brought it into Dodge."[9] At the trial, the head serving as evidence of the crime, a fast-thinking frontier lawyer pointed out that since the head had been produced in this court's jurisdiction, other body parts could be produced in another, causing legal confusion. The trail boss was acquitted.

Henry Hilton, an African American ranch owner outside of Dodge City, came into town in the company of some other cowboys. They began to tease him, one trying to rope him off his horse. Hilton pulled out his six-shooter and dispatched the tease. Arrested for murder and out on bail, Hilton got into yet another dispute, this time with another African American, Bill Smith. They were discovered the next morning, each killed by the other.[10]

Many Blacks were quite adept at handling horses and made a living at it, catching mustangs or being in charge of the remuda on cattle drives. One such was Jim Owsley, a horse trader whose stock were Texas mustangs. Leaving Corning, Iowa, by rail for Caldwell, Kansas, he followed the Chisholm Trail south, where he captured the mustangs and drove them back up to Caldwell where they could be shipped back to Iowa.

Nat Love was one of the most well-known of the African American cowboys. His story begins in Tennessee. Though born into slavery, Love was literate, helped by his father, a foreman on the plantation. This was fortunate, because Love wrote his life story, published in 1907. As a teen, Love "worked his way across Missouri . . . arriving in a typical frontier city."[11] He found work with a cattle outfit going back down to Texas who already had several African American riders among them. There he made his home for a few years, taking a herd up to Dodge City each spring.

He recalled Dodge as a wild place where he and his companions indulged in whiskey, gambling, and women for two or three days at a time. Then it was back on the trail south. On one such drive, horses this time, he had a real Indian fight, losing a horse to a skillful shot, as well as his partner, James Holley.

Another adventure: Love was riding by Fort Dodge, a few miles east of Dodge City, and, influenced by a substantial ration of spirits, tried to lasso a cannon. When he was arrested by troopers, he explained he wanted to take it back to Texas to fight Indians. At this, he was released.[12]

Of course, it should be remembered that these stories, coming from his autobiography, *The Life and Adventures of Nat Love Better Known in the Cattle Country as "Deadwood Dick" by Himself; a True History of Slavery Days, Life on the Great Cattle Ranges and on the Plains of the "Wild and Woolly" West, Based on Facts, and Personal Experiences of the Author*, was competing with other cowboy story books, and ought to be taken as thrilling but loose in factual representation.

In 1879, Charles Siringo, traveling in Indian Territory [Oklahoma], came across large groups of Exodusters [see below] on their way to Kansas. He was rather finely outfitted with a buffalo robe and a "silver-mounted Winchester," and this drew the attention of the African Americans. The Exodusters were walking; some had pack animals.[13]

African Americans were in frontier Wichita, including one who sang "plantation melodies" before an auction to be held, and others who performed on guitar while singing in saloons. There was also the murder of one Charley Saunders, a Black man who argued with a white Texas cowboy, causing both men to be arrested. This argument must have been spirited, perhaps entailing punches. Anyway, after two days in the Wichita jail, the unnamed cowboy with "the backing of his friends" shot Saunders, left him to die, and rode out of town.[14]

African Americans were just as wild as the other cowboys, as shown in this news item from 1888: "Black Friday, a noted negro cowboy of the Panhandle, was in Wichita on a painting expedition, a few days ago. He announced himself as, 'I'm from Texas—look out for me.' He attempted to kill a white man while on his visit but was spirited away before the officers could capture him."[15]

The African American cowboy's contribution to the genre of cowboy song is illustrated in the work of John Lomax, who collected "Home on the Range" (Kansas state song) and "Git Along Little Dogies" from a Black retired trail cook in 1908.[16] The ballads of the West, sung by Black cowboys, took on the melismatic and "blue" coloration of the field holler and moan, precursors of the blues. According to Alan Lomax, the music of the cowboy was comprised of "brooding songs about death . . . songs of rollicking humor, [and] the sentimental ditties of the professional entertainers [minstrels and others] who toured the western outposts."[17]

Austin and Alta Fife have made major contributions to the study of the music of the West. Their *Ballads of the Great West* contains song lyrics and poetry, interchangeable by their reckoning. The Fifes found this content "typically narrative or sentimental. . . . Sometimes there is a minstrel-like invitation to the listeners to give attention to the narrator's story."[18] David Evans points out that "Come-all-ye"–type introductions are characteristic of British and Irish ballads.[19]

Although the cowboy era lasted only thirty years (post–Civil War through the 1890s), the Fifes put the emergence of the myth of the cowboy from 1870 to 1920.[20] The innovation of the blues falls within this time frame.[21] Cowboy songs nearly always made use of existing melodies, many of which the Fifes were unable to discover. They began singing ballads about themselves, as well as events and features of life on the trail. "The Old Chisholm Trail," also recorded by Lead Belly, runs:

> Come along boys and listen to my tale,
> I'll tell you of my troubles on the old Chisholm Trail.[22]

The Chisholm Trail, of course, was named for Jesse Chisholm, who had his trading post near what became Wichita. The trail ran from Texas to the railheads in central Kansas. Black trail riders had a hand in shaping cowboy music, and this cowboy music later influenced the blues, a coequal process often noted in developing genres.

SOLDIERS (1865–1990)

The Emancipation Proclamation established the acceptance of freed slaves into the army. Before the Proclamation, ex-slaves were at risk: there was an 1850 law that made them returnable to their owners. Lincoln rectified this practice, in the process giving the thousands of African Americans a means to make a living.

The number of African Americans in the Union effort was "over 200,000 . . . principally ex-slaves."[23] Kansas shared distinction with what is now Oklahoma, in that the "first Negroes to fight for the Union . . . were Creek and Seminole Negroes in the Indian Territory and runaway Negroes in a Kansas regiment on the Missouri border."[24] This was prior to national approval. On

January 13, 1863, six companies were established as Union troops, known as the First Regiment, Kansas Colored Volunteers.[25]

On July 28, 1866, Congress increased the cavalry with the addition of the 7th, 8th, 9th, and 10th regiments. Black volunteers who had completed two years of field service in the Civil War filled the 9th and 10th. These were the Buffalo Soldiers, so named by the Indians (the exact reason unclear). The 10th was initially stationed at Fort Leavenworth. However, it appears that the post commander, Brevet Major General William Hoffman, quartered the recruits in subpar conditions, resulting in twenty-three deaths in July 1867 from pneumonia and cholera.[26] Officers were white, though several refused commissions, including George Custer, who was offered a "lieutenant colonel assignment in the 9th Cavalry."[27]

In 1867, the 10th Regiment had just over seven hundred African Americans and twenty-five officers. On August 2 Company F, comprised of two officers and thirty-four men, encountered a war party of three hundred Cheyenne forty miles from Fort Hays, Kansas. One officer was wounded, and one trooper died in the fight, the first casualties taken by African American troops after the Civil War. The Buffalo Soldiers became adept at Indian fighting, stationed at forts throughout the West. The 10th Cavalry was instrumental in Geronimo's surrender in Mexico in 1886.

John Howerton, a trooper in the 10th Cavalry from 1882–87, escaped slavery as a youth by coming to Kansas. Born in 1854 in Brunswick, Missouri, Howerton's father, from a neighboring farm, was sold down the river. When his mother learned of his death in 1864, she made arrangements to hire a wagon for a clandestine trip to Laclede, Missouri. There they were housed by a "white gentleman" for three days until put on the train for St. Joseph, across the Missouri River from Kansas. Taking a ferry across to the free state, Howerton's family was safe.[28]

Another famous Buffalo Soldier with ties to Kansas, Reuben Waller, served an unnamed Confederate general as "body servant." After witnessing General Lee's surrender at Appomattox, and admiring Stonewall Jackson's Cavalry, Waller went to Fort Leavenworth in 1867 and enlisted in the 10th Cavalry. He was present at the rescue of troops surrounded by Cheyenne, led by Roman Nose, on Beecher Island in Arikaree River, Colorado, a year later.[29]

His descendant, the late Honorable Greg Waller, served as a judge for twenty-one years in Sedgwick County District Court [Wichita], at the time one of three African American judges in the state of Kansas. Perhaps Waller's most notable case was Dennis Rader, the notorious "BTK" serial killer.

Even as late as World War I, there was still some worry about Black troops. Zornow reports that there was fear of race riots at Camp Funston [Fort Riley] when African American soldiers arrived for training. The sale of guns near the camp was prohibited for a while but no incidents occurred.[30]

COLONIES (1875–1900)

With the end of Reconstruction, African Americans found their conditions in the South again close to bondage. The Black codes enacted in the late 1870s were designed to establish social control, and in some instances prevented land being sold to African Americans. True freedom to many meant farming their own fields. The only remedy to this was migration. In the United States, the African American population of approximately four million in 1860 rose to close to nine million in 1900.[31] The African American proportion of the total count of Americans fell from one-seventh to one-ninth during those years, thanks to the influx of European immigrants. The competition for livelihoods must have been daunting, and particularly aggravating to the African Americans, who had labored in bondage for the country that now opened her arms to white immigrants. These newcomers had to bear prejudice, but a prevailing attitude that put same race above different gave assurance that the Europeans had more opportunity for advancement.

Kansas Territory in 1860 was the home of 625 free African Americans. Many African Americans found almost unheard-of freedom in the African American colonies that sprang up in Kansas and the Indian Territory. These separatists were in keeping with the sentiment of many in the country, white and Black—though colonization in Africa or South America was also put forth. What had made these African American migrants decide on the unsettled plains of Kansas?

Benjamin "Pap" Singleton, known as the Father of the Kansas Emigration, first tried to buy land in Tennessee but discovered it was sixty dollars an acre. Land was selling in Kansas for one-tenth that for the best sites, with free land still possible through the Homestead Act. As early as 1870, Singleton's agents were visiting Kansas. Anxious to resettle a group of Tennesseans, he wrote to Tennessee's governor for emigration aid, which was not available.[32] Nonetheless, Singleton established the Dunlap Colony in Kansas in 1879. Other colonies included Juniper Town, Quindaro, Rattlebone Hollow, Hodgeman, Little Coney, Wabaunsee, Tennessee Town, Mudtown, Jordan Town, and Mississippi Town.

Nicodemus, founded in 1877, is the most well-known colony in the state and still in existence as a town and national historic site. At the colony's founding, "for the first time in the history of the United States, enough black voters had gathered in a region to effect critically important decisions regarding the settlement of the West."[33] Most all the land was granted to African Americans through the Homestead Act, which meant that it likely had already been passed over by earlier white immigrants. Yet these Black settlers were fleeing something much worse. Kansas was a land of freedom. John Brown had sprung from there. Kansans fought for the right to enter the Union as a free state. Surely the state would welcome African Americans.

The land around Nicodemus was not as welcoming. The high plains of Kansas were dry, devoid of trees except along the few small creeks. A dismayed immigrant on first viewing Nicodemus wrote: "I did not think anyone could live in a place like that. There was nothing to be seen. Not a tree, not a house, not a drop of water. Except a way down to the river."[34] Several stayed only a day or two, returning the way they had come.[35]

Those who stayed learned the art of cooperation—surely a byword in successful colonies. Nicodemus had a central storage facility, and shared labor, supplies, tools, and food.[36] Of course, immigrants were taken advantage of, as from time immemorial. W. R. Hill, a white speculator from Indiana who later founded Hill City, the county seat, launched the initial campaign to lure Blacks to Nicodemus. Those who wanted to live in the city limits paid the town company five dollars. And those who wanted homestead land paid Hill [who incorporated Nicodemus with six African American men in 1877] an unnecessary location fee.[37]

The Nicodemus colonists had their own protection, too. The Kerwin, Kansas, land agent W. C. Don Carlos helped secure Abram Thompson Hall Jr.'s [one of the three resident Black leaders of Nicodemus, the other two being Edward Preston McCabe and John W. Niles] appointment as deputy district clerk of Rooks County for the unorganized area known as Graham County [which contained Nicodemus]. Hall's assistance was critical. Tragedy loomed if the settlers lost their claims through ignorance of the laws.

Tennessee and Kentucky fed the largest percentage of immigrants to Nicodemus. A typical journey: board a packet boat in Kentucky on the Ohio River, thence to a boat on the Mississippi, then one on the Missouri to Wyandotte, Kansas. Once in the state, they went on to Topeka, receiving train fare to Ellis from the Kansas Freedmen's Relief Association, a private relief organization founded in 1879 by Governor John P. St. John. From Ellis it was a forty-mile walk to Nicodemus, taking with them what livestock managed to survive the journey thus far.[38]

W. R. Hill had, as a matter of course, been quite free with his description of the bounty contained on the land around Nicodemus. Hill also had an ulterior motive. "He wanted these new African American settlers to vote for

Hill City, his proposed white community, as the county seat. Often county seats were the only towns that survived."[39] There was anger among the immigrants, probably long stored on the journey where they no doubt had to endure various indignities associated with nineteenth-century prejudice. From Charlotte Hinger's excellent book on the colony:

> When the first group of colonists realized the extent to which Hill's propaganda had misled, they tried to hang him. Hill fled to a friend's dugout. He was later smuggled to Stockton under a load of hay. Sixty disillusioned families in that first colony headed back to Kentucky the next day. Hill collected as much as $30 for locating on 160 acres of land that was being given free by the government [with the proviso of living on it and improving it for five years].[40]

The dugout mentioned above was not unique. With no trees within obtainable distance, dugouts were the initial homes built. "Nicodemus colonists, hollowed out burrows . . . Since this type of construction was dependent on hills and ravines, the settlement was scattered over an area twelve miles long and six miles wide."[41] This was true hardship for people who left the South with its moderate climate and ready foliage. And the scattered nature of the dwellings surely added to the sense of isolation.

A further complication: no horses with which to hunt antelope or buffalo that first winter in Nicodemus. The colony had to rely on donated provisions carted in from Topeka, Leavenworth, and Kansas City. There is a story that Native Americans—Osage, whose reservation was located in Southeast Kansas; or Potawatomi, located in the northeast section of the state—stopped by and gave the colonists a sizable quantity of meat from their annual hunt.

Having to haul water a long distance from nearby creeks, the colonists dug a well by hand fifty-seven feet deep. Nobody said the African Americans were afraid of work. Some of the men also hired themselves out to white settlers as diggers of wells, a dangerous occupation. The women found work in the nearest towns as seamstresses and cooks, helping bring in the cash necessary to support families. Fuel was always a problem—the legendary buffalo chips were not ideal for indoor (sod house) use. Coal was discovered and there was enough to mine for their own use.

Kansas offered the African American colonists hope and limited opportunity. As from the beginning of society, availability of resources determined which settlements would survive. In the state of Kansas, Black–white interaction was characterized largely by understanding and tolerance. This was soon to be tested further.

EXODUSTERS (1879–1880)

In 1879–1880, tens of thousands of African Americans, known as Exodusters, came to Kansas. The colonies established the migratory route from the South, a route that was followed by the Exodusters.[42] Word spread of a Utopian autonomy, and more and more African Americans became interested in the state. In 1870, the state's African American population had risen to over 17,000. This figure jumped to more than 43,000 in 1880. Many Exodusters were of practical bent, organizing Kansas clubs and sending representatives to scout the land. Kansas governor St. John, one of the Exodusters' most steadfast friends, encouraged African Americans who wrote him with questions about climate and opportunity, sending them a Kansas Agricultural Report.[43]

Emigration to African American colonies had been organized and funded to some degree. But the mass of Exodusters strained the young state's ability to handle them and demonstrated for the first time the need for cooperation between minorities and the majority. Kansas became a grand experiment of nineteenth-century cross-cultural management. Information on opportunities for African American emigration was spread by letters from those already in the state, from the observers sent by committees, and through circulars. One circular read in part:

> Attention Colored Men! . . . Your brethren and friends throughout the North have observed . . . the outrages heaped upon you by your Rebel Masters, and are doing all they can to alleviate your miseries. . . . [T]he Colonization Society has been organized by the Government to provide land . . . given in bodies of one hundred and sixty acres gratuitously. . . . [C]ome to Free Kansas.[44]

This notice, which was supposed to pass only between African Americans, was printed in a New Orleans newspaper to show the gentry why they were losing their plantation workers and domestics. It attracted the downtrodden African Americans to Kansas, but the welcome they received was most often not what they expected. "The Kansas business and professional community had serious reservations about the probable success of Black settlers. . . ."[45] White Kansas farmers held similar views. They were barely scratching a living for themselves, and most farm labor was done by the family, leaving little need to hire immigrant African Americans.

In July 1879, Governor St. John wrote in the Jackson Mississippi, newspaper, the *Weekly Clarion*: "We have received and cared for between four and five thousand. . . . The labor market has been . . . overstocked . . . to send more . . . would be a cruel outrage upon the Black man and will necessarily result in much suffering . . . for the want of food or the opportunity to earn it."[46]

In that same month, the Kansas Freedmen's Relief Association sent ten adults and four children to Wichita. These refugees were promptly sent back by train to Topeka, and a telegram informed the association that any more Exodusters would be given the same treatment. The *Wichita City Eagle* applauded the act, intimating that the people of Topeka were profiting from the immigration (which was certainly not the case).

The immigrants failed for the most part, however, through lack of capital and the unexpected severe climate in western Kansas. Yet Kansas became a comparatively good home for those people who did not give up and return to the South. Many African Americans obtained work in towns like Dodge City and Emporia. Many more remained in Topeka, the city that hosted the majority of Exodusters. Topeka was "a mecca for well-educated freeborn blacks and the center of the state's African American cultural and political activity. It was an abolitionist center before the Civil War and a major station on the Underground Railroad."[47]

Yet, "The May 1879, *Colored Citizen* advised southern Blacks never to leave home for Kansas without having money and definite plans for what to do after arriving."[48] This newspaper, which first was published in Fort Scott, Kansas, before moving to the capital, was a great booster of Nicodemus and other colonies. The editor, William Eagleson, saw the writing on the wall, but it was too late. Word was out, and African Americans had a destination. Such a number of indigent people pouring into the state would soon sour the white populace on Black immigration.

The newspapers held the same sentiment about the Exodusters, of course. The *Topeka Commonwealth* printed: "They are not needed here. There is nothing before them but hardship, privation, and beggary." But who were the readers? African Americans in the South certainly weren't. The newspaper could only be exhorting white Kansans against charitable giving. The African American citizens of Topeka shipped circulars to the South with the cold hard facts of life in Kansas—but how many were dissuaded? Hope is a thing that lives on its own without facts or practicality.

The June 19, 1879, *Topeka Capital* (still in existence) in "The Colored People," gave a brief history of Black suffering and then asked for contributions, also pointing out that Ohio, Illinois, Pennsylvania, Michigan, and Indiana were better destinations for the Exodusters.[49]

MINSTRELS (1865–1925)

The minstrel shows of the late nineteenth and early twentieth centuries brought some of the best African American musicians to Kansas. Begun in the 1840s, minstrel shows were "the first indication of the powerful influence African American culture would have on the performing arts in America."[50] White "Negro delineators," the majority of them Northerners, portrayed slaves in song and story for enthralled audiences.

What was the appeal of minstrelsy? "[P]roducing captivating, unique entertainment, blackface performers quickly established the minstrel show as a national institution. . . ."[51] Why the disguise? "With white faces the whole affair would be intolerable breaches of decorum. . . ."[52] This at least in part explains the appeal: the audience's willingness to partake in the high jinks and musical revelry of supposed African Americans on stage, which in proper white society would not be acceptable. The well-tried use of a jester had been tied to lively and sentimental music. The minstrel show was a potent release for the audience, prefiguring the use and appeal of blues today, as an emotive vehicle that transcends race.

While African Americans, for the most part, didn't get to tour until after the Civil War, when African American companies were formed, "there were hundreds of good instrumentalists, singers, dancers, and comedians who contributed to the development of this first Negro entertainment industry. . . ."[53]

Alan Lomax views the minstrel songs as "America's first popular music."[54] By the 1880s, the traditional white minstrel show had become more of a variety bill, increasing in size and incorporating acts that had no plantation orientation. For African Americans, "minstrelsy was [their] only chance to make a regular living as entertainers."[55] And there were some benefits. "[P]articipation [in minstrel shows] at least gave Blacks a chance to modify . . . caricatures."[56]

For the citizens of Kansas, the early years of statehood had an open appreciation for the stagecraft of African Americans in opera houses across the state. The fare at Emporia's Whitley Opera House is an example. The 1890 census numbered the white citizens of Emporia at 6,882, and African Americans at 667. The Whitley was located on Sixth Avenue and Merchant Street in a city that was serviced by several railways, enabling people from surrounding towns to see the shows. The Opera House was sixty-five feet wide, ninety feet long, and sixty feet high. It could accommodate a thousand, and when it opened in 1881, the Whitley was the largest house in the state. Below, a table lists the minstrel shows that played the Whitley.[57]

TROUPE	DATE PLAYED
Duprez and Benedict Minstrels	3/11/1882
Rice and Hooley Minstrel Troupe	10/12/1882
Hi Henry's Minstrels	12/4/1882
The New Orleans Minstrels (B)	12/16/1882
Haverly's Minstrels	5/16/1883; 11/3/1883
Barlow and Wilson's Minstrels	7/23/1883
Heywood Mastodon Minstrels	10/2/1883; 9/29/1885
I. W. Baird's Minstrels	2/15/1884; 2/13/1885; 4/7/1886; 4/28/1888
Calender Colored Minstrels (B)	8/8/1884
Georgia Minstrels (B)	9/13/1884
J. H. Webb's U.S. Operatic Minstrels	4/15/1885
Kersand's Colored Minstrels (B)	8/5/1885
Barlow, Wilson, and Rankin's Minstrels	6/4/1886
Smith's Paragon Minstrels	7/1–3, 5–6/1886
McIntyre and Heath's Minstrels	9/7/1886; 10/4/1887
Hicks and Sawyer's Minstrels (B)	4/1/1887; 10/2/1891
J. H. Halladay Colored Georgia Minstrels (B)	10/24/1887; 9/6/1888
Goodyear, Cook, and Dillon's Minstrels	8/9/1889
McCabe and Young's Operatic Minstrels (B)	4/29/1890; 9/26/1890
Beach & Bower (B)	2/5/1891; 1/14/1893; 2/8/1896; 12/26/1896; 1/18/1898; 2/1/1899; ?/6/1900
McCanlass' [McKanlass?] Colored Specials (B)	2/19/1891
Duncan Clark's Lady Minstrels	3/31/1891; 12/12/1899
Kusel and White's Refined Minstrels	2/4/1892
Al. G. Field Refined Negro Minstrels (B)	4/6/1892; 1/30/1896; 12/1/1897
Barlow Brothers Minstrels	2/18/1893; 3/7/1899
local minstrels	12/19/1895; 5/7–8/1900
Local All Star Minstrels	1/13, 16/1897; 2/4–5/1898
Pyramid Lady Minstrels	3/2–3/1898
Oliver Scott's Refined Negro Minstrels (B)	9/15/1898
Mahara's Colored Minstrels (B)	8/29/1899; 3/10/1903; 10/1/1904; 2/18/1907
Richards & Pringle's Georgia Minstrels (B)	10/26/1899; 1/6/1902; 1/18/1906; 11/4/1910
Black Patti Troubadours (B) [variety]	3/11/1902
local colored minstrels (B)	8/17/1900
George and Hart's Minstrels (B)	2/4/1901

TROUPE	DATE PLAYED
Gus Sun American Minstrels	10/21/1901
Gideon's Minstrels (B)	11/30/1901
Ward and Wade's Minstrels	9/16/1903
Faust Minstrel Company	3/17/1904
Elk Minstrels (local)	2/27/1905; 2/27–28/1906; 11/1–2/1909
Hi Henry's Big City Minstrels	4/21/1905; 11/9/1906
The Shoo-Fly Regiment (B) [play]	10/25/1906
Haverly's Mastodon Minstrels	11/1/1906
William H. West's Jubilee Minstrels	11/24/1906
Primrose Minstrels	10/14/1907
William C. Cushman Co. (minstrel, vaudeville)	9/11/1909
"Minstrel Comedy" (local) (B)	2/2/1910
College Minstrels (local)	4/19/1911
William McCabe's Georgia Minstrels (B)	1/29/1912 Source: James D. Kemmerling, *A History of the Whitley Opera House in Emporia, Kansas: 1881–1913.*

Minstrel Shows at the Whitley Opera House, Emporia, Kansas, 1882–1913

Sampson, Wittke, and Toll confirm the African American acts marked (B) in the legend, some twenty out of forty-eight, nearly 42 percent. However, when the number of performances per troupe is counted, thirty-seven for African Americans and forty-one for whites, the percentage of African American performers rises to 47 percent. This demonstrates a substantial presence of African American troupes at the Whitley.

The September 14, 1898, *Emporia Gazette*, under the editorship of Pulitzer Prize winner William Allen White, contain a six-inch, one-column advertisement for Oliver Scott's "Big Minstrel Carnival, Successor to The Al G. Field Real Negro Minstrel" with "40 Prominent People" including "the original Rastus."[58] Supporting members of this African American company numbered thirty, mainly in the military band and orchestra. A street parade by Scott's Minstrels is also mentioned in the ad. Admission was twenty-five, thirty-five, and fifty cents.

The touring African American shows gradually shed their minstrel trappings and took on a more representative image of African Americans. The Black Patti Troubadours played the Whitley in 1902. Peterson reports that the show "combined elements of the minstrel stage, the musical comedy, and the serious musical concert."[59] Ragtime songs were a prominent part of the presentations. Four years later *The Shoo-Fly Regiment*, with Cole and Johnson, came to the Whitley. This musical comedy "concerned the participation and heroism of Black soldiers in the Spanish-American War."[60] When the comedy played the Crawford Theatre in Wichita in 1908, it "scored a tremendous hit before an audience that filled every seat," according to a *Wichita Eagle* review. The newspaper pronounced the show "the best production ever given by a colored organization in this city."[61]

Notwithstanding the praise, after the show, African American performers were subject to prejudicial treatment. In 1902 the performer Billy McClain was arrested in Kansas City for "having too much jewelry for a colored man" (diamonds worth $7,000). He was eventually released after proving ownership.

The blackface minstrel shows performed by African Americans reinforced and capitalized on this penchant for lively and poignant musicianship. After firmly establishing their musical abilities in minstrel productions, later performers could shape their material, offering the mostly white audiences blues and rags, music that held more truth than prejudice. In the nineteenth century, African Americans were thought of as good entertainers, and this perhaps helped white Kansans accept the African Americans migrating into their state. This reputation for skill in translating emotion through song has stayed with African Americans through modern times. Compared to the majority culture, it might be that, because Africans had a less inhibited approach to the Western music they first encountered, they showed a more natural appreciation for the power of song. In many cases, the themes of their material were closer to what might be called a modern appreciation of life, unfettered by a Victorian code. This modernism fit the thinking of white society in the late nineteenth and early twentieth centuries, guaranteeing the popularity of African American performers in the days of the minstrel shows, and the later styles they developed: ragtime, blues, and jazz.

Wichita minstrel performances are looked at in the next chapter.

Chapter Two

EARLY URBAN CENTERS IN KANSAS

Topeka and Wichita

TOPEKA (1854–)

The New England Emigrant Aid Company was organized in Massachusetts in 1854, determined to make Kansas a free state. The Company founded Topeka on December 5, 1854, as a base for abolitionist operations and a model for other free-state towns. In 1859 Topeka was voted in as the county seat, and later it became the territorial capital. Topeka was sixty miles from Kansas City, a location that helped make it a railroad center. Also in 1859, the Atchison and Topeka Railroad Company—later the Atchison, Topeka, and Santa Fe—was founded. Eventually, the city became "a major center for agricultural trading and railroads . . . controlling the pace of economic growth in the cow towns on the Kansas prairie."[1]

Thomas C. Cox, in his comprehensive study, reports that the territorial census of 1855 revealed only 6 percent of the eligible voters in Kansas came from New England; Missouri contributed the largest increment, 48 percent. Settlers from the Old Northwest constituted only 20 percent. There were 151 free Blacks and 192 slaves.[2]

Republicans advocated a migration of free state farmers from the East to provide a bulwark against slavery. Republicans also believed that free labor would make its superiority self-evident, thereby awakening latent antislavery sentiment in the South and creating internal pressures for its downfall.[3] Such optimism!

The Wyandotte Constitutional Convention's free state platform in 1859 proclaimed: "The best interests of Kansas require a population of free white men, and that in our state organization, we are in favor of stringent laws excluding all Negroes, bond or free, from the territory."[4] Yet, no Black laws appeared in the Topeka Constitution.

Richard Cordley, from Lawrence, summed up the pro-Black feeling in the state, writing in *Pioneer Days*, 1903:

> Negroes are not coming. They are here. They will stay here. They are American born. They have been here for more than 250 years. They are not going to South America. They are not going to other parts of our own land. They are with us to stay. They are to be our neighbors. Whatever we may think about it. Whatever we may do about it.[5]

Senator James Lane from Kansas was a great friend to the African Americans in the state. Coming to the territory in 1855, Lane commanded the Jayhawkers as they fought the Border Ruffians of Missouri. He also was president of the convention that adopted the Topeka Constitution. "Lane began recruiting Negro troops in Kansas as early as 1861. Without authority and against instructions from Washington . . . Lane believed that Negroes might just as well be 'cannon fodder.'"[6] This sounds cynical, but it may have been said to convince those opposed to Blacks in the army. Ex-slaves returned to the North with Union troops. "In January 1865, one Lieutenant Colonel Bassett took four boats down the Arkansas River from Kansas into Arkansas on a military campaign. On his return, the boats had over 600 Black refugees on board."[7]

Cox raises an important point:

> [Kansas had] the highest number of casualties in percentage of state population in the Union. That last full measure and a final vindication of the anti-slavery crusade became enduring emblems of Kansas' devotion to the northern cause; these too were gathered into the folds of myth and reality in Kansas legacy to blacks.[8]

The gender ratio of Black immigrants was around fifty-fifty, the average family was six, one quarter were literate, and 82 percent of the children went to school.[9] In other words, these were mostly families.

The sentiment for fair treatment for Blacks in Kansas was present in both senators James Lane and Samuel Pomeroy, Radical Republicans. Senator Edmund Ross was appointed by the Governor to fill Lane's seat at his death (1866). Ross was the pivotal negative vote in the Johnson impeachment. Ross confessed to a degree of humiliation at the failure of Kansas to eliminate the race qualifications for suffrage on its own initiative.[10] Of course, in 1870 the 15th Amendment to the United States Constitution eliminated that worry.

The church played a crucial part in providing a rewarding existence for African Americans in Topeka. "Shiloh Baptist Church, founded in 1880, ministered to the residents of Tennessee Town, an enclave in the Third Ward . . . also providing channels for social interaction."[11] So postwar African Americans were on the road to guarded acceptance in the state.

Then the Exodusters hit, the majority of them landing in Topeka. Topeka's mayor, Michael Case, was against charging the keep of the Exodusters to the citizens. "Time and money would be better spent sending the migrants back to the South . . . [even though] the Board of County Commissioners were required to relieve and support all poor and indigent persons lawfully settled therein."[12]

The grasshopper plague of 1874 caused the state to marshal economic forces to aid stricken communities. While the plague was a greater economic calamity than the influx of immigrants, no similar actions were taken in 1879. "The Kansas Freedmen's Relief Association bought tracts of land carefully selected in Tennessee Town . . . [which] were divided into house lots and sold at cost to the refugees. On these they erected small frame houses."[13] So, a private concern once again came to the aid of destitute African American immigrants, sparing the government the burden.

Tennessee Town was not the best neighborhood for newly arrived families, typical of early urban planning:

> According to the *Kansas State Ledger*, Benjamin Jordan a black Dram Shop operator was a business associate of Etta Bray, a disreputable Negro woman, whose enterprise included 14 white and colored girls. Their establishments located in Tennessee Town were billed in the Black press as popular resorts for sports. Despite complaints, police raids, and closing, such businesses mushroomed in a matter of months at the same location.[14]

In keeping with minority advocacy, African American newspapers pointed out high fines in police court and long sentences. There was a bright spot: from the 1880s to 1915, one position as justice of the peace rotated among a succession of Black applicants, treating white and Black in a fair manner.[15] However, by 1896 Topeka African American neighborhoods remained little changed from Exoduster days. Tennessee Town was one of the worst. Charles Sheldon, a Congregationalist minister, stepped in to help. "Sheldon believed that poverty was not solely the evidence of sin but was the result of social and economic imbalances created by society. The preacher should preach less and the congregation work more to gain the best results."[16]

Beginning in 1896, Sheldon developed social services in the district, including a kindergarten with 210 children, funded by the Central Congregational Church. The school was absorbed into the public school system in 1908. Sheldon believed "a man who lives in an unpainted squalid gardenless place will naturally get from its surroundings a shiftless disposition."[17] So in 1898, Reverend Sheldon started the Village Improvement Society, with white parishioners in charge. The society influenced residents to have a much better environment. The Reverend felt Tennessee Town should have a say in its own governance, which the Society facilitated.

An 1899 census of Tennessee Town, conducted by Central Church, found that, of 585 residents, 87 percent could read and write and 52 percent owned their own homes. The male head of household usually was a common laborer, although a few practiced a skilled trade. Around 60 percent of adult females were employed as domestics.[18] Another Topeka neighborhood received help. "The Kansas Industrial and Educational Institute beginning in 1895, was a kindergarten, sewing school, and reading room in the southeastern section of Fifth Ward called Mudtown because of the unpaved streets." In 1919, the name was changed to the Kansas Vocational Institute, with most of the funding coming from the state of Kansas. The Vocational Institute taught thrift, enterprise, self-help, and economic development, basic to the philosophy of Booker T. Washington.[19]

In summation, Black Topeka, between 1865 and 1915, showed the collateral influence of race oppression and the promise of American life. Cox praised the Black Topeka press as a benign influence in spreading ideals of racial equality, as well as informing readers of the progress in other locales.[20] The same will be shown to be true in the Wichita African American press below.

Topeka's current (2022) percentage of African American residents is around 10 percent. Wichita's is a little above that, showing that despite the treatment of the Exodusters sent from Topeka, the city finally became a welcoming home for African Americans.

WICHITA (1870–)

The first African American neighborhood in Wichita (founded 1870) occupied Main, Water, and Wichita Streets north of Central. As chronicled in *African Americans of Wichita*, by the 1890s, a community of over twelve hundred African Americans had founded businesses, churches, and newspapers that stretched along North Main and North Water Streets. There was also an ox yoke factory, blacksmith, barbershop, undertaker, barbers, and

Katherine Geeder with Music Students at L'Ouverture School, the L. K. Hughes Photograph Collection, Kenneth Spencer Research Library, University of Kansas Libraries, Lawrence, Kansas.

seamstresses. Among the community were police, firemen, railroad porters, and the clergy.[21]

During the 1890s, the African American community had several weekly newspapers, among them the *Headlight*, *Wichita National Reflector*, *Wichita Tribune*, and the *People's Friend*. The *People's Friend* (May 24 to September 28[?], 1894) was a lively weekly published out of offices at 150 N. Main. W. M. Jeltz, editor and proprietor, put forth a statement of purpose in the first edition: "You never hear any good news of colored people unless you hear of someone raping, stealing or fighting."[22] Along with national news of importance to the community, the *People's Friend* used its editorializing capabilities to encourage subscription, patronize advertisers, and congratulate the African Americans who had broken the color barrier to join Wichita's police and fire departments. In a subsequent issue, Jeltz pointed out that the paper was one of eighteen weeklies in the city and railed against "chair warmers and loafers who said that no Negro had any business publishing a paper for the welfare of the Negro race."

Under the heading "City and County News" that was used for notices of social events and illness, the June 14 edition stated: "A number of colored people from the South are expected this week. Let's make it pleasant for them." It could not be determined whether this meant émigrés or visitors. The same edition exhorted, "Let every man that calls himself a friend to the Republican party, vote the right ticket this fall."[23] Despite the sizable ad content—the front page held 50 percent advertising—the *People's Friend*, like most other African American papers, folded after a short run.

The 1899 Supreme Court decision in *Cumming v. County Board of Education* allowed for separate but "equal" accommodations, stating that they did not infringe upon the civil rights of African Americans. Beginning in 1912, African American children were sent to segregated schools in Wichita until ninth grade. African American elementary schools were Douglass (615 N. Water), Grand (Boston and Mosley), 18th Street (18th and Riverside), and L'Ouverture (1539 Ohio). Dunbar (923 Cleveland) was established in 1927. L'Ouverture also taught all African American seventh and eighth grade children. The percentage of African American students at L'Ouverture as late as 1960 was 99.7 percent.

The following table gives US census figures for the African Americans in Wichita and percent of total population:

YEAR	POPULATION	PERCENTAGE
1880	268	3.5%
1890	1,247	5.2%
1900	1,389	5.6%
1910	2,457	4.7%
1920	3,545	4.9%
1930	5,623	5.0%
Source: US Census 1880–1930		

US census figures for the African Americans in Wichita 1880–1930 and percent of total population.

1920S

In 1924, the majority of African Americans lived in northeast Wichita in an area centered around Wabash from 3rd to 21st Streets, as well as the old downtown area west of Main and north of 3rd. The 1924 *Wichita City Directory* offers the designation "(c)" presumably to denote African American businesses and residents. The designation is not accounted for in the abbreviations legend. The (c) appears on North Main from 503 to 632 ½. The Sedgwick County Jail is listed at 634 N. Main. Included in the African American entries are barbers, shoe shiners, tailors, lunch counters, cleaners, and physicians.

The Knights of Pythias Hall is listed at 615½ N. Main. This structure, as well as the Kansas African American Museum, are the last remaining buildings of the once thriving African American community.

Addresses on North Water are also given the (c) designation, beginning at 414 and continuing intermittently until 935. Douglass School is listed, Calvary Baptist Church (now site of the Kansas African American Museum) is at 601, St. Paul's AME Church appears at 523, and 517 N. Water is listed as "YMCA (c)." The 1924 *City Directory* applied the (c) on North Wabash beginning at 530 and ending at 2630, as well as on the several adjoining streets.

In 1920 African Americans in Wichita engaged in gainful occupation were counted at 1,207 males (ten years and older) and 433 females. One percent of Wichita whites were illiterate, with African Americans at 4.4 percent.[24]

During the 1920s, Black Wichitans read the *Negro Star*, a weekly that carried national and local news. The *Star* subscribed to the Negro Associated Press and had a circulation of 28,000 in 1922. There was continuing news of the Dunlap and Nicodemus settlements, as well as African American communities in other Kansas towns. An example of local social activities is reported in the July 9, 1920, edition: The Excelsior Club of Wichita held a picnic in South Riverside Park on Independence Day; a "young band" performed, most likely brass instruments. African American music researcher and musician Lemuel Sheppard, in his study of Black nineteenth-century Kansas, could find no distinctive African American form of music. The musicians played whatever was popular.[25]

By 1922, Roscoe Robinson had invested in a movie theater on North Main Street, an important aspect of the Black community. And there were voices of protest—the newly formed [1919] Wichita chapter of the NAACP collected signatures on petitions and spoke out against segregating African Americans, who were outnumbered by 6,000 KKK members.[26]

Black-white relations were under strain nationally and locally during this time. There were several articles in the *Star* on lynching and the activities of the KKK in other parts of the country. The July 7, 1925, *Star* had a front-page story decrying a *Wichita Beacon* ad for O. J. Watson Auto that read: "1923 Overland, shines like a n-----'s heel."

The African American neighborhood was growing apace; the 1927–28 *Wichita Colored Directory* counted:

7000 Negroes, 65% own or are buying their own homes and property; 15 churches with 3100 members; one YMCA, one YWCA, NAACP with over 200 members; the strongest and only African American American Legion in the state with 84 members; 24 fraternal

organizations; one orphans home; and three public schools employ-
ing 25 teachers with almost 3000 students.[27]

Sports played a large part in the community. The Negro League's Monrovians were the city's best-known Black baseball team. Part of their fame
came from a show game they played in June 1925 against the team of Wichita
Klan #Six. White Catholics served as umpires, so chosen because the Klan's
enmity to Catholics would supposedly even up any racial favoritism. The
Monrovians won 10–8. Playing at the old Island Park Stadium surrounded by
the Arkansas River,[28] the game was partly a publicity stunt for the Klan. In a
preceding piece, the June 21, 1925, *Wichita Beacon* announced: Strangleholds,
razors, horsewhips, and other violent implements of argument will be barred
and umpires are "instructed to rule any player out of the game who tries to
bat with a cross," a seemingly lighthearted look at the Klan.

By that time, the State of Kansas wanted the Klan out. In January 1925, the
Kansas Supreme Court ruled that the Ku Klux Klan was a sales organization,
not a benevolent society (no surprise there), and it had to get a charter.
Just a few days before the game, the KKK's application for a charter was
turned down.[29]

Wichita had a home for African American orphans—the Phyllis Wheat-
ley Home. The Home was "part of a national movement to provide settlement house services to African Americans. . . . Some were affiliated with
the YWCA."[30] Wichita's home was independently administered and could
accommodate as many as forty-five children.

1930s

Even though the community had Black police, they were unable to arrest
white offenders, and could only detain them until a white officer came to
the scene.[31] If Wichita's African Americans needed a social service, fraternal
or sororal organization, they had to provide it themselves. They could not
eat in majority-culture restaurants or go into nightclubs, and hospitals were
segregated, to mention a few of the indignities. The enterprising members
of the community developed "beauty schools, cleaners, groceries, taxi companies, contractors, [and] an ice plant."[32] Since Blacks were excluded from
most parks and skating rinks, their YMCA had sock hops and skating. There
was one Black-owned skating rink: BFW in the 1800 block of Wabash, open
on Thursday and Fridays. There were good-time houses, residences or small
buildings where people could go after the clubs closed for illegal gatherings

where alcohol was sold. The "blood and gut clubs" were around 15th St. The American Legion was strictly for war vets. In 1938, the new business district around 9th and Cleveland held twelve restaurants, five grocery stores, eight barber shops, seven billiard parlors, and a taxi service.[33]

Willierein Thompson had vivid recollections of growing up in the city. Her family migrated from Oklahoma in 1915. She recalled Wichita's streetcars, and unfair treatment in education. "All the kids from Douglass [School], next to the old Calvary Baptist Church, had to walk to L'Overture to attend home economic and shop classes. And they passed a lot of White schools to get there."[34] Thompson remembered, during the Depression, the trains running on coal, with people gathering the fuel from railroad tracks for home heating. "There weren't a lot of jobs during that time. Kids had to drop out of school to help their parents. . . . Women went to work in kitchens and as maids and the young men worked odd jobs." Her family survived the Depression with a garden and chickens, as well as the bounty of Wichita's fruit and pecan trees.

1940s

Lea Johnson recalls:

> The Dunbar Theatre [1007 Cleveland, built in 1941 for the Black community] only showed old movies. Downtown, there was a Hires Root Beer Barrel set on the corner. Blacks were not allowed to go beyond that barrel. Buck's [Department Store, downtown] sold clothes, but Blacks were not allowed to try the clothes on. Black-owned restaurants: Mr. Rosco's Barbecue. Miss Dunbar's, Steve's Chicken Joint. Ralph Bons was where everyone hung out after the Y [closed], and Miss Juanita's. Blacks preferred not to go to St. Francis [Hospital] because they were treated on the same floor with dead people. Wesley [Hospital] would not give rooms to Blacks; most were served in the hall. Ambulance service was not offered Blacks. Sometimes one of the two black mortuaries, Citizens and Jackson's, would offer service to the hospital. Yellow and Checker cab companies would pick up Blacks.

The recollections of Jackie Lugrand Sr., whose family were pioneer inhabitants, are powerful.[35] "Richard and Sarah Robinson, my great grandparents, came to America from England . . . indentured servants of the Throckmorton family. They were brought first to Harrisburg, Pennsylvania where my grandfather, George Walter Robinson, was born." In 1870, the Throckmortons and

"Merry Christmas Baby": unidentified Wichita woman, the L. K. Hughes Photograph Collection, Kenneth Spencer Research Library, University of Kansas Libraries, Lawrence, Kansas.

servants came to Wichita. The Robinsons were paid wages and given space to live in the rear of the dwelling. "It was almost like slavery . . . The Robinsons stayed in those quarters for 30 years until the Throckmortons saw to it that they had their own homes. You know we always had to have a White man behind us to buy anything." This was in the 1,200 block of N. Main, a little north of Wichita's original Black neighborhood.

Lugrand's father came from Topeka after finishing high school and attending a training school. "My dad always went to work in a dress suit. He changed into his uniform after he got there. It was for self-esteem." Her grandfather was the first African American firefighter in Wichita, rising to the rank of captain. "Everybody called him Cap."

Being one of the oldest Black families in town, Lugrand had a special upbringing. She had her friends chosen for her, and "We had certain ways we could even walk to school. We weren't allowed to go down 9th Street because that was where all the beer parlors were." Good advice for all children. She reports that, in the Black community, physicians had a ranking: "Dr. Farmer was first, then Dr. Bell and then Dr. Jeter." Dentists received similar treatment, as did houses of worship: "Calvary was first, then St Paul and St. Mary's." Of course, this is one person's assessment.

"Teachers were considered upper class. That was about the only decent job Blacks could get." Lugrand moved away from hierarchy, ending her interview with this sentiment: " I learned you have to judge people by their character. Treat everybody with respect to get them to respect you. Everybody has something to offer to society."

1950s

Willierein Thompson did not learn to swim at East High School because Blacks were given last hour in gym when the pool was drained. She was also barred from dining downstairs at Grant or Woolworth. In 1958, "Wichita University students boycotted Woolworth. My sister-in-law was one of those students. They were the ones to stop all that. The old folks were too scared, due to slavery."[36]

Wichita had few gangs then, one being the Vamps. There were car clubs: the Road Lovers and the Flames, who would race and have dances. The *Wichita Beacon* had the reputation as very prejudiced, with disparaging reporting on Blacks, resulting in a boycott of the *Beacon*. Prejudice might be detected in the *Beacon* story of the Monrovians vs. Klan game.

There were stirrings of protest even in the earliest days of African American settlement. Note the early formation of the NAACP chapter. During the 1950s, the women mobilized; the wives of doctors bought several items at upscale stores that wouldn't let them try on clothing. When the statement came, they refused to pay it until they were allowed to try things on. "These same women refused dental appointments on Thursdays, once they learned that white dentists would see black patients only on Thursday."[37]

Chester Lewis Jr. was famous in the city and nation. He "led the Wichita NAACP from '57 to '68. In 1953, he brought the first civil rights suit against the city and achieved the desegregation of both city swimming pools and Wesley Hospital."[38] Mr. Lewis was a national figure in the NAACP, one of the Young Turks in 1962. This was "a national movement within the NAACP that sought to shift the organization's traditional focus of seeking change through court action and legislation to include strategies of non-violent protest and direct action. The movement also advocated

Wichita Bluebirds, unidentified group, the L. K. Hughes Photograph Collection, Kenneth Spencer Research
Library, University of Kansas Libraries, Lawrence, Kansas.

greater NAACP emphasis on the issues of poverty experienced by African
Americans in the urban north."[39] When their goals did not succeed, he
resigned from the NAACP in 1968 and put his support behind the Black
Power movement.

1960s

The 1950s brought big changes to the Black business district and original neighborhood, and the 1960s followed that trend. The new Sedgwick
County Courthouse was built at Elm and Water, and a block-long parking
garage would follow on the other side of Water. The community's first
Black churches, St. Paul A.M.E., Tabernacle Baptist, and Calvary Baptist
moved out, although Calvary Baptist's building was left standing.[40] Yet
things were slowly getting better. In 1965, East High, the high school with
the largest African American student population, enlarged its cheerlead-
ing squad from six to eight, including a Black cheerleader, Anita Guidry.
However, in 1966–67, the school decided to reduce the squad to six again,
all of whom were white. This precipitated a large student fight in the spring
of 1967 at Sandy's Drive-in across from the school.[41] African Americans at
Wichita State University also demanded a Black cheerleader in April 1967.

Black athletes threatened to boycott practice until the university acceded. This was accomplished when Joan Huff was added to the squad.

ENTERTAINMENT

1870–1920s

Lots of minstrel troupes played Wichita. From the 1870s through the 1920s, there was a minstrel show at least two or three times a month. These were national touring productions, as well as amateurs. One of the earliest acts, in April 1872,[42] was the Frontier Serenaders (later Minstrels), a local group that played in the "school house." Wichita was two years old at the time. On May 7, 1873, the Crystal Minstrels performed at Eagle Hall, corner of Wichita and Second St.[43] The hall also served as meeting room for the First Presbyterian Church. The Georgia Minstrels #2 came to Eagle Hall on June 24, 1874.[44] This was a national touring company of some renown. In June 1877, the New Orleans Minstrel Troupe played Eagle Hall, paying the city $10 in taxes.[45]

On January 2, 1878, Healey's Hibernian Minstrels performed in Eagle Hall. This was a departure from the usual show of Ethiopian Delineators. There were two Irish "end men," nineteen vaudeville artists, and "the beautiful scenery of Ireland." A later tour had "Dutch musical sketch artists J. E. Henshaw and May Ten Broeck." Of course, Dutch meant Deutsch or German caricatures. After all, someone had to be made fun of. A review of the performance from the *Atchison Champion* was reprinted in the *Beacon*:

> Corinthian Hall was well filled last night with an audience to see McEvoy's beautiful panorama of Ireland and the wonderful comicalities and sketches by Healey's Hibernian Minstrels. Ed and Alice Murray, in their original Irish musical sketches, were very funny and entertaining, but it was the great and only John Henshaw who made everybody laugh until the tears ran down their cheeks. He is unquestionably one of the finest talented men in his line on the minstrel stage. We have heard nearly all of them, but John E. Hinshaw, stands head and shoulders above all. . . . Billy McCann's clog was another excellent feature that the audience enjoyed.[46]

Not all press notices were glowing, however. From the *Wichita Herald*:

We received a call from Mr. George, our more advanced agent of McEvoy's Hibernians, who informs us that his troop will be here about April 1. He showed us several very complimentary notices from various country exchanges, but . . . We endorsed that troop of bell-ringers last December, on the strength of some such encomiums and those two from some religious journals, and as a number of deluded victims will remember when, we were badly fooled. . . . We dare not do otherwise than state in all kindness and candor, that we fear that McEvoy's Hibernians is a snide concern. We won't get tickets now, but our religion and the reputation of the Herald as a religious journal, is more consequence than half a dozen tickets to their show.[47]

Further examples of touring minstrel shows include Haverly's Minstrels in April 1879, and Sprague's Original Georgia Minstrels in September 1879, both at Eagle Hall. In 1882, Wichita had the newly built Turner Opera House for touring shows. That year, Duprez and Benedict in March and Oakes Musical Minstrels in November played the Turner.

In 1887, the city had a new, larger venue, the Crawford Grand Opera House, leaving the Turner to host more mercantile ventures. In 1885 a large display ad in the *Eagle* for the Crawford Opera House lists three minstrel acts upcoming: Kersand's Colored Minstrels, Barlow, Wilson & Co. Minstrels, and McIntyre & Heath's Minstrels. Also listed is Thomas W. Keene, a well-known actor.[48]

On Valentine's Day 1893, Barlow Brothers Minstrels performed:

Barlow Brothers minstrels are in town and will present their performance this evening at the Crawford Grand. The company in its entirety numbers over thirty people. A number of specialists have been engaged in Europe and are said to present something entirely different from anything ever seen here. . . .

Al G. Fields Minstrels will be at the Crawford Grand February 22. This is one of the best minstrel aggregations on the road. . . .

Barlow Brothers appeared on the street this afternoon with a very creditable parade participated in by about thirty people.[49]

What better way to show your affection than taking your valentine to see old-time entertainment?—which is what the minstrel shows were becoming nationally. Vaudeville was stepping in. Yet, Wichita, a city that was rightfully suspicious of fads, still liked the reliability of minstrel shows. In 1914 the Al G.

Fields Minstrels again played the Crawford. The Harvey Greater Minstrels played the Crawford on February 27, 1919:

> Minstrel fans will be pleased to learn that one of the very best and largest minstrel organizations on the road is to appear at the Crawford Theater. Possibly certain people have forgotten that they are minstrel fans because it has been so long since they saw a really first-class minstrel. . . . The amusement question has by some people always involved the "questionable amusement" question, but that theme is never aroused by the coming of a high class minstrel. Base ball games, a good circus and an up to date minstrel seem to be at least three forms of amusement which are never questioned even by the most scrupulous. . . .[50]

The questionable amusement likely refers to the coarseness of material, rather than racial stereotypes.

So, the local press was on board to extol the qualities of the touring shows with hyperbole of the period. The times had changed of course, and in April 1922 Mamie Smith, first blues singer to record ["Crazy Blues," 1920], appeared at the Crawford. A display ad in the *Star* calls her the Queen of the Blues.[51] Along with her Jazz Hounds, the show offered "Boots Hope, the lying bootlegger, and Hamtree Harrington, comedian." The paper also carried a short article: "Mamie is a reigning favorite in the world of syncopation. . . . She is to this generation what Black Patti was to the last." The newspaper called the production "the cleanest and most wholesome colored attraction now touring."[52] As the *Star* was the official organ of the Baptist Convention, this meant a lot.

The Fisk Jubilee Singers appeared at the Forum, the city's municipal auditorium built in 1911, for Wichita's fiftieth anniversary in 1920.[53] The October 15, 1920, *Negro Star* has a display ad for Harvey's Greater Minstrels, performing at the Crawford Theatre.[54] The troupe featured Harry Fiddler and Noah Robinson and boasted fifty singers, dancers, and comedians. Seven acts of vaudeville were offered. "First and 2nd balcony and Upper Box Seats reserved for Colored." Other shows mentioned in the early years of the decade were: "The Smarter Set" at the Crawford,[55] the Sunflower Minstrel Entertainers at Philharmony Hall on N. Lawrence,[56] and J. M. Busby's Colored Minstrels— "Watch for Street Parade"—at the Crawford.[57]

Blind Boone, the pianist, played the Calvary Baptist Church in May 1926 and caused a stir. A front-page article in the *Negro Star* took the church to task for allowing ragtime, dance, and popular music, included in his repertoire, to be played in the sanctuary. Such practice "worshipped the follies of Satan."[58] The production of *Shuffle Along* played the Crawford in March 1923, with a "New York cast."[59] Drake and Walker's Bombay Girls, with the Cyclonic Jazz Band, played the Crawford in December 1923. It was billed as the "Big Musical Revue of 1923," with thirty people.[60]

In 1923 W. C. Handy, then engaged in his publishing firm in New York, appeared at the Crawford Theatre. "Both balconies for colored persons."[61] Sara Martin, another of the classic blues singers, was also on the program. The blues and vaudeville were replacing minstrel shows. Segregation was still in effect, but at least the performers were playing their music.

There is a front-page story in the *Star* on the Crawford return appearance of the Harvey Greater Minstrels in 1924. "This is 1924. . . . To characterize a young woman as a 'High Yellow' is the essence of courtliness."[62] The 9th Cavalry Band came to Wichita in September 1924 for a show at Central Intermediate School.[63]

In 1928 Wichita had a very large local African American music event:

NEGRO MUSIC FESTIVAL

The beauties of Negro music, when properly developed, are being more and more recognized. Paul Robeson and Lillian Evanti have demonstrated in Wichita what first-class artists the race can produce, but it remained for the expert hand of George L. Johnson, composer and concert tenor, to organize the voices of 200 colored citizens of Wichita into as fine a chorus of amateur singers as is to be heard. Mr. Johnson . . . was brought to Wichita by Arthur Gossett Post of the American Legion, with the cooperation of the Wichita Park Department . . . A number of Negro spirituals were sung. . . . There were also solos, including some by Johnson himself. . . . The Afro-American Quartet and the Community Glee Club also gave selections.[64]

This was undoubtedly well-deserved praise for an event held in Wichita's Municipal Auditorium. The city appreciated her African Americans who lifted their voices in song.

Sheet music could also be had by mail. *The Folk Songs of the American Negro*, the Fisk Jubilee songs for choir, was sold for $.55 a single copy by the National Black Young Peoples Union in Nashville. Films and stage productions were viewed at the African American Melrose Theatre, 632 N. Main. A December 23, 1921, Melrose ad offers the film *By Right of Birth* featuring an "all Star colored cast" (which included Booker T. Washington), as well as vaudeville every night. There were also ads for the Regent, showing *Isabel*, and the Marple Theatre (417 E. Douglas), presenting *The Avenging Angel*.

RECORDS

1920s–1980s

Recorded music was obtained through the mail from the Colored OKeh Record Store, Shaw, Mississippi. Mamie Smith's "Crazy Blues" is listed at one dollar. "Just write a letter . . ."[65] The Kansas City Record Shop, Missouri, ran a display ad in 1921, offering OKeh records. Paramount also offered records by mail. Eventually, Wichitans got their own record stores: the Pastime Music Shop at 611 N. Main, which offered Black Swan and Paramount Records, and Hattie Eslinger's at 632 N. Main, which advertised "Blues & more Blues."

Jenkins Music Company of Kansas City opened a branch store in Wichita in 1922. As well as musical instruments, it offered 78 rpm records. Jenkins sold to African Americans, although it is uncertain if they carried race records. The 1970s were a good time for record sales. Denise Sherman, interviewed by Dr. Robert E. Weems Jr.,[66] reports, "As a small child, I remember lots of record stores around here and appliance shops." Maaskelah Thomas, also interviewed by Dr. Weems, recalls: "My first job out of high school was at J D's Record Shop, which was on 17th Street. It was the place to go to get vinyl. I mean, we'd pump music out into 17th Street, and it was just always happening." Music and More, 2429 E. 13th Street, was in business at least through the 1980s.

This is the history that laid the groundwork for Wichita blues performers, as will be seen in the following chapters.

Chapter Three

THE 1930S

Walton Morgan, Shirley Green, Perry Reed

The decade of the Depression hit Kansas as hard as any other state, with the added burden of the western half being in the Dust Bowl. In Wichita, census figures show the 1930 Black population at 5,623, 5.1 percent of the total. The end of the decade saw 5,686 Blacks, 4.9 percent, thus depicting a fairly static percentage.

In 1930, Black employment in Wichita was found to be 41.9 percent of females fifteen and older, and 81.6 percent of males ten years and above.[1] Figures for the state of Kansas reveal ninety-three African American male musicians and teachers of music, with thirty female.[2]

In the 1930s, Wichita's Black population heard music in church groups, at social organizations, and similar functions. After 1937, there were beer gardens that provided live music along North Main, and on the outskirts of town at 29th and North Santa Fe.

One of the most important groups that played Wichita in the 1930s was the Syncopators. Walton Morgan, Perry Reed, and Shirley Green all played with this young, local group.

WALTON MORGAN (1919–1996)

Saxophone

"I was born in Altoona, Pennsylvania, in 1919. Grandpa was a fellow who liked to move around. He came to [Wichita] Kansas in 1923 and we came with him."

There was some music in his family. "My sister was great on the piano but she didn't go too far with it." As a boy, Morgan wanted to play the bugle. A friend gave him a C-melody saxophone, a beginner's instrument that did not require transposing. This served him for a while.

Walton Morgan, photo by Arthur Kenyon.

"Then Uncle went to Jenkins Music Store and bought instruments—whatever we needed. He played baritone sax, his wife played piano and his daughter clarinet. Every Sunday afternoon we would practice at his house." Morgan played alto saxophone.

"We had a teacher in the 9th Cavalry who came down from Fort Riley."

Soon afterward, Morgan formed the Syncopators. "We had Perry Reed on drums, Elmer Jones was on bass, James Streeter on tenor sax, Wendel Turner on tenor. Henry Powell, tenor player, was with us.

"Russell Emrick's folks gave us the house to practice in. This was in '34 or '35. We started playing for Black dances. We played at the Masonic Hall on Main. On Friday nights the Syncopators had it. Ten cents and twenty-five-cent dances. That's where we had the blow out.

"We had a cleaners, Ed Sexton, who furnished us uniforms. He said, 'You won't have to pay me much.'

"It was a community effort. There wasn't much for us to do. Look at what the kids are doing nowadays. Shootin' and carryin' on. The families worked with us.

"While I was at North High, we played North and East High School dances [Wichita's two high schools at the time]. And we played the Hollow Inn.

"World War II broke up the band. Perry left us and went to the army. I said, don't go, Reed. I graduated in '39 and went to Fort Sill, Oklahoma, and joined the band. I was first chair clarinet."

Over his lengthy career, Morgan associated with local and national musicians.

"Charlie Parker lived with me for two weeks. Jay McShann brought him down here. That didn't last long. Jay McShann had a bass, and Parker; just a trio. Charlie was good. He was nice to live with. I couldn't understand what he was doing. I used to ask him how he got those notes. He said, 'If you learn a number, learn to play it backward and forward.' I never could do that.

"The clubs that let Blacks play were on South Broadway. Gilmar Walters, Harold Cary—I worked with them. Harold, you never could make him mad. Gilmar played piano and trombone. When we had our union, he was vice-president. The old Dunbar Theatre, that's where we had our meetings."

This union was a short-lived attempt to obtain better working conditions for Black Wichita musicians.

"At that time, you couldn't join the union here.[3] You had to get to Kansas City or Tulsa. We formed a union here—701. We were bona fide. James C. Petrillo sent a man down here and gave us a lot of help. Twelve musicians were in the union and then other musicians would come in and join."

The Syncopators also played neighboring Kansas towns.

"We never had an agent. Price Woodard's [Wichita's first Black mayor, elected in 1967] dad told us, 'Anytime you guys play, I will write the contract.' We played the Wichita Club and Lawyer Woodard was there to see that we got our money. He'd stop the band halfway through until we got half our money. It wasn't very much. Back then three and four dollars [a man] was good money."

As the musicianship of the members progressed, the Syncopators experienced personnel changes.

"Most of those guys would leave Wichita. But they had families here. They would go to California and come back. The Syncopators stuck together. Off and on, it was a regular jumbled-up thing because we had to get together and do it."

Morgan comments on the camaraderie he witnessed in the 1930s.

"Alonzo Mills was a drummer. He had a group and did a lot of boxing. He'd help us. If we needed a drummer, he'd come and sit in. And they had a lot of jam sessions. Start at nine and end six o'clock the next morning."

There was little blues in the style of music the Syncopators played.

"We tried to copy Duke. We got all of Duke Ellington's music, and Count Basie's. We learned to read the stocks. Bought the music at Jenkins. We played some blues. McShann had some blues. We'd learn that through listening. Most of it was jazz. We liked Duke, Count, and Fletcher Henderson. We used to catch him on the radio late at night. But Duke was the man.

"Count Basie came here all the time but it was so expensive. We saw him at the Forum. They would let us in at 12:00 and we would get to listen for half an hour, and then the show was over.

"All in all, it kind of wiggled away. But Morgan, I taught school for thirty-one-and-a-half years. I got my teaching certificate at WSU [Wichita State University] on the G.I. Bill of Rights. I taught L'Ouverture first. We only got them from the fourth and fifth grades to teach music. I taught in all the Black schools—Dunbar, Douglass.

"I retired in '86. Since then, I played in church and taught music, private lessons. I have twenty students. Now I play with the Morgan Mid-Towners. There are eight of us, all over fifty-five, playing care homes and churches. All this is volunteer through the United Way. We play a half an hour. We go anywhere in Wichita.

"As it stands now, jazz in Wichita is pretty nil. The high schools are doing a pretty good job with it. I think it can be built up if we can hang in there together. The best time for music here was before World War II.

"The main thing about it is we don't get together enough to keep the music going. We catch it in the churches and that's where it's going to be. I'd like to see more individual instrumentalists. I just wish that all the musicians in Wichita could get together. Mostly they're in trios. We're divided here.

"We can do better. All these kids comin' up—stay in school and stop runnin' up and down the street and form their own groups.

"I think an alto sax [professional] is $3,000. That's where it's going to hurt. Music lessons are $20–30. If you have an old horn, parents should get it fixed up and stay behind the children."

SHIRLEY GREEN (1917–1998)

Saxophone

"I was born in Hutchinson, Kansas, 1917, January One. My dad was a hotel man. We moved over here when I was seven years old, to 910 Ohio."

Why did he move to Wichita?

"To better his condition."

Green attended L'Ouverture. "That was in the old building. We went to eighth grade and then we went over to Central [Intermediate]."

Shirley Green, photo by Arthur Kenyon.

Green had four brothers and sisters, all older. "My sister played piano, and my mother played piano, just for amusement. I started playing in the Wichita East school band, 1933, clarinet and the alto saxophone. We played the football games, all the meets like that. We rehearsed quite a bit."

What did your uniform look like?

"It was blue and white. They were hot."

Did you get tired marching?

"No, I had plenty of energy then. I worked at the Wichita Club after school. I used to wait tables."

Did the school furnish your instrument?

"They gave me a clarinet, and I made enough money, I decided to buy me an alto saxophone from Jenkins Music Store, on installments. I think it was $85. It was a Olson, a used one. It was in good condition, though. I bought some music and took it home, then got some from the school."

How many hours a day did you practice?

"Oh boy, so many, many, many."

Did your brothers and sister encourage you in that?

"Yes, they liked it. My mother liked it also. My brother played violin."

What was more influential on you back in the early days, jazz or blues?

"Blues, gutbucket, man."

When did you first start playing outside school for people?

"I played at this club called the Little River Club, way up north. We had a kitty and I think they paid us something like two dollars a night. We'd get most of our money out of the kitty."

Who was playing with you in those days?

"Homer Osborne, and Junior Johnson, so many different guys. Homer Osborne had a friend out in Denver who had a band, Sticks McVey. He wanted a first alto player. I was eighteen."

McVey just heard you were good?

"Yes, well, Homer pushed me along. He'd vouch for me. I went out there in '35, maybe along there."

You had just graduated from high school and were pretty young to be out there on your own.

"Yeah, but I made it though. I was determined. My mother and dad were proud of me. They wanted me to look forward. I would contact home writing."

Denver was a pretty good-sized city.

"Yes it was and they had some good musicians there, too. William Thalee, Johnny Hartsfield, tenor player. I got right in there with them, though."

You had only been playing two or three years.

"Yeah, I know, but I had it. We played six nights. And we used to broadcast from there. We had a salary. It wasn't too much, twenty-five maybe thirty dollars, then our tips. The main thing I wanted to do was learn how to play. They had nine pieces.

"I stayed there until Floyd Ray come through from Los Angeles. He had a big band, eighteen-piece band. They come out to the club and heard me playing. He said: 'Come on, go with me. I'm going to New York.'"

You got out of your contract with McVey?

"I got out of it. I was lookin' to better myself. I been there a little over a year. Playing three, four hours a night at the Tiddly Terrace Club. Big place; it was the best one in Denver at that time."

Did you ever get any photos back then or newspaper articles written about the band?

"Yeah. I wouldn't know where, but I know we did. In the Denver newspaper. You know, I had a picture of myself when I was with this Floyd Ray

Band, but I had some company over here one night last week, and I was showing them this picture and the gal took the doggone picture. I was nineteen years old, and we had a big band, you know. She had been beggin' me for pictures."

Did you have your own style of playing back then?

"I liked Charlie Parker at that time."

Did the rest of the guys in the band let you get away with Charlie Parker stuff?

"Oh yeah. Well, I mean I was the first lead man, you know, alto lead second. They respected me."

This was all in New York?

"Yes. We played Savoy [Ballroom]⁴ most of the time, and the Apollo Theater. This was '39, '40."

You were at the top of your profession.

"I was. I played at Smalls Paradise. I was in the union, 802. You just about had to get in the union to play around there."

Did you play with Charlie Parker back then?

"Oh yes, yes. I worked for him right here in the beer gardens over there on Main Street. The two to three hundred block was full of beer gardens. They could just sell beer. They got wild at times. We used to play for Don Holladay. That was in the thirties, before I went to Denver."

What did people think about Parker?

"Oh boy, he upset them. Yes, I used to see him in Los Angeles with Mack Sand. And I seen him in New York with Mack Sand. Everywhere he was, he upset everybody."

But you knew what he was doing?

"I knew what he was doing, yes. He had a real fast tongue. But he was a genius, man, absolute genius."

How did you feel when you found out that Charlie Parker had passed away?

"Oh, I felt bad. I mean it hurt me, it struck me. But I knew it was going to happen, because he was doing everything."

What did he think of Wichita when he was here?

"He thought it was a no-good town. There wasn't nothing—at that time the town was dry. Everything was bootleg then. Charlie was here a long time."

Where did he stay?

"Let me see, where did Charlie stay? Oh, down on Main Street, the hotel."

He stayed with Walton Morgan a little bit, didn't he?

"I doubt it, but he could have. Walt knew him."

How is your style different from Walton Morgan?

"Walt is mostly a book man. He reads. I'm just the opposite. I read a lot, too."

Talk about some groups you were in.

"There was so many. Let's see, I was with the Sunset Royal [Serenaders], they were from Florida. Then I was with Cootie Williams and Lucky Millinder. I worked with Eddie Vinson and Cootie Williams. Illinois Jacquet."

Could you describe a typical evening playing at New York's Savoy in the forties?

"We start early, you know eight o'clock, nine o'clock or something like that, but they had three bands. They had three bandstands. Each one had a set time to play. Savoy Ballroom, big huge, huge; all of the musicians would be there."

And then you'd play mostly dance music?

"Yes, yes. We would broadcast. I played with Ella Fitzgerald when she was startin' out. She's seventy-eight, I'm seventy-nine. I stayed in New York fifteen years. I was roomin' in a house."

Did you go to any jams or after hours?

"Yeah, we'd go to plenty of jams. All of us."

What type of music influenced you that you liked to play? You were playing dance music, but what about for your own amusement?

"I like ballads a lot. But I played it all though."

Did you ever have any younger musicians come and want to study with you?

"Yes, yes, Bud Powell. He taught me a few things too because Charlie Parker was his idol. He liked to copy Charlie Parker playing."

Did you play any blues in Denver, before you went to New York?

"Oh yes. A boy named Eddy Moore was singing with us. I think he's from Tulsa."

In New York, did you still play the blues?

"Still played the blues and the jazz. But more jazz at the Savoy."

What about boogie-woogie? Did you ever play that?

"Oh yes, all of that. That was real popular then. Pearl Bailey was in the band too. She'd sing 'St. Louis Blues' all the time. She danced too.

"Then I went on up to Andy Kirk. We worked out of New York. We were mostly doing one-nighters and we stopped in Chicago at the Three Deuces, or something. Oh yeah, he had a good band. All these bands I'm tellin' now, we worked out of New York."

When you were playing in New York, you were making pretty good money, weren't you?

"I suppose to be. I made $50 a day. I thought that was a lot of money. It was then at that time."

When you came back to Wichita, did you retire from playing?

"Yes, I did. I got married."

Where did you meet your wife?

"Here in Wichita. She passed ten years ago."

Did she have a musical background?

"Not really, but she enjoyed music."

Why did you pick Wichita to come back to?

"This is where I call my home. This is where my mother and father and brother and sisters were, where I went to school."

Wasn't it tough to come back?

"Yeah."

What did the people in New York say when you told them you were going to Wichita?

"They think Kansas City. They call Wichita Kansas City. 'Oh, you going to Kansas City?' I wouldn't tell them the difference because Wichita wasn't very well known."

Do you think it was ever well known as a jazz town?

"Not too much, no. It was just one of those stops."

Did you play after you came back?

"I played so many clubs. I went up to Kansas City and got William Fisher, piano player. Just went up there and lingered around and found him. And said, come on let's go. And he came. William, he was a good piano player too."

Where did you play?

"Oh heck, these clubs. Lancers, and the Aces Club, along Kellogg up there. Then we played down there on 9th Street, at the Sportsman. Esquire also. It was a little nicer than the Sportsman."

You came back to Wichita in 1955?

"Yeah, somewhere in there."

Did you have to get a job?

"I got a job down there at the Gas Service Company. That's where my dad worked and my oldest brother."

Is that the first job you had since you were playing music as a teenager?

"Oh, yeah, really."

That must have been a change?

"It was a big change. I was forty years old when I got married. And I started working there. Then I went to work with the Board of Education. I was a custodian, Mueller School."

And you still played two or three nights a week?

"Yes."

That must have been rough.

"It was kind of rough, but I mean, heck, I was young, I could take it."

Could you make a pretty comfortable living playing music?

"I could, if they would let me play. It seems like it was always something happening, I don't know."

You mean clubs change hands?

"Yeah, they'd change hands. It was a little rough then, but I made it, I was happy."

Did you reunite with some of the guys you played with before leaving town, like the Syncopators?

"Well yes. Perry Reed and another one named Howard Martin, he's out in Denver, he played drums too. Perry's quite a drummer, but he can't play anymore, you know. His foot's bad."

You recently injured your hip. You were doing volunteer work and fell off a ladder?

"No, I didn't fall off no ladder. I was on the floor. I have high blood pressure, and I just got dizzy headed. I was coming from lunch out there at the children's home."

What do you usually do there?

"Nothing. Just watch them boys. I'm a foster grandparent."

Did they come over and help you pretty quick?

"Yeah, when I fell, boy, they all swarmed in, put me in the chair. They were good boys, they liked me."

Did you encourage them to do something?

"I encouraged them to act like gentlemen. You know they'd do little ol' silly things, but they were young boys, fifteen, sixteen."

Any of them play music?

"No. It sure would be good for them."

What did they think about you playing jazz?

"They liked that, man. They say, 'Did you ever play with B.B. King?'"

What's the appeal of jazz over blues to you?

"I consider it all the same. Of course, I know blues is twelve bars."

Do you have a church?

"Calvary Baptist. I was baptized in that building when I was twelve years old. I've played in church several times."

Did you keep going to church through your musical career, or pick it up after you moved back to Wichita?

"When I moved back here. Yeah. I enjoy it. You don't smoke do you?"

No.

"That's good."

I used to.

"Just fire one of them questions."

I'm pretty nosey, aren't I?

"No. Well, you're trying to do whatever."

You mentioned your horn needs some work.

"It needs an overhaul. That'll run better than a hundred dollars."

How often do you have to have that done?

"Not too much, about once every two years maybe."

That's because you use it a lot. How many hours a week do you usually play?

"Oh heck, I don't keep track of it. There's a bass player, Luther [McDonald], he plays piano. I go over to his house."

And you play with Harold Cary.

"Oh yes, I enjoy playing with him. All in D-flat. So many horn players that can't play with him in that key."

Is that the horn that you've had all these years?

"Naw. I've had it for a little while, not too long."

What brand did you play in New York?

"Martin."

What happened to the Martin?

"Oh, I got rid of it sometime, sold it, put it in on that one. I've had four or five horns."

Do you have a piano or did you ever work things out on keyboard?

"No, no. That's one thing I wished I had done. No sooner I open my eyes, there was a piano in the house. Because my mother played piano, sister played the piano, but I never fooled with it. All I wanted was a saxophone."

Could you make a distinction between blues and jazz?

"Blues is only twelve bars. But now jazz would be sixteen bars."

The same feeling that makes somebody play the blues would make them play jazz?

"Yeah, that's right. It's all in your heart, the soul."

How many of the players that you used to work with could read?

"All of them could read, everyone but Harold [Cary]."

What was the main style of music in Wichita in the thirties?

"I would be playing like Fats Waller, let's see 'Honeysuckle Rose,' that kind of thing."

What kind of blues?

"We'd play all the blues. Oh shoot, all the blues is alike, only different beat or something."

When you came back in the fifties, what kind of music was Wichita playing?

"Well, we was playing 'Moonglow,' 'Chinatown.'"

Were you just with a piano player? You never really ever got back with the big band?

"No. Well, I did play with Ernie Fields down in Tulsa after I came back. I made a tour with him. We went down South."

How long was the tour, a few months?

"Yes, something like that. That was the good days. The people liked it."

Did you work very much with guitar players?

"I played with Florence Smith with Andy Kirk. He played good guitar. And Ernie Fields had this one, Rene [Hall]. He played good guitar. He could write nice too."

Did you ever do any writing?

"No."

Was there pretty good feeling between musicians back in the thirties and forties? Did you take care of each other?

"Yeah, they respected each other."

Which do you think is more popular today, blues or jazz?

"They run neck and neck, I would think. It just depends on the locale. Of course, country music is big in Wichita. Yeah, country music, boy they got it. Now that's what throwed me out of a job, that Western music."

Could you play it?

"Oh yeah, I've played it."

But they usually don't have a sax with a country band.

"No, you don't have no sax, not with them damn ol' guitars."

Did you ever play with a Hammond B-3 organ?

"I played with Bill Doggett, in New York."

Are you on any recordings?

"Yeah, I did a lot of recording. I did recording with Sunset Royal. 'How 'Bout That Mess' was the name of the thing. Kat Anderson was on it also. And I took the tenor solo."

Have you got those?

"No, I don't have."

Where did they record that?

"At Decca, or Capitol, in New York."

Was that your first time in the studio?

"First time in that studio."

How many times have you been recorded and released on a record?

"Heck."

You haven't kept track of them?

"No, I haven't."

What other groups were you recorded with?

"Well let's see, Cootie Williams. I recorded with Andy Kirk."

What was that like to hear yourself playing on records?

"Sounds all right. I mean, you know where your weak parts were, your stronger parts."

Did you used to buy those records and send them home to your folks?

"Well, yes. I kept a whole bunch of records out there in my garage, and I got rid of them like a fool. I had 78s and 45s also. Had so many records, man, I don't know. Now Eddie Davis, Lockjaw Davis, he and I worked together with Lucky Young."

What is the future of jazz and the future of music?

"It'll be here. It'll get better. But this stinkin' ol' rap, I don't call that music now."

Some rap tunes are starting to use jazz in there.

"Well, they should. It needs all the help it can get."

Is playing music helpful to the people who play it, or does it hurt them?

"I love to play jazz. I love to play jazz and blues. I love it. I love it. It's in me. Yeah. And I like to see people that are playing it to enjoy it."

And if people get up and dance?

"Then I know they're feelin' good."

Do you have any comments about your life?

"I have had a good life. But there's all ups and downs, and you know? I mean that ol' country western, that's what knocked us out of work."

When you came back here, did you join a union?

"No, I didn't have to. At one time here, they wouldn't let you in. All them drawbacks."

But they let you join in New York.

"Oh yes, sure."

Was it a segregated union?

"No, 802. That's the biggest one in the country. In Chicago, it's 208. Them people, they're not like these people here, no. This is your downfall, this segregation shit. But New York isn't like this. Oh, it's another world."

When you came back here, how were you treated?

"They didn't have too much of that old country western shit going on when I first came back. These people just went and fell in love with that crap, man."

PERRY REED (1922–2006)

Drums

"I was born in Wichita April 12, 1922, at a residence, 1615 N. Wabash. Those were very old homes. I've got two sisters and five brothers, one deceased. My father worked at DeCoursey's Cream Company as a stationary engineer. Mother looked after the children. In those years everybody pulled together and looked after each other.

"Everybody knew each other in the neighborhood. You didn't have the worry you do now. Out of my family, I was the only one that took to music. When I was small, I used to listen to quite a bit of march music, John Philip Sousa. The drums kind of fascinated me.

"I was fourteen when I got my first set. I got it at Jenkins Music Store downtown. At that time, a full drum set—bass, snare, two tom toms, a couple of cymbals, and a high-hat—a lacquer set cost $170.00. The payments weren't very high, so my mother and father consented to get me the set of drums."

Reed helped make the payments. "When I was fifteen, I was with some high school kids; some of us went to East High, some went to North High. Walton Morgan got together a few of these guys and we named ourselves the Syncopators. We played for little dances and assemblies at the schools.

"My first professional job was with the Black Barons, leader and owner Doug White, in Hutchinson, Kansas. One winter month, a telegram was sent to my home. They had heard I was playing drums with this high school band. They needed a drummer. My mother consented to let me go over there.

"I stayed with this band four or five months. It was ten pieces. They did a lot of traveling. We played odd jobs in and around Kansas, Oklahoma, Texas, and Kansas City. I was the youngest member in that band. I came up the hard way. Nothing came easy. Doing a lot of one-nighters. This was the late thirties.

"They had their own sound system, nothing like there is today. Some days it worked, some days it didn't. Some clubs you go to, they might have a sound system. Either way, people could hear us and dance to the music we played. The clubs and halls were not enormous. They were normal-sized dance clubs.

"We played a little jazz, and a little blues. We had a vocalist. He sang danceable tunes, blues and jazz. There again, it depends on where you're playing, what town you're playing in, what crowd. The band geared itself

Perry Reed, photo by Arthur Kenyon.

to the crowd. If it's blues they like, we can accommodate them. If it's jazz, same thing.

"With the Syncopators, we were playing a lot of stock music. At that time, Lionel Hampton was going, Benny Goodman's band was going, Artie Shaw's band. We were playing that kind of music because that was available.

"The Syncopators didn't do any kind of contractual work. They would want us to play and say, 'We only have this amount of money in our treasury.' Fine with us. If not, fine with us.

"When I came back from Hutchinson, friends of mine had joined the army in Ft. Riley, Kansas. I happened to see them one weekend when they were home on pass. They told me they had a terrific band, the 9th Cavalry Band. Of course, what really attracted me was the uniforms. I went up there—my mother didn't even know anything about it—on the third or fourth of March in 1941. I was too young to enlist. I had to get my mother's consent to join, and it wasn't until the twentieth of March that she signed. I was up there all that time.

"In a few months, we happened to come home on leave and got as far as Newton. We heard on the radio that Pearl Harbor was bombed, and all servicemen were to return to base."

After basic training, Reed joined the 9th Cavalry Band.

"You just couldn't walk in. I went to the bandleader and told him I wanted to join.

"'What instrument do you play?'

"'Drums.'

"'Well, we need a drummer.'

"At that time, they had what you call try-outs. This band was geared to playing march music, like John Philip Sousa. Like I told you, when I was a kid, I used to listen to 'Stars and Stripes Forever' and all those different marches and I memorized them. So, when he gave this interview, I played it. The music was on the stand, and it was Greek to me. I was looking at it just like I was reading it. That's how I got in the band.

"It wasn't until a year later that I had a very good friend who was a drummer also, and he taught me how to read. The band consisted of twenty-one men, including the warrant officer who was the leader. In our duties, we played for all military functions, ceremonies, and parades.

"We're now called Buffalo Soldiers. The 9th and 10th Cavalry, back in the early settlers days in the West—if you read anything about the history—helped pave the way, settle the hostile Indians. I am a member of the 9th and 10th Cavalry Association, Buffalo Soldiers. They have a reunion once a year."

Reed was sent to the European Theater.

"We were still in the band but when there were no ceremonies for the band to do, we were attached to medical units, hospitals, things like that. When the war was heavy, we never saw our instruments. It was only when they were ready to send the soldiers home, that we played departure ceremonies, military funerals, and burials.

"I was discharged in 1945 and came back to Wichita and stayed here for a year. Jobs were hard to find. I enlisted in the air force, November 1946. After quite a few reenlistments, I retired a master sergeant.

"I joined the Air Force Band in Columbus, Ohio. Then I was stationed at Wright-Patterson Air Force Base. Horace Heidt had a radio program, a talent show. Some of the guys said, 'There's some talent scouts on base. Why don't you give it a try-out?'"

Reed auditioned, a number featuring drums.

"I was selected. We traveled, mostly on the West Coast. It was sort of like a contest. Whoever the winner was, he won money. I won first place four months in a row. This was temporary duty.

"The Armed Services were segregated until I was in Columbus. We had real good accommodations, as good as the white units. We were just separate. I knew segregation wasn't going to last. Overseas you didn't pay much attention because you were busy. It's only when you get back here that you noticed."

After retiring in 1952, Perry became a technician in the operating room and moved to Kansas City. For thirty years, Reed did not perform.

"The medical profession took over where music left off. Music was not so much in demand. Clubs were closing down. I never thought about music until '83 or '84."

One day a friend came by from his old army days.

"'Do you still play drums like you used to in the 9th Cavalry?' I told him that I had not played music for many a year.

"'Come with me to the Mutual Musicians Foundation. A gentleman down there is rehearsing a big band and he needs a drummer.'

"Once I saw that big band, it just got me. I was right back into music again. I was introduced to the leader, J. R. Williams. He had played baritone sax with known big bands on the West Coast and East Coast. I joined this big band, the Kansas City Jazz Brokers."

When Williams passed away in 1985, Reed became bandleader.

"Kansas City has festivals, the Jazz Festival, 18th and Vine Festival, June-teenth. We did a lot of playing for senior citizens. When Jay McShann had something big going on, he would hire our band. While we're talking about Jay McShann, blues, jazz [performers], you name them, they were all there at one time in Kansas City.

"Years back when I was younger in Wichita, I played with a trio or quartet, piano, bass and drums, very seldom a horn. Everything was head tunes. The clubs and things we played around here, blues was the main menu. There wasn't so much jazz until jitterbug came in. Mainly it was blues: slow blues, medium blues, fast blues.

"They had what you called the Hollow Inn Supper Club, located on North Hillside, past the old Swallow Airport. They had another place we played, a blues place called Hancock's. We also played the Esquire Club.

"We played a few functions for society clubs and high school dances. There weren't that very many clubs. At that time, people worked hard all through the week and they wanted somewhere to go on the weekend. They were kind of starved for entertainment. I won't say any kind. People in Wichita, they know good music, good blues when they hear it. They knew exactly where to write and call to bring different bands in.

"To me, Wichita never did have a style of jazz, in comparison to Kansas City. All the greats started in Kansas City. There weren't that many blues and jazz musicians in Wichita.

"There's a great deal of difference between Kansas City and Wichita, because Kansas City is known for its style of jazz. Wichita, Emporia, Topeka— you branch out from Kansas City and go to these places. Everything came back to the hub of Kansas City. That's where it started.

"When I was in Kansas City, I used to ask my brother what's happening in Wichita. What happened to the jazz when I was there?

"He said, 'It's no more. There's a lot of country and western going on.' He was telling me about Old Town [Wichita's current entertainment district]. They do play some good blues, the jazz-like blues down there. There are some guys who get up and sing the blues, but it's nothing like the old masters used to do it.

"Back in the days when jazz was going, there was jitterbug, then music went on and Dizzy Gillespie came in with bebop. Bebop was popular for a while but there weren't a lot of musicians who could comprehend it until Charlie Parker came by. Parker set the trend on saxophones. Finally, there was no one in to keep that up until it died down. Jazz was moving and blues was on hold.

"Now we've got some artists around here who play blues and are studying blues. Blues was just like day one. There are some blues singers out there who can sing and can remind you of your troubles. That's what blues is all about. As these young people come up, they need to do research and find out what is blues—what makes the blues, how do you play the blues, when do you play the blues, and who's playing the blues.

"With jazz, you'll find that you've got a lot of young men coming along now, in high school and college. They start putting names on jazz, this type of jazz, that type of jazz. It's technique. They are electronically playing a lot of parts in jazz.

"Back in our days, we used to listen to Thelonious Monk and other guys like that, and we never could understand them. These days, you get a little bit to where you can tap your feet, and the other part, you've got to lend an ear and see what he's doing, what he's playing.

"Long as there's blues, somebody's going to play it. Long as there's jazz, somebody's going to get a group together. All you have to do is look back over your shoulders and see the old masters and see what they were trying to tell us.

"One of the things I have been thinking about for quite some time: I've been involved all these many years in music. And all the experience I went through musically, I feel I want to give something back. I chose to work with the young kids in high school in the jazz bands. I was accepted at West High School. I plan to start a clinic in jazz on Saturdays in June and July.

"I contacted the Kansas City Jazz Brokers, the leader and librarian, and told them what I wanted to do. They were really enthused. They have been sending me some of the professional charts out of the Count Basie library."[5]

Count Basie is Reed's favorite artist. "There is just something about the rhythm and the style Count Basie plays. This will give the students a little experience on how the big boys were doing it."

Chapter Four

THE 1940S

Gene Metcalf, Harold Cary, Arthur Bates

During World War II, Blacks were drawn to Wichita's prospering job market. Many followed a sister or brother who had come to Wichita, found a place and a job, and wanted to share the wealth. Census figures for 1940 show 5,686 Blacks in Wichita, 4.9 percent of the total population. In 1950, this number increased to 8,802, but the percentage fell to 4.8 percent, due to the general influx of aircraft workers.

The years after the war found Wichita a crowded and separated city.

GENE METCALF (1925–2004)

Drums, vocals

"I was born here in Wichita, 1925, in a home on a street now called 8th Street. It was called Eagle Street when I was born. Right over there off of Mosley. No brothers and sisters. All my family loved music, but I was the only one who played music. Well, I had an uncle who played trombone but he didn't pursue it too long.

"My grandmother started me out on piano in 1936. I learned piano but I didn't like it, so I went to trumpet. A friend of mine that liked me real well, named Squench Davis, gave me a big yard trumpet. And I taught myself how to blow it. That's when Slim Gaillard was coming out with 'Cement Mixer (Put-Ti-Put-Ti),' 'Jeepers Creepers,' back in the middle thirties. I was about ten or eleven years old.

"My grandmother, Sally Adams, ran a rooming house on 9th and Mosley and all the musicians would come here from Count Basie, Duke Ellington, Jimmie Lunceford bands and stay with her at the house. I ran into some that taught me a lot. It was a wonderful thing. One of the musicians was a tenor player—I can't think of his name—and he told me to take up drums. I went to drums and I really like drums.

"I got my first set from Jenkins Music Company. My grandmother signed for me and I think back in them days you only paid about fifty, seventy-five cents a week on them. A drum set only cost about two, three hundred dollars complete and that was a Ludwig set. They were very good drums."

Metcalf played with Ted Mathews, Glonquez Brown, Vernon Duke, and Shirley Green. His first professional gig was at Flagler Garden, 820 E. 29th.

"Around '42, '44, Lionel Hampton came out with a song called 'Loose Wig.' We took that as our theme song. Everybody called me Loose Wig.

"Flagler was a good place to play. We had the house band, had it locked up. This was before the Esquire [Club]. They had a place called the Hollow Inn on 27th and [North] Hillside. There was nothin' but woods and fields out there. Earnest DeFrance owned it. Another place was called Shadowland on Hillside. In 1941, when the Syncopators had their band, I had a tin can band.

"We had a guy on bass, an inner tube with a stick. I had chitlins buckets, cut the tops out of them and stretched an inner tube across the top, cut the bottom out and made a cymbal out of it, stuck it on a post with a nail. We had a lot of variety shows back then. They gave away prizes for the best performance. We were playing one night. I hit the cymbal and it flew off into the audience. Everybody thought that was in the game." He laughs.

"Back then, we didn't have no problem with police. At Flagler, Vern Miller [later Kansas state attorney general], when he was a rookie on the sheriff department, was a bouncer out there. They had to have a bouncer. At Shadowland they didn't have no police, no bouncers. Everybody got along pretty well.

"Fifty cents went a lot farther than fifty dollars today. This was during the war. I was still going to school, East [High]. I was working up at the Wichita Flour Mill in the evening to buy my clothes. We had real nice clothes. They didn't cost that much. You could get a whole suit tailor-made for thirty-five dollars.

"I never did play in church. Back in them days you didn't have too many musicians in the church. Piano player, organ player, that was about the size of it. They played tambourines and so forth like that. No guitar, no drums. Everything was what they call sad sermons. Preacher was the only one who would liven it up. They sing songs, 'Old Rugged Cross' and stuff like that."

You belong to the Elks' Lodge. Any other lodges or unions?

"I formed a union here in 1945. I don't remember the number, it was too long ago. James Petrillo was head of the main union at that time. He sent a representative down here to help us. It lasted about three or four years. Clubs didn't want to honor unions back in those days so it went to pot.

Gene Metcalf, photo by Arthur Kenyon.

"At that time, our band had from four to five pieces. We were playing boogie-woogie and blues and a little bit of jazz. People didn't care for jazz. They wanted to jump. If it wasn't the blues or boogie, forget it.

"We just had horns, piano and drums. We didn't have a bass at the time. Our piano player had a good left hand. Glonquez Brown. Everybody call him Flappysack then. He had a game left foot, but he had a heck of a left hand.

"The only thing that came close to jazz back in those days was Count Basie but he was doing blues, but it was sixteen-bar instead of twelve-bar blues. Duke Ellington came out with 'Sophisticated Lady,' and they didn't care too much about that. Billie Holiday was a favorite around here at that time."

Did you have any good women singers who emulated her?

"We had some who could sing but they wouldn't come out. We had one girl named Lena. She was about the only one who would sing. She was a nice-looking girl. She'd come out and sit in every now and then. She only knew about two or three numbers.

"Back in them days, we was playing at least four nights a week, sometimes five. We'd start around nine o'clock at night and play until three or four in the morning. There wasn't no carefree [curfew] on the clubs in them times. They play until the people stopped spending money and it would be packed.

"We played out in Planeview there at Roosevelt and Hillside, called Smitty's.[1] He made a whole house into a club. We didn't have a PA I could holler loud enough. Drumming and singing. I had big lungs. We didn't know what a PA was in those days.

"We got our material from different musicians like Louis Jordan, Jay McShann. Jay McShann had a band who played here. Walter Brown sang with him in 1939. They played out at a place on 3400 West Douglas, the Trocadero. Charlie Parker was playing with them and he fired Charlie Parker that night. They did 'Confessin' the Blues.' Charlie Parker went up to take a solo and went to be-boppin' and Jay McShann fired him right there. Didn't nobody understand what he was doing. He was way ahead of his time.

"Jay McShann was here a lot. Jimmie Lunceford, Count Basie, and all them old bands, the Carolina Cotton Pickers and so forth like that. They played at the Forum. And later on, they had a place upstairs on West Douglas, the B.E.T. Playhouse, Beech Employees Center."

What is the blues to you?

"The blues is what you feel, and you have to experience it. All the blues is a story from experience. For instance, you might have a bad relationship with your woman. Well, you get over that by expressing your feelings through song. You write some words to it, and there you go. That one I sing, 'I'm Not Comin' Back Home Anymore,' that's original. I haven't copyrighted it yet but I think I will. I better get on it 'cause somebody be done stole it. I've had quite a few songs stolen, because I didn't have sense enough to copyright it.

"But during them days, we were just happy-go-lucky to be playing. We just loved music. Everybody in the band loved to play. We played all over town."

Your aunt had a bar, didn't she?

"Yeah. She had a place down on East 9th around Mead. That was the uncle who used to play trombone. Polk Jordan. His wife was named Della. He played in bands before he came to Wichita in 1923. Our family moved up here in 1922 from Waco, Texas."

Has that influenced you, the Texas sound? What kind of blues do you like to listen to?

"I like contemporary blues, not the Lightnin' Hopkins. I like the blues like Little Milton, B.B. King, Roy Brown. Louis Jordan has been an influence too."

Where did you get your records back then?

"Jenkins Music had them on Decca. They catered to the Black community too. Jenkins had more Black trade than they had anybody else. Back in 1945 when I first heard Billy Eckstine's big band, 'Blowin the Blues Away'; boy that's a bad record. It was on a big 78. That got away from me. They had them big 78s on the jukebox at the old [African American] Masonic Hall on Main Street. It's still standing there."

Did you just play in Wichita?

"We played in Hutchinson, Sterling, Salina, Topeka, Junction City. We played all over the little towns. I booked myself. We didn't know what a booking agent was.

"I went with the Brownskin Models in '44, for six or seven months. That was when Wes Montgomery was with them."

Was it pretty good money?

"It was supposed to have been. But you know how it is when you on that road. In those days, the booking agents collected all the money. Now the booking agent gets a percentage, 15 or 20 percent. When I quit in Montgomery, Alabama, I had to go back to Indianapolis to get my money. The Ferguson Brothers had the booking agency then."

How did you get hired by them?

"They came through Wichita. They needed a drummer. But I wouldn't go unless they took my piano player, Glonquez Brown.[2] He went with me, too. They had a good piano player, Miller Lee. He was playing more of a jazz thing, and Glon was rocking the people, playing for the shake dances and so forth. They had some too.

"In 1948, I moved to Denver. I formed a band out there and we played all over. We had the only band that played blues and boogie. That was the days when Nat King Cole was real popular. We locked up all those places out there, seven days a week."

How did you find the musicians?

"Went to the musicians hall and picked them up. They gelled right in. That was something they wanted to do. They'd never done it before.

"I stayed out there until Grandmother kept calling me. I came back here around '56 or '57 to come back and look after my grandmother. I found this out—if you ever leave Wichita, you're going to end up coming back to it. Something about this town draws you back."

What about a tradition of blues in Wichita, a style?

"Blues goes back, that I can remember, to 1939. We had [were listening to] Lil Green 'In The Dark.' That's the traditional type of blues that we been playing ever since. Walter Brown 'Confessin the Blues.' And 'Black Gal.' I can't remember who played it."

What kind of style did you guys play?

"Give the public what they wanted to hear. We'd play two or three songs till we hit the right thing, then we'd go from there. We'd feel out the public."

Was there a Wichita style?

"We had a style. It's hard to explain what type it was. You'd have to hear it [he hums a boogie beat]. From there then we'd go down to a natural blues, something like Roy Brown, 'Rocks on my Pillow.' Fast and slow, back and forth. They liked slow dance, then they liked jitterbug."

What was Wichita like during the war years and just afterward?

"Really, it wasn't that many clubs that opened up until the fifties. Back in the forties and late thirties, we had quite a few white clubs but they were bootleg clubs. You'd go there and get your whisky."

What kind of drinks did they have at the Shadowland?

"They didn't. You brought your own from a bootlegger."

Were you ever in on a raid?

"No they never raided because, well, I better not go into that." He laughs. "Max Cohen and Bob Brunch controlled all the whiskey in this town.[3] So therefore you didn't have to worry about no police. Police wasn't bad on them. People just wanted to have a good time and they knew they was just going to have a good time."

You relied on bouncers to keep order in the clubs?

"They were on top of it right quick. Take them outside. If they didn't want to act right in there, they put them out in a minute. And they wouldn't do it in the parking lot."

What was the group name in the fifties?

"We were still the Loose Wigs."

What about in the 1960s?

"Blues kind of went out. Everything was rock 'n' roll back in the sixties. I wasn't playing then. Every now and then I'd go down and sit in at the Starlight on 9th. We had more fun sitting in. They weren't paying that much no way. Disco come in and that knocked the bands out of money. People found they could get by with disco without paying the bands. I can stay home and play records. Why would I go to clubs? Don't make sense. But that's fads."

What about in the eighties and nineties when you started playing again?

"I started in '88. King B had the club opened down there. I went down there and said, you ain't making no money. Let's have a blues session. We got it started. We were the house band. Gene Metcalf and the Blues Machine."

How often do you play these days?

"Not too often. These old bones won't let you move so much. When you get seventy-one years old, you kind of slow it down. It's just more or less something I enjoy doing. We're trying to get it set up at the Elks' about twice a month, Blues at Sunday at the Elks."

How has the blues affected you?

"The blues has inspired me a great deal. You learn a lot from the blues. You learn about life, you learn people. It's a great experience. A lot of people need to get off into that. You feel the public, you feel how things go."

Who do you like to listen to in town?

"They knocked down King B's and you can't go there anymore. And that was the traditional blues. A lot of white musicians came out of King B's learning the blues."

What about Wichita's taste in blues? It seems pretty popular.

"In the last five or six years, blues has caught on 190 percent. The Blacks and the whites love blues. Blues comes from way back. Blues will never die out. It may fade down some but it will come right back. Once a person gets hooked on it, he'll never turn loose. It's the roots of everything. They were playing blues before they even knew what jazz was. And this rap stuff, back in the slave days, the chanting they had there, that was the beginning of the rap. He would say something, and then they'd echo it. Really, rap ain't new."

Did Wichita have a good community for blues musicians?

"Oh yeah. Back in them days, musicians took care of one another. There's a lot of animosity amongst musicians nowadays."

Just like you took your piano player with you into the Brownskin Models.

"He had to go with me. I wouldn't go if he wouldn't go with me. They was hurtin' for a drummer so they had to do it."

Have you ever been recorded?

"We did one song with Alonzo Mills called 'Vera' back in 1943. He was a drummer but he quit drumming and went to singing and put me to drummin'. He had his own band. Back in them days, if Alonzo needed some of my musicians, they'd go with him to play. We worked together. He was an amateur boxer. He could box, too, with his big fat self."

HAROLD CARY (1922–2001)

Piano

"I was born in Texas in 1922, in a place called Atlanta, really a hamlet. There were 3,000 people, whites and Blacks. They didn't call them Blacks then anyway.

"My parents at the time did what most Blacks did, domestic work and farm work. Mother wanted to keep us in school. I have a brother, Richard. We did the little things, like delivery for the drug store. I took tickets for the movie theater, rather than being out picking corn and peas. I was about fifteen. I came up during Hoover's days, and in the cow kills.

"Hoover was letting the cows rot in the field, because the farmers couldn't buy any feed for them. Roosevelt came in and bought up all those cows and had cow kills. He put it in the paper saying such a such a section, big cow kill, bring your own deal [implements and transportation].

"You had to find your own cooling. If you couldn't keep it cool, you didn't get very much. But they had icehouses back in those days.

"My mother was a musician. She played for the church. That's how I got interested in music. I didn't play by [reading] music because there wasn't very much tradition in those days anyway. I didn't realize how important it would have been. If I'd known, I would have gone along with the program. But being a brash little kid with a little bit of talent—by the time I was eight or nine years old I could play as well as grown people—I figured I had it made.

"She was a mother alone. My father died when I was two years old. My mother and my grandmother raised us.

"I could play when I had to reach down and look for the pedals. There was one piano player that used to come through with the minstrel shows. He roomed at our house. That was another way Mother made a little money.

"I used to call him Jake. I don't know if that was his real name. He was interested, talking about how cute I was, sitting down there playing. They would come on tour. A year or so they'd come back—they'd call me Billy in those days—he'd ask, 'How you doing, Billy?'

"He played in five flats [the black keys on the piano]. He couldn't read. I don't remember him singing. Usually we didn't hire the minstrel shows. That was all done by whites. To tell you the truth, I'm not sure we were even able to go to the minstrel shows. There were no integrated shows.

"If you happen to be lucky to be working around the place, you could see them. They didn't put on shows for Blacks. Blacks generally didn't have any money.

"Our school at home only went to ninth grade. I had to go fifty miles from home to finish high school. I stayed with one of my cousins in Marshall, Texas. That's where Wiley College was, that's where Bishop College was. This was a big high school. It looked like the white high school at home. It was all brick and everything. It had civics and music.

Harold Cary, photo by Arthur Kenyon.

"I helped around the house. Didn't have a job. Mama would send money. She would work in the fields. I can remember just as well, Mom gettin' on the trucks coming around early in the morning. Everybody was crawling on with their long sacks. Black-eyed peas was a staple we used to have around our area. Pea-pickers.

"She was a domestic also. Go to white people's house clean up, cook, take care of the kids.

"I had fun down there [in Marshall]. They could play a lot of music, the kids could. They had a band. Their fathers were doctors, lawyers. It was a college town. They played traditional music, things you'd expect to play in high school.

"Music teachers in those days didn't want you to play anything like blues. They didn't want you to play jazz either. They didn't want you out playing on the streets. They frowned on you going out playing gigs at night.

"In the neighborhood, they had a lot of blues. It was a little bit farther along than what I call cotton patch blues, with the overalls and sitting on a tin roof."

Cary graduated in 1938. Following a year at a junior college, Cary worked as a dental technologist for a year and a half. He came to Wichita in 1941.

"Back home, I could walk two miles and be dead in the middle of the woods. I came up here and they had all these paved streets, buses, bowling alleys. But money was very sparse. We had to help out with the food and things. I worked cleaning up bowling alleys, busting suds at the Broadview Hotel. The regular old things if you weren't born to the money. My uncle, Charley Reed, was very instrumental in getting jobs for Blacks. He said:

"'Well, I tell you what. You get some meals over there [at the Broadview], you can eat.' He came from Texas in 1921.

"At home there was nothing you could do but go to church. That was about the biggest thing. And we had all those baseball teams, little Black leagues. We had the 19th June feast; it was a rural thing.⁴ Baseball games were rampant. You would practice all year for that Juneteenth game. I didn't play. I was playing that old boogie-woogie.

"We used to barbecue. The traditional was barbecued goat. Everybody raise that goat all year. On the 19th of June, those dudes in the city get up early in the morning, get those pits dug out there and get those spits ready. Get that old goat." He laughs.

The music was "just getting into boogie-woogie. I remember my first job, I was fourteen years old. There was another kid there. His mother had a cleaners so he had more money than we did. She cleaned up white folks clothes. He had a saxophone and we used to play together. We played for the white country club. It was just plain old boogie-woogie, all made-up stuff. We made twenty-five cents apiece.

"I got drafted in 1942. With my dental background, I was put into the medics." Cary was sent to India.

"I was a dental assistant all the time I was over there. Then I decided I want to drive the Burma Road. I got tired of sitting around looking at teeth all day. We used to drive to different outfits with the dental truck. Our unit was all Black, 45th Quartermaster Truck. We had white officers.

"Monsoon. That's what you had to worry about. Rain a whole month, every day. The heat was so hot after the rain got through, you'd see steam coming off your clothes."

"I had one close call, almost ran off that mountain one night. During the blackouts, you had to use blackout lights, fluorescent things about as long and big as your finger. The only headlights were on the truck up front. That's the only way you could get to China, on the Burma Road. When you think about thousands of trucks driving over that road every day and every night, that doggone stuff was just like talcum powder.

"One night I was driving along and had a Chinese guy we were taking to China. All at once I heard him jabbering away. He was having a fit. I looked over there and I was headed right off that doggone road. I looked down and there was nothing but air."

While stationed overseas, Cary got to perform in a USO production, *Hit the Road*.

"MacHenry Boatright was my dancing partner. He married Duke Ellington's sister. Paul Gonsalves, that great tenor man with the Duke Ellington band, was head of the band in the show.

"We had singers, tap dancers, cross-dressers, so we would have skits with boys and girls. Wonderful Smith—I can't remember who he was with, Red Skelton, or somebody—was in the show.

"When I first got out of the army in 1945, I came back here and started working for Cessna. Stayed here for about a year, then I went back down home [Texas]. I started working for an eleven-piece band in Texarkana, the Jay Franks Band. They were playing Basie charts and Duke charts, Lucky Millinder, all these guys.

"Bands back in those days couldn't live anywhere. If you went to a town so small you couldn't find a place where ten people could stay, you slept out on the ground.

"We traveled all over Louisiana, all the way to Saint Angelo, Texas, Brownsville, Abilene. We had a '46 Ford and the bandleader had a great big Cadillac. Put the old bass fiddle on top of the car and strap it down. We got about seven guys in a Ford with all our instruments—no trailer. People were sitting on things; you couldn't get the trunk lid down.

"We'd get to the place where we were going, if we had shirts and things dirty, we'd go to a filling station and get buckets of water soak them up and down, get on the road again and hang them out the window. By the time we'd get there they'd be dry.

"We'd sleep under the car. Everybody had their own blanket. Those filling stations were great. If it started raining, we'd run to the filling station, sit out under the canopy. We'd get to the job and start wailing. I'm telling you, we had a good band."

Cary returned to Wichita in 1947.

"I wanted to come back here and go to school. Not a heck of a lot of African Americans at Wichita U. After the war, there were more. You were glad to see each other. When I started working out there [playing piano on campus], that was different. They had no Blacks playing on the other side of Third Street. They had one guy named Junior Johnson. He used to play piano around here. People were always comparing us. His mother was a domestic and he used to play sometimes as a lark.

"I was playing at the university in the CAC [student union]. I broadcast over KMUW [university station] twice a week remote, during lunch hour. The fraternities and sororities would talk to their people about me. They wanted me to play at their parties, at their homes. That turned out to be sort of a hit.

"I did a back door thing on them, getting across Third Street. I was playing at the homes. From there I started playing the country clubs. First one was Wichita Country Club. This was around 1948."

Cary also played on a commercial radio station, KFH, and at the (white) Danceland and Swingland Clubs.

"That was during [Kansas] prohibition. Got to the point that school just happened to be too much. I quit and went to playing music.

"Back in those days I came in and started playing the things Kenny Cole was playing, also interspersed rhythm and blues. At that time, I could sing. Used to do 'Kansas City,' also 'Peg o my Heart.' My repertoire had broadened out. To tell you the truth, I guess they had never heard a Black man doing that kind of music.

"I played Black clubs too, before I was running that thing at the school. I played where I could. I played many a club down on 9th Street, like the Downbeat Club, and the Dunbar Theatre. And Flagler Garden. Played with Shirley Green; Big Sam Williams, he was playing drums. Fiddlin' Pete Garrett was on bass. I needed a good bass man, who could play in five flats, and they're hard to find.

"We had quite a good group. Just called it the Harold Cary Trio. Gilmar Walters played bass with me. He had his own group for a while. He played piano with his group.

"I could play blues, but at that time I had added to my repertoire. I could play a lot of things that white people knew: 'Don't Get Around Much Anymore,' 'Sometimes I'm Happy,' 'September in the Rain,' 'A Train.' I could jazz it up and put a little bit of pepper on it. I'd use my dancing talent, because sometimes we had a little floor show just before the intermission at the Candle Club on East Kellogg. I used to do those flying splits.

"I worked more as a group but I would take single acts, like a birthday party or around the pool. I played every country club around here. Eventually I worked into a job after I dropped out of the university. I was playing of course, but I had to have a job. I went down to Pearce-Turk Dental Laboratory. Stayed there for thirty-nine years."

Cary talks about playing in color-conscious Wichita.

"At the Bulls and the Bears [100 block N. Market], we had to take our breaks outdoors. We'd just go back and sit in the car in the back alley out there. If it was real cold, they would let us go sit in the office. It was bad news. There wasn't segregation but it was still segregated in the clubs. The money wasn't very good—$10, $15 a night, sometimes $5, $6 a night.

"One of the funniest things that ever happened to me—show you what kind of things you can get into in a deal like this—I ended up playing on one of those joints on South Broadway, late forties, early fifties. If you think that ain't redneck country down there in those days. You cross Kellogg, you're in trouble. I don't know if it was the Wagon Wheel or one of those other places. I was playing solo piano. I didn't know they had a stripper. I'm sitting there playing along, playing along. I couldn't see behind me. All at once everybody's looking at me in the face.

"This woman back here was stripping buck naked. Instead of looking at her, they were looking at me, seeing if I was going to turn around and look at her. You talk about somebody scared to death. Everybody's looking at me, she's coming up putting clothes on my grand piano. I was glad to get out of that place.

"It's funny now but it sure wasn't funny then. I didn't know whether somebody was going to come up and tell me to get out of the room. Because that has happened. I've been playing at nightclubs and they had strippers. She brought her own records because she wanted her own music. They told us no, you can't sit in here. You have to go out to the kitchen until the stripper's through." He laughs wryly.

"I'm in show business all these years and still get treated like a kid or something. Those were some funny days."

Cary talks about the style of music offered in Wichita.

"At the time, we didn't have very many big bands. It wouldn't be boogie-woogie. 'Going to Kansas City,' 'Perdido.' Wichita had its own style from the standpoint it had pretty good rhythm and blues. Secondary would be ballads.

"I didn't work with too many jazz girls. I worked with a girl named Judy McCord for a while. Iris Dean [pianist], she was very good. She's still around but I don't think she plays as much as she used to. Millie Foster sang with me for a while, at the Candle Club in the eighties."

What about the musicians who influenced you?

"The first was Erroll Garner. People like Willie the Lion [Smith]. Used to listen to a lot of his stuff. Meade Lux Lewis. Nat King Cole, Ahmad Jamal.

"I recommend music for young people if they play it from the standpoint of it being an asset instead of just a fad. Not everybody's going to be the Beatles."

ARTHUR BATES (1920–?)

Bass

"I was born 1920, in Waxahachie, Texas. I grew up in Tulsa, Oklahoma, with my mother. She worked and got me started in music very early. She took a few piano lessons. No brothers or sisters.

"I was about eleven years old, and started on a fiddlet, a beginner's instrument for a violin. It's about three inches wide. I didn't like it. I didn't want to play an old violin.

"When I got to junior high school, I decided I wanted to play the sousaphone. So they started me out on the E-flat. After one march, I decided I didn't want to play it. It was heavy. And I went to the bass fiddle."

You didn't have to carry that in the band, did you?

"No, but I walked on the weekends with it, 'bout fifteen blocks one direction, and it was heavy. It belonged to the school. I didn't have one, so they let me check it out on the weekend and practice.

"I'd be the first kid at school when I started, and the last one to leave. Because I wanted to get in the high school symphony orchestra, and I finally got in it.

"I was a doorman for a while, where the jazz orchestra would practice. I would kick the other kids out. One day the instructor wasn't there, and I was lookin' at the guy playing and I said, well, I can do that good. So I went and picked up one of the other basses and started practicin'. And when the instructor got there, he never told me not to, so I ended up in the band, the Booker T. Washington High School Band.

"It was close to around forty of us in that band. When I finished school, I wasn't thinking about playing anymore, because I didn't have an instrument. I knew a young lady who played in the high school dance band. And in 1941 an all-girl band came to Tulsa and she was in it, the Sweethearts of Rhythm, Pineywood School [junior college], in Mississippi. I saw those young ladies, and I say, hey they got a boy's band?

"They gave me the address of the Don Clifton Collegians. I wrote them, they told me where to meet them. I wrote and told them how broke I was, didn't have a bass fiddle. I forgot about it. About two weeks later they pulled up in front of the house, and that was the beginning of my after-high school career.

"The first dance I played was Coffeyville, Kansas at the Port of Entry. I was with the band 'bout two months before we ever went to school. We had about a fifteen-piece band.

"If my mother tried to send me to Mississippi, I wouldn't have gone. The war was what broke our band up, in 1942 in Junction City, Kansas. We had some pretty good musicians in there. Our piano player ended up doing some things with Dinah Washington, Howard McGhee. The Five Blind Boys. Bud Archer. We all went to school together in Mississippi."

When you traveled around and played with the Collegians, what kind of music did you play and where did you play?

"All kinds, in dance halls and everything. We had a lady named Miss James that was bookin' us. She drove about thirty-five miles an hour, and that's no joke.

"Before I got drafted, I had talked to Benny Carter, out on the West Coast. I was living there then.

"'I'm glad you're here; my bass player got to go to the Service. Come on up here and try out some.'

"So one night we worked out a little bit and he told me when to come back. A few days after I had seen him, I got my greetings [from the draft board]. I went back almost with tears in my eyes, because I call that the big break."

Bates tried to get assigned to the army band.

"Not only me, some other guys couldn't get in the band. One guy, a heck of a trumpet player out of Cootie Williams's band, they didn't take him. He would get up every morning and play, 'I Can't Get Started.' That trumpet was disturbing. Up on the front lines! And he's going to get up playing that thing! Finally they got tired of him and shipped him to the band."

Bates was sent to Italy. When the war was over, he went back to Tulsa.

"Been home about a week and I got a job with the Eddie Lawrence band. He had some musicians that was as good as you wanted to find. In fact, one of them was a brother of the great Oscar Pettiford."

Did you ever run into Charlie Parker?

"Yep, in 1941. He wasn't famous then. It was in Arkansas City, Kansas. He sat in with this Don Clifton Collegian Band. They say, 'There's Charlie Parker; he played with Jay McShann, and he and him kind of put a record out.'

"He soloed on it, but he played just a number solo on that. He blowed about three or four numbers with us. He use to be here in this town at one time. The blind drummer, Homer Osborne, told us Charlie Parker use to play with him in, he called them, greasy spoons. Guys see him coming and they'd put their horns in their case."

They put their horns in their case because they knew he could play so well?

Arthur Bates, photo by Arthur Kenyon.

"No, he wasn't playing that well then. But when he came back off of this tour, he'd got his stuff together."

What did you think about bebop when that came out?

"I liked it."

Did you play it around the Midwest?

"Oh yeah, we were playing it pretty heavy in Tulsa. Of course, when I got to Wichita, I was going to use some. Those guys stopped me, say 'We're not there yet.'

"I went to Langston University and I ended up in a band out there. I majored in industrial arts. At that time, I realized from what I had been reading, big bands were going out. And I knew there was going to be too many musicians on the street."

When were you in Clarence Love's band?

"After Eddie Lawrence, in 1948. Ernie Fields had the classification of number one, but Clarence was paying more money. We played the Big Ten Ball Room in Tulsa. It would hold about 4,000 to 4,500."

How did you make a sound with your bass to fill that whole hall?

"Back in those days, you wasn't miking them. There was a trick to it. You would go to the corner and turn your bass to the wall. Several musicians would do this with horns. See mikes wasn't a big thing until, I'd say in the fifties, and now you don't know how a band really sounds. I love some of the older ways to know how a musician really sounds.

"Now it's too loud. That's one of reasons I backed off. I couldn't stand it. Ruth Brown and [Hank Ballard and] the Midnighters came here once, right over here at the old Mambo Club. I played a dance with them. They needed a bass player. The Paul Williams Band was behind it. They asked me, do I want to make the tour. I said I wouldn't last three days, because it was too loud.

"The drummer said if he ever made it back to St. Louis, that's where he's going to stay. It was killing him, that loud stuff. And it's doing a lot to hurt musicians today.

"In the fifties, I got with another band called Stack Walton, he was a saxophone player. And that's who I was playing with when I come to Wichita in '52. I come here to play two dances and I'm still here."

Why did you choose Wichita?

"I was looking for a job. In 1949, playing with Nat Towles band, those one-nighters wore me out. He didn't record any while I was with him. There were so many of the bands that didn't get to record."

These records that you were on with the Love band, can you tell us what the titles were?

"No I can't, because that's been too many years. These were just some guys down in Tulsa that was recording it. And just like the Homer Osborne band, we went over on Main Street [Wichita] once to record, it was a trick to the thing. Iris Dean was playing piano, Jimmy Taylor was on it, and we might have had a trumpet. There was about five or six of us. We went back to check on the man, and there wasn't anybody in the building. And we did quite a bit of recording that day. I don't know what happened. They could have been released somewhere, under a different name.

"After I came to Wichita in 1952, I went out and got me a job at Boeing. I stayed with Boeing, had thirty-three years seniority when I left. For seventeen years, I played music till it got too rough for me working. A lot of that time I played with Homer, because Homer had things sewn up here."

How did you meet him?

"The first place I rented a room was at Homer's. I stayed there about three weeks, 917 Indiana. He had a big two-story house, he rented some rooms."

And he was blind at that time?

"That's right. He was married. I stayed there three weeks and I went and got a room where I could cook and do everything else. You need that.

Unknown celebrants at the Mambo Club, the L. K. Hughes Photograph Collection, Kenneth Spencer Research
Library, University of Kansas Libraries, Lawrence, Kansas.

Shortly after that we started playing together. For about seven years straight
we played together. Then we had a little break and then a couple years later
we played."

When you were playing with Homer, how many pieces did you have?

"Most of the time it was three or four, piano, bass, drums and the saxophone. Sometimes, on some dances, he might add two more. On piano we
had Wilbur Chapman. Then the next one was Geneva Taylor."

Where was Homer Osborne from?

"Really, he was born in a small town in Oklahoma. I can't think of the
place there, right now."

How did he get to Wichita?

"I think it was music. Clarence Love asked me a question right after I
first come here. In fact, I was living with Homer when I went back home.
Clarence Love say:

"'You ever see ol' trombone player Homer Osborne up there?'

"I sees Homer Osborne up there, but he's a blind drummer. He says,
'That's him. He used to play with King Oliver.'

"I got back, I say, Homer, what is this about this trombone playing? He say, back in those days, if you lost your teeth, you found something else to do, if you blew an instrument."

When did Mr. Osborne pass away?

"At least fifteen years ago. And one fellow told me that Homer was older than what he said he was. I said, man that would make him ninety-something when he died."

Did Homer ever talk about his days with King Oliver?

"He never talked about that hardly. He did a lot of travelin' before—let me see, Homer went blind in '27. The doctor told him wouldn't be safe for them to mess with his eyes at that time. Well nowadays, it's different."

According to Joshua Yearout in his book *Wichita Jazz and Vice Between the World Wars*, Osborne was working with King Oliver Band in 1919, playing the Plantation Club, the Vendome Theatre, and the Savoy. The personnel: Oliver and Louis Armstrong cornet, Lil Hardin piano, Johnny Dodds clarinet, and Honore Dutrey trombone. Baby Dodds played drums on recordings. Osborne acknowledged that Dodds was superior on drums.[5]

By 1927, Osborne had left Chicago for Wichita and played in an eleven-piece dance band at the Arkota Ballroom. Then—"I was walkin' home Decoration Day evening with a couple of suits hangin' over my shoulder, when all of a sudden, everything went black." Somehow, he made it home and a doctor was called by his mother. Yearout continues: "Osborne promptly got up, dressed, slipped out the back door and made his way downtown to the Arkota, where he led the band through the night's gig."[6]

"Homer was playing more of the dances than anybody else. Sometimes Walton Morgan would play with him. Jimmy Taylor played with Iris, me, and Homer.

"Duke Ellington came to town, we were playing up here on 21st Street at the Aladdin. Paul Gonsalves stood at the front door and hollered:

"'Jimmy Taylor, you going to play.'

"Paul kept pushing Jimmy. I knew Jimmy could blow, but I didn't know he could blow as good as he blowed that night. Paul, before he left, put his horn in his case. He said, 'I done cussed Jimmy for thirty minutes for staying in Wichita.'

"Jimmy was real sick with sugar then [diabetes]. He said, 'I wouldn't go across town with nobody.' He stayed here till he died."

You saw some drug use in your years of performing?

"Oh my goodness, from word say go! They were using marijuana; some of them was using heroin. I didn't hear the word 'crack' then. I heard of canned heat [Sterno]. And they used aspirins in coke a lot. I don't think you can get it anymore, was the pure vanilla extract. And bay rum. I know they stopped selling bay rum during World War II. Man, there's so many things that people have used."

Why do you think musicians were prone to use that stuff?

"Well that's who got accused for it, because they're in the limelight. More people would see them."

In Wichita more than in Tulsa, or about the same?

"I wouldn't say one place more than the other. Even some of your smaller towns were just as bad."

How about rate of pay—what you were making in Tulsa compared to what you got for playing music up in Wichita in the fifties?

"It was more in Tulsa, $12, $15. At that time some of your big bands wasn't paying too much more. In Wichita I made a little less, about $10. We played in some of the best places they had here. We played the Esquire Club, but not in long series. In fact, when I was playing with Gilmar Walters sometime out to the Esquire, Jerry Hahn would be on guitar. We used to play the old Bomber Club. We used to play at another place called the Blue Note, and what used to be the Mambo over here. All the top bands that come to Wichita would end up there, from Duke Ellington on down."

Let's talk about the blues a little bit. You had arrangements on blues?

"We used arrangements, head arrangements, and B-flat blues is one of the most popular blues in the business. Just like Duke says, some of your top jam numbers are blues. And people get the misinterpretation of blues, they think blues is all gutbucket. I say huh-uh. Blues is a feeling. Count Basie played a lot of blues. They were jump, slow."

When you were playing with Homer Osborne, how many of your tunes were just the blues, and what did Wichita audiences demand back then?

"Well what we did, we tried to play as much of top numbers. I don't know what the height of our repertoire was. Any dance that we played, somebody would come up and request the blues. I don't care whether a farmer or what. Just like so many musicians I've said, you can't lose if you play the blues."

What about when rock 'n' roll came in? Was that a change from the big bands?

"That was just a name that come in. We had been doing the rock 'n' roll umpteen years."

When people asked for the blues, did Homer have a good feeling for the blues?

"Oh yeah. He didn't sing, he would talk sometime on it. We always had somebody in the band can sing some. One thing about some of the musicians I played with. We didn't just copy, we used our ideas of the way we wanted to do something."

Did younger musicians ever come up to you and ask for performance tips?

"In Tulsa, and very little here."

Do you think there is a particular Wichita style of blues as opposed to Tulsa blues?

"No different. Just long as you do a good job of it. The main thing is, you have to watch your crowd. Most crowds go for medium jump blues. Now, in olden days, somebody would ask you for a slow drag because they want to talk stuff. We used to play three different tempos to see how the people reacted on it. Pleasing the crowd is the main thing about playing a dance. If you don't, they will get up and walk out on you."

Would you encourage younger musicians to get into music today?

"Yeah, if they're going to play right. I mean play something decent. Learn an instrument and not try to be the one-man show."

When did you stop playing?

"About 1970. The stuff was getting so loud I had to get away from it. We were accused of playing loud in my day."

Chapter Five

THE 1950S

Franklin Mitchell, Jerry Childers, Henry Walker

According to the Bureau of the Census *County and City Data Book of 1962*, Wichita gained 48,534 in civilian migration 1950–60, growing by almost a fifth. The population of Blacks in Wichita more than doubled during that decade, from 8,802 to 19,861, reaching 7.8 percent of the total population.

In 1950, Wichita's ranking in residential segregation "was fourteenth from the top among 211 cities."[1] African Americans who fought for their country were returning to find their country unwilling to give them a hotel room or a main floor seat in a theater. But integrative forces that were being felt in the rest of the nation slowly made their way through the city. The music of African Americans aided this process, just as it had done in the days of the minstrel.

FRANKLIN MITCHELL (1943–2000)

Bass, guitar

"I was born here in Wichita in 1943. I started playing music professionally at the age of twelve, down on Main Street with Berry Harris, Harmonica Chuck, Jerry Childers, Sam Franklin and Charles Walker, Donald Dunn, those fellows. Plus a few more; I really can't remember all the names.

"There used to be an old man come by when I was about six or seven years old, sit on the porch and play guitar to me. His name was Bill and he played 'West Texas,' 'Bow-Legged Woman.' He's the one that got me really interested in playing music.

"He wasn't a professional musician, just loved to play and sing. He was a old Oklahoma boy, a friend of my family.

"We were on the 1800 block on Ohio Street, right across the street from a club called The Green Frog. I heard mostly jukebox from that club. A lot of the times, the musicians would get together at McKinley Park and sit up under the shade tree and play, and after hours in the bootleg houses and stuff. This was in the early fifties. I'd be outside listenin' and trying to be one of the big boys, and they would teach me a little. Then my mother eventually bought me a used guitar.

"One of the first songs I learned was 'Honky Tonk,' then 'After Hours.' When I reached the age of twelve, I met a lady by the name of Kathryn Smith. Her and her husband Bob Smith used to manage bands around here in town."

Kathryn and Bob Smith [Aunt Kat and Uncle Bob] were a vital recruiting and managerial force in Wichita. Their names occur repeatedly in the interviews.

"I got so involved in music, till I was playing down on 13th Street one night at a club called the Blue Note. My mother came in there. She ran me out of the club. Every time she turned around, I was going somewhere trying to follow the boys to play music. They would sneak me in the club. So I left home when I was the age of twelve.

"I had three sisters and one older brother. I was the youngest. It was just my mom and stepdad. I had a good life as a teenager, always worked. Never really been in any serious trouble. I was staying in another friend of mine's car, until his mother come out and made me come in the house. Then Mother would take me back home. But I told her I wanted to play the blues. I wanted to be a big time musician. Kathryn and Bob Smith kind of took to me. They adopted me as one of their own, along with fifteen or twenty other musicians that just come out of Muskogee like Herbie Welch, Donald Dunn, and Willie Wright, Carl Wright, and these guys.

"It was all in a little one-bedroom house up on 1200 block on [N.] Minnesota. Sometimes there would be ten or fifteen musicians in there sleeping everywhere we could sleep, and playing. We thought we was doing good if we could make just enough to put some jingle in our pocket then. I started playing on bass. Guys got to coming and asking me, if I wanted to play on a gig. Upright bass is what was popular then. I originally learned how to play on a big upright from a janitor at my school, L'Ouverture. His name was Mr. Garrett. First time I ever seen somebody play a bass. They had these here park shows out to McKinley. He used to play with a jazz band. I thought the bass was for like opera or classical music. I'd never seen a Black man play a bass like that.

Franklin Mitchell, photo by Arthur Kenyon.

"The deepness of the tone caught my fancy more so than the treble on the guitar. I got one from Jenkins Music. They had a bunch old instruments that was secondhand and they wasn't very good. You could pick them up for fifteen–twenty dollars, but fifteen–twenty dollars then was a lot of money. Sometimes I had to work two or three weeks just to get enough money to buy a set of strings."

Aunt Kat didn't help you out? They didn't buy your instrument?

"No, they didn't buy my instrument. They had some instruments but everyone pretty much preferred to buy their own.

"We played the Mambo Club, and at Jack and Jill, down on Murdock. Down on 9th Street, the Sunset Club, North End Club, and Bunny Club, and Chicken Shack, Smart's Palace, just about anywhere we could play to make a quarter. Wichita was full of musicians back then.

"This was late fifties, early sixties. We had a band called Jive Five, and then the Finger Poppers. We started going to Junction City, Hutchinson, Salina, Newton, and McPherson, Topeka. We had an old station wagon or else we would rent a trailer. We had more fun than we did anything else. During that time, you grew fast because you meet a lot of people doing a lot of different things.

"I got an electric bass, a Kay, at a pawn shop. We started going up to Junction City. And up in Junction City, there's Fort Riley. I got to meeting other musicians from other parts of the United States, because it was a military base.

"There was a guy who come out of Omaha, Ray Price Jr. It was like a twelve-piece band. One night I sat in with him on electric bass. I had real good timing and a real good ear. Anything that I'd hear, I could play it. It didn't matter if it was blues, or jazz, or country. That's mostly the three popular music going on then."

Did you take music lessons at L'Ouverture?

"I took violin from Mr. Morgan. I think I was in the third grade. I didn't take it a year, I don't think."

How was he as a teacher?

"Mr. Morgan wasn't strict, he was easygoing. But he was exciting to watch, to learn under, because he had a certain air about him. He could bring music out and make it exciting to you. He was an excellent musician. He would always encourage young musicians because he used to come to different clubs and play on the jazz set. He'd yell at me: 'Boy, where your mama at? Do your mama know you're out here?'

"I was pretty headstrong. My mother always told me, whatever I do, take care of myself. My mother installed a lot of morals in me and they kept me up until this day. I always had some kind of little job, deliverin' papers, work on the trash truck, or cuttin' yards, or doing something. Always kept my own little money, so she always told me: 'Since you're going to grow up and be who you are, just remember to take care of yourself, respect people. I'm always there when you need me.'

"But she knew I was going anyway. She tried to break me, to put fear in me. But then she really found out how serious I was, and then after she found out how good I was, she used to come and listen to me play.

"I remember when I was smaller, she used to keep a lot of old gospel music around the house. That's mostly what she had. My mother didn't work. She was on welfare. And my stepfather was a meat packer.

"It used to be a carnival that came through with an all-Black show, *Harlem in Havana*.[2] It was a stage show, like dance and show band. I got a chance to go with them, left Junction City, went to Cocoa Beach, Florida. And the carnival went from Cocoa Beach all the way up to Anchorage, Alaska. That's where I got to meet a lot of name musicians, a lot of studio musicians. And them older guys, they took to me. When I make a mistake or something, they would say: 'No, young man, it don't go like that. It goes like this. Music is not rude, music is always subtle. Music is always in tune, music is always correct. Music has a language of its own and a life of its own, and music is always decent and in order. And if you want to be a good musician, you always have to have perfection in your music.'

"We had black and white tuxes. We had one portion of the show was called the country show; we wore old coveralls and old straw hats. And we had dancers, singers, comedians, magicians and everything that went with the show. We stayed in a boxcar. Every now and then we'd get a hotel room. We traveled by train, trucks and buses.

"The whole show had like forty, fifty people in it. I was the youngest. A lot of older women, older men helped keep me out of trouble. When you're on the road like that, you run into all sorts of people that's doing anything, some selling drugs, some prostituting, some hustling, some gamblers, some murderers. But I thank God that I really never had any problem with nobody. I was only interested in my craft and playing music. I wasn't in it for the money. I think we made like $50 a week in the carnival.

"All expenses, all our food. Every day they would feed us breakfast, lunch, and dinner. They had three or four cooks. But it was a hard life too, because you had to get there. You had to have set-up. You never got a chance to really get attached to nobody except for, it was like one big family. And that one big family, couldn't too many people penetrate their family.

"Then after we leave the carnival, we always go to town, found a jam session. That's where I met a lot of musicians on jam sessions. I met groups out there like Ike and Tina, and the Temptations, Lou Rawls. I seen Billy Eckstine on stage; I didn't get to play with him or anything. We had a big band. And those musicians were from New York to Florida, from California to Mississippi, Chicago, Detroit, St. Paul, Minnesota, Texas, and Wyoming and New Mexico.

"I called home once a month. Never did write too much. No one ever did wonder where I was. Half the time, I didn't know what city I was in. That's a hard life, but I enjoyed it, I loved it. You didn't eat right, you didn't get no sleep half of the time, because you was young and you wanted to see everything going on. I believe a lot of that helped me today to go from the blues to the gospel.

"After that, I got a chance to go with the Ray Price Jr. band in Omaha. He was playing mostly contemporary show tunes and blues and jazz. I wasn't reading then. But his piano player, Ted Anderson, taught me how to read.

"After I got off the road band, I come back to Wichita. Berry Harris and I used to travel a lot down in Oklahoma and down through the backcountry, little country bootleggin' joints. Berry played his harmonica and guitar, and I was playing bass and doing most of the driving, because Berry didn't drive too good, because he was always wanting to get loaded. I'm not saying nothing bad about Berry, now.

"Berry was pretty known then. He would call Oklahoma or they would call him. Most of the time we would pick up musicians there—drummer, piano player, maybe a saxophone player, another guitar player. Sometimes we would take some of the local musicians with us.

"In 1960, Berry and I moved to Rock Island, Illinois. He had some relations up there. It didn't take very much to talk me into it. I had the urge to go."

In the carnival, you had to play a lot of different kinds of music. When you came back to Wichita, what could you play around here? Not too much, because most of them was still playing blues and R&B. The R&B I had got used to playing was more on an upscale. So, it had got boring to me really, just playing the three-change blues thing. That's what Wichita is all about."

Do you think Wichita has a blues style all of its own or does it borrow from other styles?

"Wichita is a melting pot. It come from everywhere. Everything comes to Wichita eventually. A lot of musicians was coming through from Tulsa and Oklahoma City, Kansas City and St. Paul, bringing bands through here. And then Wichita got to advancing into the big band era. And that's when the organ got popular. And when the organ got popular, and they wasn't using bass players anymore, that's when I switched to the guitar. The organ [foot pedals] took the place of the bass.

"When Berry and I went to Rock Island, Berry stayed about three months. We run into a guy out of Chicago, his name was Floyd Edward, something like that. I started traveling around in Illinois, Iowa, Wisconsin, Missouri. That's when I come across Ike and Tina Turner, B.B. and Freddie King, and Sam Cooke, did some things. Not on the stage with Sam Cooke, but the front band. Temptations. I played a show with Lou Rawls."

So you were the opening act?

"Yeah. Eddie and the Finger Poppers. I played guitar. Over one year, I played 109 one-nighters. I played bass and guitar with the Ike and Tina Revue for about four months. Ike Turner was very hard to play with. I didn't like Ike. He was temperamental. He was bossy.

"I was twenty or twenty-one when I played with Ike. Then we done some shows with B.B., Freddie King, and a lot of musicians who never leave Chicago. Little Milton, I played with him. Bobby Bland, played a show with him. Then I got into the studio field where if a band come through and they needed a musician, they would send me out.

"I signed with Ace Recording Studios. So when you go into the studios and do tracks, there's a lot of songs I probably was on, and didn't know whose track they was. They'd give me the chart and say, 'Heh, play this track.' I'd either play it on guitar or bass, and then I'm gone. I may not go to the studio for another week or so, but in the meantime, you played with different bands come through town.

"Then I worked too. See, I had me a job at the refinery. I worked for John Deere for eleven years. I got married, had kids."

Didn't the factory get in the way of your playing music?

"Yeah, because it hurt my hands. I had a beautiful career in music. I never made it big or famous or anything, but that was okay."

Are you listed on any credits on albums?

"I don't even know. Because we'd just go in there and make the track. Pick up our check and go home."

How was Ace to work for as a record company? Did you ever think about going over to Chess?

"No, because Chess was just getting popular and this was when I was out of Detroit. Well the Temptations, Stevie Wonder was with Motown. Motown was just on the grow then. I went to Detroit and played a lot of shows. We used to play a lot of balls. We'd travel from Chicago, from Rock Island. A lot of socials, picnics, gambling boats.

"I never was approached by anybody from Motown. I was just so wrapped up in excitement of the big city life: the clothes, the cars, the money, the music, and the travel. The things that musicians do. You meet people that you never see again in your life. I met a lot of big name musicians just at a party, at jam sessions. Up and coming musicians that hadn't made it big then.

"A lot of young guys fell by the wayside. I seen a lot of young musicians, women and men get taken away—talented musicians. But there is always someone out there more talented than you were. And I learned at an early life, if you're going to play, play the best you can and play right. You can experiment, but there are only certain areas you can experiment in.

"The band leader or the name musician wanted to remain the top, so he limited you in certain areas. The only time you really got free, was at a jam session. I went to those every night. There was so much more that you could absorb, so many different talents, so many different sounds, so many different runs and notes that you knew was there but you couldn't find yourself.

When did you really decide to begin doing God's work?

"I come back to Wichita in '74, because I wanted to settle down. I was burned out; twenty years of being a musician, hard-core. Uncle Bob had started preaching at Shilo Missionary Baptist Church. Kathryn had got out of the club thing too, and was in church.

"I just quit playing music. So I went to visit the church and joined. I started playing guitar in the choir, then I become the choir director. Then I had to learn what I was teaching. That's when I went to the Bible.[3]

"Now all the energy I put in the streets, I reversed that energy and give it all to God. Now I give Him all the glory. So all the things He gave me, all the things He taught me, all the blessings He gave, now I'm putting it all back to Him. I'm using it for His glory. I'm still not in the forefront, thank God. Now God is the head of my life. Jesus is everything.

"Even today, let the young musician come here. I'm still helping young musicians now but on the gospel field. These young men is a blessing to me and the church."

JERRY CHILDERS (1939–1997)

Organ, vocal

"I was born in Wichita, right by North High School on a little short street called Sherwood. I've got a brother that's two years older than me. I heard my mother just vaguely mention that she used to play the piano.

"I went to L'Ouverture. I lived in a predominantly white neighborhood. Had to come past all these other schools to go to school back then, and I couldn't figure out why. I suffered with asthma when I was in grade school so there was no need for me to ask my mama about a horn or a wind instrument of any kind. There was no need of asking about any drums because that wouldn't have worked either. She wouldn't have wanted that racket around.

"I took Glee Club in school at Horace Mann [Intermediate]. I didn't really get interested in music until I was more or less out on my own working at Boeing at the age of seventeen. They had the shop paper and there was a set of Slingerland drums in there. A trombone player told me, said, 'Jerry, you buy those drums and I'll teach you how to play them.'

"So I bought the drums and I played until the time I got married. In the meantime, I heard Jimmy Smith playing the organ and around 1961, I started taking organ lessons, unbeknownst to anybody.

"I took lessons for about six months. I'd just be missing in action about couple hours every day, because I worked night shift at Red Ball garage. I had so many women in my house, my grandmother, my mom, and my mother-in-law was up from Louisiana and sister-in-laws, and my aunties, and never got a chance to hold a baby. I said, I've got to get out of here. I'd go out to the Hammond organ dealer and play his organ and he was trying to coach me to buy one. And back then, just a Hammond spinet run you 'bout $1,800. Then with the finance, you're talkin' about enough money to buy a car. I took my wife out there, played that organ for her, and she said: 'Where'd you learn to play this organ?'

"'Well, when your sister was telling you that she thought I had a chick on the side, that's what I was doing.' I played drums from '57 to '61. I had some good teachers and mentors—Elvin Forrest, he's long gone now. He introduced me to Homer Osborne, who padded my drums. I was just the timekeeper, I wasn't anything fancy but I played with a lot of guys, like Henry Powell, tenor saxophone, John Gonzales, he was tenor saxophone. I understand he's down in Oklahoma now. Alonzo Mills, I used to buddy around with him.

"Sam Williams, he was a drummer. He started playing drums with me years when I switched to the organ and he's a very good friend of Perry Reed. We were playing a whole lot of blues, and rhythm and blues, and maybe a few standards. They were doing stuff like 'Take the A Train,' and maybe 'Honky Tonk,' and 'Night Train' by Jimmy Forrest. I was always busy, because I was reliable, and I had my own self-transportation, a great big ol' 1954 Buick four-door Super.

"I went to North High but I didn't graduate. I went and took a GED test later on. I was working at Zongker Drugstore at 13th and Waco, deliverin' drugs and playing music at night. There was a lot of places to play, the Sportsman's or Flagler Garden. I'd play with Berry Harris, Tricky Marvin, Kid Thomas. They were out of Chicago, one of them played drums and one played the harmonica and guitar.

"Two brothers had a couple clubs here, the Bomber Club, George Washington and Oliver [Street], right behind McConnell Air Base, and another downtown called the Tic-Toc Lounge. Oh, there was a lot of venues back in the late fifties, early sixties."

Did Tricky Marvin and Kid Thomas play Chicago blues?

"Exactly. House rockin' music. They put on quite a show. They did a lot of covers and they had their own stuff too, but they were dynamic. Flash Terry use to play out at Rhythm City. Gene Franklin and the House Rockers, they was another group that used to come through here.

"Those days, where the courthouse is, that was all Black businesses. You had the Water Street Hotel. That was the only place the Black musicians could stay, like [out of the bands of] Count Basie, Duke Ellington, Little Richard, and Preston Love. Marvin Gaye would come here and walk the streets and talk to people."

Jerry Childers, photo by Arthur Kenyon.

Are you active in the church?

"I got baptized in the Catholic Church in 1954, over there at St. Peter Clayvern, 11th and Indiana. I don't never know where I would have been headed, if I hadn't gotten into the church. I was pretty active up till the time I got about seventeen, then the music took over. But I still would go to Mass on Sundays.

"I had a chance to go to California in '62, and I run into another organ teacher, Mr. Neal. I had this little old Hammond spinet.[4] I guess I did a pretty good job. All the other students told me 'Boy, you going to make it, you going to be a fantastic organ player.'

"I met people like Charles Kynard out of Kansas City, an organ player. I used to go and see Jimmy Smith play and Johnny Guitar Watson play. Me and Johnny "Guitar" Watson played the same organ.

"Billy Preston, when he went on *Shindig!*[5] back in the sixties, was playing at a club there right off 54th and Broadway, below the 54 Ballroom. They had a room called the Organ Room. My landlord managed that place, and he said, 'Jerry, we need an organ player.'

"So I went down there and I started playing that organ of Billy Preston. And then Johnny Guitar Watson, he would come in and play on the weekends. I'd play the happy hour and just kind of fiddle around on the organ.

"I never will forget when I went to see Charles Kynard at Marty's Club. I'd never seen him in Wichita or in Kansas City and I told him I was from Wichita. We knew some of the same people because he played in churches and clubs here back in the late fifties and early sixties.

"So he said, 'Do you want to the play the organ?'

"'No, I just want a lesson.'

"He said okay. So he went on about his business because he's on break and he got him a drink and talking to his crowd and his fans and he went back up there and he played a couple numbers. And he said: 'Now ladies and gentlemen, we have a fantastic organ player in the house.'

"He went on with this here hoopla and I just looked around. I thought maybe Jimmy Smith or McDuff or McGriff was in the house or something, or Wild Bill Davis. And he said: 'From the Midwestern part of the United States, ladies and gentlemen, put your hands together for Jerry Childers from Wichita, Kansas.'

"And I tell you I wanted to disappear. I mean I wanted to just slide up under the booth. But the people looked at me like they just knew I was Jerry Childers from Wichita, Kansas. So I had to go on.

"I went up there and I started playing this big B-3 [the Hammond B-3 has two full keyboards and more pedals]. I mean, it frightened me to death and then playing with these here good players, because he had Grant Green on guitar, Jimmy Forrest on saxophone, and I think Kenny Dickson was on drums. But these guys just enveloped me. They just took me in and I played the blues and I was ready to get down on my knees, and my hands were shaking.

"And they saying, 'You're doing a good job, baby.' They kept me up there for about thirty minutes. The crowd liked it. They encouraged me on and I felt real good about that. That's the way those professional musicians do. If they think that you might be competent, they want to see what you can do and they'll just front you off like that."

Would you consider yourself a blues player?

"My best suit is blues, because that's what I started off on. Jazz is just something I kind of graduated to. I would say if you can't play the blues, you can't play anything too much. You'd have to play the blues or gospel, before you could ever graduate to jazz. That's just my theory."

How would you define the blues?

"The only way I can define it, it comes down through ancestry. Just like the guys over way back in the plantation days and out in the cotton fields, they started singin' the blues. If they had an old guitar, they'd sit on the back of the stoop after they'd get off from work and moan and groan and speak about the way life was with them. They would put it into words and emotions and music. Blues and gospel is closely related. Blues is the beginning of the Black culture.

"I've played and hollered the blues for thirty years or more. I played for a lot of different people and different walks of life.

"I come back to Wichita in '67 and stayed here until '71, when I went back to California. A friend of mine, Jesse Price, was a drummer out of Kansas City, used to play with Count Basie's band. He said he had a job for me out there in Beverly Hills playing a campaign party for Wilson Riles [board of education] and Tom Bradley [mayoral candidate].

"I didn't believe either one of them had a chance of winning, because both of them were Black. But they had the money and the people behind them. We had to take my organ up the steps at this house. It was on a hill, naturally in Beverly Hills, and through the house, through the living room, the kitchen, and then out the back door down the back steps and put it on a gazebo which was about twenty, thirty, fifty feet from there. That's fine, I said, but how am I going to get this organ out of here?

"They said, 'Don't worry about it. We'll get it out.' I says, 'Anybody going to be sober by that time?' Because the booze was flowing; but that was an interesting gig.

"Then I played at a ski resort up in Bishop, California. That was something different."

On your own?

"Yes. You do the bass line with your feet, of course."

Do you use an electric drummer?

"Yes, I have and for quite a while I done that. I had a drummer, Leroy, the electric drummer. We made a lot of money together and played a lot of jobs together, just me and that drummer. I had a chance to play with a lot of good musicians too, when I was out there in California. People like Eddie 'Cleanhead' Vinson, and some of the people who played with Johnny Otis. I used to catch all the acts at a club there called the Skillet.

"When I was working for United Parcel we had some safe-driving days accumulated. So they said, 'We got to spend this money. Jerry, we would like for you to play for us, if you can get a band together and tell us how much you going to charge. We're going to rent the banquet room at the Queen Mary down in Long Beach.'

"You mean the ship? 'The ship, yeah.' I went and asked Jimmy Forrest, he wrote the song 'Night Train,' would he play with me. He said, 'Sure, baby.'"

What about some of the national blues performers you heard in Wichita in the early days?

"We would go out to the Mambo during the last act, because we had Black policemen that didn't allow us to go in there because we was under age. They had a patio outside where you could kind of stand and look in there and hear the music and stuff.

"We'd sit up there on the corner at 9th and Cleveland and then those guys would ask for a ride out there [to the Mambo] and I'd taxi them for a little bit of gas money. Then maybe around about thirty minutes 'fore it was over, Bill Lambert, one of the Black policeman, would let us come in.

"Now downtown, at the Forum, that's where the big bands would come, like Count Basie and Duke Ellington. The crowd would be mixed. This was way back in the forties. Mother used to take us down there to listen to the big band. I guess that kind of rubbed off on me, too.

"When I got my B-3, I started learning all over again how to play the organ because there's quite a difference between the spinet and the B-3. I ate and slept with that B-3 for the better part of my life, and I still do. I turn it on every chance I get, because there is always something to learn."

What is the main style of blues that you think is around Wichita?

"Anymore, you got such a mix of it; you've got the Chicago blues, which is very prominent here because of Jesse Anderson. Then you had a mix of Wichita blues that come in. Oklahoma blues is yet a different style. Berry Harris can vouch for that."

Who did Texas blues in this town?

"Back in those days, Riley Joe Terry. He was another guy who used to play with Berry Harris out to Flagler Garden. These out-of-town musicians were very impressive. When someone would come in, we felt that they had a little bit more on the ball. And of course, there is always something to learn from anyone that plays. A lot of it influences you.

"Just like with my organ playing; it's a mix. When I'm playing blues, it's a mix of the Wichita where I got my roots. And I had a chance to listen to a lot of good blues players that would come through here. When I went to California, I started leaning my ear towards jazz. Naturally I got a West Coast sound on the organ. Geographically, there's a distinct difference between the blues or whatever it is in any part of the country you go to."

Talk about the Hammond organ.

"There's a lot of electronic equipment they got that kind of duplicates the sound of the B-3, but anybody that's been around one for any length of time, they'll tell you there's nothing like the B-3. And it seems as though most musicians fall in love with it, irregardless what instrument they play. When I pull that organ out and set it up for jam sessions or something, I mean the musicians just come out of the woodwork.

"I learned that early on, back in '71, when I was playing in Wichita at the Camelot. We'd have jam sessions that start at twelve o'clock on Sunday afternoon, and we wouldn't get out of there until three o'clock Monday morning. Rock Green, he was the bass player, and of course, Mike Finnigan and the Serfs, Smitty, and Larry Faucette would play. It was a B-3 at their disposal and I didn't mind anybody playing it. We just kept it hot all of the time."

Is Wichita a good music town?

"You got a very wide array of musicians from different ethnic backgrounds and all. I can learn something and listen to anybody as long as it's done well, and there's a lot of groups around here that's doing it well. I'm glad to see that live music has come back. There's been two or three lulls in my lifetime—the go-go girls back in the sixties, and disco in the seventies. But now blues has really caught on again.

"It's a type of music that's just been introduced to the young generation that they'd never heard. The blues has always been dominant. You got the dominant seventh chord. You can't beat it. When you can't do anything else, you play the blues and you be alright."

Has there always been a pretty good community of musicians in Wichita?

"Oh yes, as far as I know and as far as I'm concerned. Just look at it this way, musicians have always gotten along with the public, because the people adore you whether you playing in an all-Black club or all-white club. One thing about musicians be they Black or white, if you can play, that's all the cat is interested in. Musicians get along quicker than anybody else because they don't see no color."

HENRY WALKER (1935–)

Guitar

"I was born in Pine Bluff, Arkansas, 1935. My folks were sharecroppers. My old man demand you work. That's one thing; I couldn't get to sleep in the daytime. He catch you sleeping in the daytime, he would find something for you to do. I have a bunch of sisters and brothers, eleven. I'm second from the top. I went to school in Pine Bluff, and here also at East High. I was in Pine Bluff until I was seventeen. I had an uncle who lived here. It was a quiet town, real quiet."

What kind of music was down in Pine Bluff?

"Basically, real old-fashioned kind of blues. My favorite was one of the guys named Amos Milburn out of Louisiana. And B.B. King, naturally, Big Joe Turner."

What about the tradition of music in your family in Arkansas?

"Believe it or not, it was spiritual. I didn't get interested in music till I was way up in my twenties in Wichita. We lived at 1010 Wabash. It was a very busy area, kind of the core of the Black neighborhood. Couple blocks from the Dunbar. That was my hangout. The 9th Street Drugstore, that was the spot. You could get on the corner there and meet anybody you wanted to meet. You had the Sportsman, the Flamingo, and several other clubs on 9th street. But the Sportsman was mainly the club. It was the happenings. It wasn't a real big place, but it was nice, it was a comfortable-size club.

"I didn't graduate. I was living with my uncle. He got married so I had to go to work full-time. I was on my own. From '52 to I'd say about '55, I worked for Stoney's Market, 1111 East 9th."

You got interested in music later than a lot of people.

"Yes, very late. I kind of just slipped into it. A friend of mine came by and told me he could play. And which he couldn't, you know, but still, he take me over to this guy's house and showed me this guy's guitar. He said:

"'Let's go down and get us a guitar.'

"I said okay. So, we go down and get a guitar. I think I bought a little ol' Stella. I kept this a month or two, and he said, 'Let's go get each of us a electric one.' So, I goes get a electric guitar, a Les Paul Jr., at Jenkins Music. It was quite a bit of money for somebody just picked up a guitar.

"I always been a person, if I buy anything, I want the best. I don't like to buy something and then later on I just decide I want to get something different. I drove people crazy practicing. I always been a kind of a jazz enthusiast. I ran into a very knowledgeable musician, Billy Bruce. He was from Wichita but he spent about twenty years in Chicago. He kind of influenced me to swing a little jazz."

Why did he come back?

"I really don't know. This is his home, his mother lived here. He worked inside at the post office, and he stayed here until he passed. I took a few lessons from him. He's one of the few people that really influenced me for music. Otherwise, I don't think I ever became the musician I am, because I started late. So, what I've done, I developed it by work, by hard work.

Henry Walker, photo by Arthur Kenyon.

"I'm a person who always worked one and two jobs all my life. Playing became work for me, because I had to get it when I could. Right now, I'm working seven days a week, playing two nights a week.

"My first job was playing bass for Berry Harris. I believe at first, I wind my string down and played on my guitar. Later on, I bought me one.

"Berry was popular when he came here. I been to Oklahoma with him and I been to places here in Kansas. People called Berry. We head out. We used to go to Great Bend some nights, rain, shine, sleet, or snow."

What kind of response did you get from the white audiences in Great Bend?

"Very good. It went very well. We played just what we playing now, blues and rhythm and blues. I played just about every joint here in town, and we always got good response. Somethin' about music is universal."

Now you're with the Regents?

"Right. I founded it. Ray Valentine named it. Ray worked with me about ten years or so. Berry stole him from me. Some time or another we all done play with one another through the years. They use to have jams at the Esquire out here on North Broadway. That's the way you meet a lot of musicians and get ideas and start playing together."

Even though you don't get paid at these jams?

"A lot of times we didn't. A lot of clubs acknowledge you, and a lot of them don't. They don't buy your drink. You run into some cold moments. The musicians have paid their dues, don't think they haven't. The very first night you get a crowd, the owner's attitude change, and go down there next week, he got somebody else in there. You sit there week after week and build the place up and then all of a sudden you out, just because he want to get somebody cheaper. He rather pay somebody else that didn't build the club.

"I've been let out for five dollars, after playing for a guy for a year. He says, 'I got guys in here every night lookin' for a job. I can get them, I don't need you.' Two months, the guy went out of business. Do you believe he had enough gall to ask us to come back down and play again? A lot of time we go. But I don't want to get on that."

How do you learn material, through charts or do you just pick it up by ear?

"I do both. I don't have the real good ear, but I can read a little bit. Billy Bruce drilled me into learning how to read."

Do you think the audience appreciates you?

"Some people show their appreciation, and then some don't. You likes when people acknowledge you."

What about church membership?

"I was a member of Elm Grove Baptist Church until I moved here. A time or two, I went to a couple of churches here, but I haven't been back in church since I left home."

What other bands did you work with before the Regents?

"I had a group years ago called the Impacts. And I had one called Times. These are groups of my own that I managed. We played basically the same thing, a little jazz every once in a while, rhythm and blues, and blues."

Was there ever a time in this town when you couldn't play blues?

"No. Right now, we're probably doing about 10 or 15 percent blues. We're doing a lot of rhythm and blues, which a lot of people call blues."

What about funk, do you get into that at all?

"A little bit, not a whole bunch. It all depends who we were playing for. If you're playing for a younger crowd, you probably get into more funk, but if you're playing for a more mature crowd, you tend to stick to rhythm and blues, and blues."

Who was one of the most popular bands in Wichita?

"Willie Wright had the most popular band that ever hit this town. The Smart [Brothers] Band was pretty popular. But Willie Wright, they played for a long time."

Have you given some thought to what the blues is?

"Yes. To tell you the truth, it's life. It's a feeling. It's an expression. It's all them things wrapped into one. That's all the blues is, and you have to play it as such."

You're not playing too much blues in this current band. Do the people in your group just want to move away from the blues?

"You might say that. I don't think you ever move completely away from the blues, because it's just too deeply rooted. You just get away from the basic down-home stuff. You change. You have a tendency to add different things. This is one reason I keep playing. I hate sittin' around and not doing anything. So I keep playing. Maybe somebody come along and get inspired by what I'm doing and take it to another level."

Do young musicians come up to you and ask you to teach them something?

"Yes, you get that all of the time, but sometimes they show up, and sometimes they don't."

You have a wide range of audience.

"Yeah, we been playing for a large range, older peoples and younger peoples, kind of mixed. Basically, we play for a mature crowd."

Did you ever work with Aunt Kat and Uncle Bob?

"Oh yes. All of the musicians in town have worked for Aunt Kat and Uncle Bob. They put a lot of time in working with the young musicians. They did a lot for us. I can't say anything negative about what they was doing."

What about rehearsals?

"We rehearse probably about once a week now. I'm on everybody about it all of the time. Because I think a person should be the best they can. I don't care how good you get, or how good you think you are, music is something you never quite accomplish. You always demand more out of yourself."

Did you ever work with a Hammond organ?

"I bought a Hammond organ, brand new, $6,000. That's how deep I was off into it. Couldn't play a lick. I just liked the sound and I wanted it in the band. I had a guy named Steve Williams play it, and Horace Gwynn. If you didn't have an organ in the group, you didn't hardly have a group."

How were things during the disco years?

"I'm one of the few bands that kept working clear all these years. Maybe you were called not as often."

Do you use a lead singer most of the time?

"I like vocalists. But there's times I have played without vocalists. One of the most popular bands I have played with, we didn't have a vocalist because nobody in the group could sing. But everybody played very well and we got by."

What's the wildest thing you ever had happen when you were playing?

"Somebody shot in a club on 9th Street. I don't know what it was called at that time. They teased me. We kicked the sound off [at the moment of the gunshot], my guitar went twang, they looked around and said I wasn't there but my guitar just going. They looked around and thought I was still there, when they heard the guitar hummin'. They say:

"'Henry, we going to go back and finish the gig?'

"Nope, we done; we finished.

"From then on, I stayed away from the rough clubs."

Who are the main influences in your music?

"I think George Benson is one of the most accomplished guitar players there is alive right now. Speaking of stars, I don't think I've seen any stars in Wichita. I seen Kenny Burrell in LA. He's good, he influenced me quite a bit.

"I went out with a friend of mine, Jerry Childers. We played together for about eight or nine months."

Did you have to join the union out there?

"No, I got by that. But if I'd got caught, I'd been in trouble. There ain't any union pressure back here."

Would you like to see a union in town?

"It might work. But only thing I see with organization, people don't work them to the maximum. We tried to organize a union right here years ago. It was around the sixties or seventies. We was going to do it locally and then plug into it nationally. But we couldn't even get it off the ground at a local level."

What did you hope to achieve?

"Get these club owners to let go of a little of it. My main thing is making all the musicians to play up to their potential. They just throw something together and go do a gig. But if they was playing up to their potential—we have some dynamite musicians around here. You wouldn't believe how good some of these guys are. I guess they're just not interested, maybe because they can get by and the crowd will accept it."

Is Wichita a good town for money as far as playing goes or is it break even pretty much?

"You might can break even. It's not a good town for money. I would say fifty to seventy-five dollars a man, about the most you going to get locally in clubs."

Did Wichita have its own style or was it influenced by Texas or Chicago or the West Coast?

"I would think it would come out of Chicago. And you got some Texas style blues."

Do you think Wichita is forming its own musical sound?

"It's a possibility that we could get a sound out of here, because there is enough good musicians around here to develop a sound. It would take more people interested in what they're doing, playing up to their potential, not only for themselves, but for the younger generation. The musicians here are just kind of lopin' along, influenced by Chicago and maybe Texas and just playing."

What kind of blues were you playing when you first started?

"I was just to trying to make any kind when I first started. Billy Bruce kind of steered me into the jazz field. I found a little more depth in jazz. It makes you think."

In Arkansas, did you hear music on farms, guys coming through with guitars, or was it on a Victrola?

"We had gentlemens played guitars 'round there from time to time. You'd pick up jazz, and a very good blues station coming out of Mississippi and New Orleans on the radio. John Lee Hooker was hot back when I was a kid."

Blues seems to be pretty popular these days.

"Yes, it is. It's really coming back and I think is more popular with the whites. That makes me feel great because I seen a time it seem like nobody was listening. If you a musician, you're going to enjoy playing, period. There was a time, I sit here two o'clock in the morning not knowing what time it is; didn't even care. I had to go to work the next morning, but I sit here and get off."

You don't use stage suits anymore, do you?

"We got one and we need more. Musicians should be doing something a little different from what his audience is doing. And another thing, I'm pleased to say, I got a dope-free group. I think I got one guy drinks beer."

Did you ever play with any people who would be drinking and let you down?

"Oh yes. Had a guy named Charlie Toran. He's from here. He's an older guy, playing ever since he was fifteen years old. He drank quite a bit. He was a good musician but once he start drinking, he might just pass out on the keyboard. You will find that most of your best musicians got some kind of problem. I've seen musicians who couldn't hold you a conversation, but they could play."

Would you recommend that a young person get into music these days?

"I wouldn't recommend it, unless they are really talented, because it takes a lot out of your life. I wouldn't recommend it to my boys. If they pick it up, fine. I got a son now want to go fishin'. I have no time to take them fishing.

"This is another reason I think where all the drinkin' and all the drugs come in at. You lose so much time and never get paid for it. Sometimes people lose families and never got paid. Just sittin' in there drinkin.'"

Henry Walker is still performing, occasionally with Lady Dee [Deanna Custard], at the Bootlegger's Ball in Wichita.

Chapter Six

FOLK ARTISTS IN THE 1950S

Harmonica Chuck, Albert Tucker

The rural blues was the type of blues most rarely performed among those interviewed. Largely ignored by those musicians and fans who are less concerned with tradition than social progress, this folk blues is, in one regard, the most appealing and worthy of study. It accentuates the rural roots of two Oklahomans who came to Kansas and who were unwilling to leave their past in a sophistication process. The simple charm of farm living, along with the demands of a slowly integrating Wichita, are expressed in this chapter.

HARMONICA CHUCK CHARLIE PHILLIPS (1935–1998)

Harmonica, guitar, vocal

"I was born in Morris, Oklahoma, in 1935. I had six brothers and five sisters. I was out on the farm, three miles east of Morris and a quarter mile south. It was about a forty-acre farm we stayed on but we farmed another forty, and then we had an eighty. We was pretty well filled up and occupied.

"When I first begged for my first hoe, my dad made me a little bitty hoe. I guess I was about six or seven years old. I couldn't hoe a whole row but I could be out there and cut a piece of grass down. I'd mess around there and it got where my dad would ask me:

"'Where's that hoe? Come on boy, let's go.'"

Are you the youngest family member and was your family supportive of your music?

"I'm the fourth from the bottom. All of them like it, brothers, sister, and all. I've got one brother, he blowed harmonica. He picked it up first. He got it sort of from my dad and other relatives. I picked it up from him. He supported me in harmonicas. If he didn't, I would caught myself stealing. I'd

95

ride two or three miles with him to get it out of the glove compartment. And then he would turn around and give it to me, and tell me, say, 'I brought it to you in the first place.'

"But harmonicas didn't last very long back then. I had to take the sides off of them to see what made the sound. They was mostly Old Standbys, and Marine Bands, M. Hohners. Cost about seventy-five cents; that was the good one. You could get them round about forty-five cents, twenty-five cents.

"My mother, she played piano, sung in the choir. My dad, he played piano and organ, guitar and blowed harmonica. It's in the family. We had a piano that stayed with us for a long time. I used to could play the piano. I couldn't even see the keys. I'd reach up there and push that top up.

"Mother would tell me, 'Charlie, get away from that piano. You're going to mash your fingers.' I just had to do it, till that top fall down on them fingers.

"'I told you.'

"She never gave me lessons. I just picked up on it from hearin' my brother and other guys blow. There were some Payne boys down there, Floyd and William, some brothers and cousins. All of them was talented. They could really eat a harmonica up. My brother, he was long around age and he took it up.

"You heard nothing but the blues—'Baby, Please Don't Go,' 'Black Gal,' and 'Long Legged Sally,' 'Caledonia.'"

Did you pick them up on radio or go to people's houses to listen to records?

"We had them old Victrolas, we had them records and stuff. It was wind up. We didn't know what electricity was." He laughs.

"I was about eighteen when I moved away from the farm. I started school at Long Tree. Then I removed from there and went to a little school called Wayside. It was off in the bottom. It's about six or seven miles. We had to walk three or four, five miles to school.

"I was off into school but I had one of them teachers that kind of broke my pride. I was very smart but she had her picks and choose. I'd get a whupping if I knowed my lesson; I'd get a whupping if I missed a word. She discouraged me a lot. She broke me down a lot. I was just that one out of the bunch. I don't know what it was. At the time, it seemed that Mother and Dad didn't do nothin' about it."

This was a segregated school?

"It was a one-room schoolhouse. Thirty-five, forty, fifty kids. I did pretty good when I first started. I don't know what really happened. Then too, we had to work a lot.

"My mother and daddy separated. My mother she was sickly. I had two brothers and a sister under me. They was too small to do anything. I got

Harmonica Chuck, photo by Arthur Kenyon.

me a job in taking care of them. I started to running a dairy, and plowing ever since I was about fourteen, fifteen years old. I was running the dairy, taking care of the farm, me and this old maid. I did the hiring and firing, picking cotton, chopping cotton.

"On a weekend, this old maid she would milk the cows maybe on a Sunday morning, and I'd come and milk them on a Sunday evening. Or if I wanted to go to town on Saturday evening, she would milk them that evening and I would come Sunday morning. We kept balancing. I really enjoyed it.

"When I went to town, I'd mostly get my mother and carry her to town to get food and chicken feed. I had an A-Model Ford. I traded a pig for an A-Model Ford. I plowed for a guy. I was really too little for that. I didn't have a tractor but I always stayed out there trying to do something. So, he just gave me the pig. Supposed to been the runt. She growed to be a pretty pig and had couple of a little pigs. I traded the pig to Mr. Ross Gassineux, a white guy who used to pump oil wells, for an A-Model Ford. I wasn't big enough to drive. He kept it until I was able to drive. I messed around and finally got my driver's license.

"I still stayed with my dad, help him out. He was still farming. We milked like sixty-five–seventy head of cattle. When my mother was going to move up here, I had my choice. I could have stayed down there. They was going to buy me a '49 Ford, no payments, place to stay, room and board, something like forty dollars a week, furnish me gas. But I just couldn't part from my mother, so I come on here.

"She came here because this was where all the other kids was at. All the kids chipped in a little. I just stuck with her. Finally got me a little job. I'm still on it." This was at a salvage yard.

Why did your brothers and sisters come up here?

"They came here for work. There wasn't any work back there at that time. My oldest brother came in '41 or '42. John came up here in '45. Then my sisters started coming.

"I didn't like Wichita at all. Kids wasn't doing things here like we was having fun there. Kids didn't have cars, which wasn't very many had cars down there. I was fortunate enough, and a few of my partners were fortunate enough. We always had some pie supper going on, or picnic or something or social going on at the schools and church."

What church did you go to?

"Well, I got a few things to tell you about that. Antioch Baptist Church. Now that's another place I found a hard time in. Me and kids growed up together and I joined the church. Every time they'd be having revivals, I'd go up to them. Always saying something about the family. I didn't give up on it. I kept going. Just seemed like the church people held me back from it. My mother was deep into it. All of us were religious.

"When I left Oklahoma, that's really what I wanted to be in, is the church. I tried to get into church here. I could go and carry my sisters to choir practice. The preacher would just cut the quiet and get on me because I didn't belong to the church.

"'You living in God's world. Wearing His clothes, eating up His food.'

"I was about eighteen. I'm getting invited now. I've got a tape I made up of that—I didn't make it up, it was a God-given thing. I made it once and somebody broke in the [904] Club and stole it. And then it kept beating on me to make another one. I'd set my tape up, every night when I'd get everybody out. And then I'd say, 'I'll do it tomorrow.'

"One night, I got everybody out, and I said I was going to do it tomorrow. That's when a voice came in the club: 'Do it now.'

"I thought somebody else was in there. I looked and when I got back behind the bar, He said: 'I said do it now.'

"I reached over and punched a button and started talking. And just like He turned me on, that's the way He shut me off. I've got it here. I'd like for you to hear it. It's really the foundation of my deal. But like I say, just like the music. Everything Charlie try to do, somebody put their foot on it. They like it, but then they smother me. I just have to bulldoze and go on. I don't have confidence but somehow or other I get the job done."

Is this tape about your difficulty with religion?

"No. From a child. Otherwise what it's saying is: you can't really play a little baby cheap. Because I wasn't played cheap. My mother and them didn't know. A lot of other people didn't know. But see, I was looking way, way north ever since I was a little bitty kid. You got a minute?"

We listen to the tape. . . .

"The only hobby, well like different other things that I can do? I can do carpentry."

He has lived in his home for twenty-five years.

"It's four lots. I mow it myself."

Do the neighborhood kids want to mow it?

"Man, they drive me crazy. They all—just anything they just want to help. If it ain't nothing but pick up the leaves. They so many of them. 'We won't charge you nothin'. We'll do it for nothin'.'

"They got them a sack. They'll get them a sack." He laughs. "I got some sweet kids over here."

You know everyone in the neighborhood?

"We don't visit a whole lot, but, we're all neighbors and know each other. I ain't a big visitor, but I'm going to look out there and see how you doing. I'll walk out and we'll have a conversation. Stand out there in the street or go over in their yard and talk. They come over here and talk. We all get along good."

A neighbor lady just came over and borrowed some aluminum foil. What was her name?

"Well, she ain't been too long moved over there. I know her other family, you know the older people. Very few of them don't know me. Just so many I can't remember all of them."

When you came to Wichita, how did you get friends?

"I started out with the older group, like guys that work on the job with me. I'd go out with them. I never have been too tight with the younger generation, going out partying and doing stuff like that. Older people just took me under their arms. Then I had older brothers. We hung out together."

How about the music? Did you bring that up here with you?

"I had a harmonica. You didn't find kids around playing music like we did in Oklahoma. We'd take rub boards, gallon buckets, wash tubs, sticks. We'd make some music, a lot of spirituals. We would sing. I used to could sing pretty good spirituals. I never did really think I could sing the blues.

"If you've ever been down. Those women can make you sing the blues. And actually, the blues, that's just the same thing as religion. You know, you go to church to empty your sorrow and pray. And I take the blues, pray, and talk to my Man. There's not a minute when I leave Him out. When I go to bed, I'm taking to him. Sitting up here talking to you, I'm talking to him. I'm out there on my job, I'm talking to Him. I just never leave Him out of my like. He has done some wonderful things for me and He has whupped me. He's stubborn. He'll put the hurt on you. You don't talk back to Him, either.

"In that room right there, I begged Him to take me one night. That was with a stomach ache. I was hurting so bad. I couldn't even call my wife in this room to call the ambulance. I couldn't call my daughter in that other room to call the ambulance. Every time I opened my mouth, He'd tell me to shut up. He finally let up off me a little bit. I came in here and got a bottle of Maalox that I just had bought. Normally it has the seal on it, but that one didn't. I took me a swallow. If I had to open it, I never would have got it open. But I still couldn't say nothing to my wife.

"When I got back to the side of the bed, I got back in that joker and I kept talking to him, and He put me to sleep. When I woke up, I mean I had *been* there. I felt just like a fresh born baby. I don't really knows how a fresh born baby feels, but anyway I was scared to move a limb. So, I asked Him: is this the way you feel when you are dead?

"I said, well, let me get up and see if I can go to the bathroom. I got up and went to the bathroom and came back and set on the side of the bed. Man, it's just like I ain't never had a pain in my life. I told Him I'm going to lay back down. Because I couldn't believe it. After I seen I was really alive, you know what I asked him?

"I don't want you to hurt me like you hurt me before. But could you just semi-get me back up there and let me see again. And I laid flat on my back and I was right back up there.

"It's nice up there. They spent all that money trying to find out in all those years and it don't take but a few seconds to find out what it's like. I've experienced a lot of things and you can't talk to people about it, because they think you're crazy.

"But anyway, when I came here and met my first wife, I was blowin' harmonica a little bit. Just mostly around the house. Me and my brother

John, we would set up and blow and play around. Then after I got married, my wife, she didn't like it. I'd be blowin' down there on the job. The boss man came out and told me say:

"'Charlie, your work is good but your singing got to go.'

"Well, that hurt my feelings. That's when I stopped through town and bought me another harmonica. I started to learn to blow all over again which I just about had forgot. After I got to doing that, then I went to getting back pretty good. Then I was messing up the TV. So I'd go into the bedroom, then it was time she wanted to go to bed. Then I'd go into the bathroom. It sounded better in the bathroom anyway. Then she wanted to go to the bathroom." He laughs.

"Then finally after I met a lot of friends, I started blowing at house parties. Then I went to the Sportsman down on 9th Street and got on the stage. This was the first time I ever got on the stage and blowed through a mike or anything. This was about '55, '56. When I walked off the bandstand, I had thirteen one-dollar bills in my pocket.

"Shoot, make money like that, I'm going to keep on blowin' this joker. I blowed for five years and never made another dime.

"Then I started building my courage up. I'd take my harp and go to white clubs. Some of them I'd get in, some of them I wouldn't. I didn't really want to go in noways. Well, I went back to my childhood in Oklahoma when you wasn't allowed in the cafes down there. See, me being little, this is a strategy I would use.

"'They can't hurt a kid, because a kid don't know.'

"So, I played like I didn't know no better. My dad came and get me, I was sitting up there eating a hamburger." He laughs.

"This is the way I got into a lot of the white clubs. I used to play down on 37th off of Broadway. I used to go east on Central. I can't think of the name of the club. There was a bunch of clubs. Some of them I got in and some of them I didn't.

"Finally, I was making money then. I'd hit one or two clubs and there was a lot of half dollars and quarters. People would throw money out on the floor. I never was no good at pickin' up change. Some of the women, some of the men would get up and help me pick it up. I walk out of there with six or seven dollars and that was big money then. I'd go on to another, and by the time I make it home, I got me twenty dollars in my pocket and I was only making a dollar an hour on the job.

"I was mostly just blowin' harmonica. I didn't know but two songs, or three. And they was all about the same song. But I'd blow it fast, then I'd blow it slow, then I'd bring it back to moderate. About that time, I was ready to get out of there.

"Then I got hooked up at the [N.] 37th Street Inn. The lady that owned the club was Big Angel. It was a white club. She always sung that song, 'Hot Nuts.' She had to sing it every night. So, I started to working five nights a week out there with [a white band] Jim Swillney, Roger Balterman, and Tommy, and I forget the rest. They played rock 'n' roll, piano, guitar, drums, and sax. I don't remember what they called themselves. That's where we started the Sunday evening jam sessions. We'd show up and start and then the other talent would come in. Once we'd get the show going, we was gone but we still got paid.

"That's where I come up with the idea when I had my club for the Sunday jam sessions. This was about '58 or '59."

This was when you were playing at the Sportsman?

"This is what it was. That's why I was out there. They wouldn't let me play with them at the Sportsman. They might let me play and they might not. That's when I branched off by myself. That's during the time when this scout was out for talent. And I had a chance to go to Hollywood then.

"I'm pretty sure he's got tapes of me and everything. Like he told me, say, 'You ain't got no business down there in that junk yard. You've got too much talent.'

"I tried to show him to the place to where I couldn't touch Little Walter, Muddy Waters, and them. And like he said, 'There ain't no two people the same. Where they get on the bandstand and show you something, you get up and show them something.' But see I was just young. I had three kids and I didn't want to leave them."

Did he want you to go out West?

"Oh, yeah. He told me my family would have been well taken care of and he would send me to school. He would want me to record. And something like at the time I would have got 2 percent. That was back then. He even came to the house and asked me four times. He said, 'It'll be a long time before you see me again.' And I ain't seen him since. I've seen people who looked like him.

"I was out [in California] for a while. I'm the first guy who got little Don [Dunn] a job playing out there. Henry Walker, I got him out there. He used to travel the road with me.

"After the band started breaking up, Tommy and them, then it come to country and western. I blowed some of that for a while."

Was the 37th Inn crowd white?

"It was all white. It wasn't but two blacks out there, the bartender and me."

You were accepted in some clubs.

"Most clubs I didn't get in, because I hadn't never been in them before. After I met the white musicians and then they'd be playing somewhere and

I'd go and maybe I'd get turned around at the door; but if one of them seen me before I got to my car, I was brought back in there."

When did you start playing the guitar?

"That was in the seventies. Actually, the way guitar came along, I never could make a third [chord] change. I always said if I ever made a third change, then I would play it. One night my guitar player didn't show up, but his guitar was there. I picked it up and I played. I had a house full of people. And I played that joker that night, played everything they normally played.

"Next day I couldn't hit a note on it. And then it happened again. I picked it up and played and then couldn't hit a note. After I finally learned the third change, that's when I decided I got to sing. I started to learn how to sing with the guitar and the harmonica. I got me some tape and taped the harmonica on the microphone and that's how I came by all that."

You had a drum machine at one time, didn't you? You were a one-man band operation.

"I could hold a conversation but the only thing I couldn't do was go into my pocket and make change [for a waiter] for a twenty-dollar bill and don't miss a beat."

What kind of blues were people listening to around this time, '58–'60?

"They were listening to Muddy Waters, Slim Harpo, Bobby Bland, B.B. Back at that time, they was coming through at the Mambo [Club], they used to call it. James Brown, Hank Ballard and the Midnighters, the Coasters, all of them used to be out there. There was a dance at least two or three times a month."

So you got to see Muddy Waters. Was he an inspiration to you? When I came in to do the tape tonight, you were listening to him.

"I used to blow a lot of his songs. When I started my own band, I met a guy by the name of Johnel [Nero]. We made a electric guitar out of a box [acoustic guitar] just like that one on the wall. I had an amplifier. We started auditioning over the telephone. We'd call ourselves the Noisemakers."

You'd call a club up and put the phone down and play. Was that pretty effective?

"Sure it was effective. We made more money then—fifteen dollars a man."

What is the blues to you?

"Blues to me, it's a relaxation. Otherwise, blues is something you can sing, or play, or listen to, and that'll take your mind off a whole lot of other evil things. Otherwise, blues can keep you out of the penitentiary. Blues can keep you from hurting somebody. You can sing one of them or take an old raggedy guitar with a key out of it, and you take all the spite out on that. When it gets through whupping you, then your mind is all ready to relax some way else. That's why I play the blues. If I feel upset about something, or feel down and out, I reach and get my harmonica, guitar. When I get through, I feel good."

What about the act of performance?

"Well, I really feels it, when I get up there. It's something that just comes out of me. I might get up there and can't even think of a song when I first go to the stage. Once I get there, it just explodes. It's like I used to tell my mother. I'd say, 'Mama, I'm shy.'

"'Oh, Charlie, you ain't ashamed of nothin'.'

"'Yes I is, Mama. People think I'm really working and the sweat be runnin' off of me. I be nervous. Half the time I don't know whether to say this or say that, or don't know whether they like the song or not.'

"She said, 'Charlie, just open your mouth and whatever come out of it, let it come.'

"You know, I started doing that and it's so much easier."

Was she pleased that you were playing music?

"She was really proud of me. She was 100 percent behind me. But one thing she always told me: 'Charlie, you could blow it in church too just like you blow it out there.' A lot of deacons want me to blow in church. But that little tickly-tickly is still there. I can do it. One day, one day I'm going to surprise them."

Let's talk about the Cavaliers.

"After we got my brother with us, we got a set of drums. Then we got two amps and we named ourselves Harmonica Chuck and the Cavaliers."

How did you get the name Harmonica Chuck?

"I picked that name. There was only in my hometown, one guy who called me Chuck. His name was Chuck Magnut. He was an older guy. One day he asked me my name.

"'Charlie.'

"'I don't like that name.'

"'How come you don't like it?'

"'Because my name is Charlie. I'm going to call you Chuck.'

"That's what he always called me until I came to Wichita.

"My dad-in-law, when I started dating his daughter, he asked me what was my name. I told him Charlie.

"'Oh, I don't like that name.'

"'How come you don't like that name?'

'My name is Tollie,' Tollie say.

"'I'm going to call you Chuck.'

"Then when I got to blowing harmonica, I named myself Harmonica Chuck."

Has that name helped your career?

"Oh yeah. People don't even know my real name. You can hear that, I don't care where you go, the first thing they going to holler, I can be driving down the street or they see me: 'Hey Chuck, Ol' Harmonica Chuck!'

"When I go to Denver and all them places. 'There's old Chuck, Harmonica Chuck. He's *still* blowing that harmonica.'

"Actually now, I brags about it because there ain't now another in the world. Then I brags about the 904 [Club], because there ain't another in the world. There's a 409."

When did you decide to go into the bar business?

"In 1962. I played for this Mexican guy on 15th Street. It was a [beer] tavern. He had about a month to go before he could switch it over to a club. I just had came in off the road. The lady, my booking agent, Aunt Kat, what she would do, she would rent the instruments, and she'd take out for the instruments. Nights she wouldn't have stuff for us to do, we would pick little jobs around here.

"After, Joe Garzelas—I think we charged him $85. It was me, Earl, Johnel, and Jerry Burns. We borrowed Aunt Kat's organ and stuff. Then we got paid, she wanted the pay for using the instruments, plus half what we made. I told her, Aunt Kat, I'll just hang it up. I got a place to play here.

"And we broke it down to just three instruments. Me, Johnel and Earl; we had our instruments. I played two years for Joe Garzelas. He sold the club to Gene Mickey, a white guy. At the time, Gene wanted us to play for him, but we was playing at the Starlight. Johnel Nero, my brother Earl on drums, and Hollis Pridgett on guitar. We played there one Christmas and we went in and played for the door. They wouldn't pay us what we wanted but we knew at that time that we'd pack a house. All it took is two weeks, and shoot, you couldn't fan flies. We built a crowd up there and we run nearly two hundred dollars on the door.

"On New Years Eve, me and my wife, we called different clubs and found out what they were charging. We didn't have to charge that. All they wanted us to do was pack the house. We dropped fifty cents under what the other clubs were charging. We packed that joker. New Year's Eve we went down there to play and we had to pay to go in there and get our instruments. Berry [Harris] and them had done took over. So, we partied that night. Then we went on back on 15th Street and played for Gene Mickey and pulled a crowd back there.

"Gene told me, say, 'You need this club.'

"I said, 'Oh man, I don't want no club.'

"Say, 'You really need it.'

"All I did was took over the lease. He left his furniture and everything. It just so happened I saved up a little money. I could buy my license. I didn't know nothing about running a club, but I knew how one should been run. I seen how other people, traveling around, did to customers, seen how they treated them. I told a few of them, one of these days, I'm going to get me a club and I'm going to show you all how to run that joker. All of a sudden it fell to me. I sewed up things around here. Stayed there twenty-two years."

But you had to move from 15th and Mosley to 9th Street.

"Urban renewal come through and bought all that out. It was a club. You couldn't sell liquor by the drink but you could bring your bottle in and put your name on it. I couldn't sell beer, but you could bring your beer and I could cool it for you and put your name on it. You had to put somebody's initial on every can."

How did you make money?

"There's always a way." He laughs. "The law just passed after I got on 9th Street where you could serve liquor by the drink [1986]. It wasn't as big as the place on 15th."

When Chuck got his own club, he found that the blues band's popularity led to difficulties. "I used to have people out of Ponca City, Hutchinson, Salina. I drawed a crowd: Mexicans, white, Black. I was mixing the crowd and people was getting along but the city of Wichita didn't go along with that. The police used to give people [traffic] tickets on the way into the club and on the way out."

Tell me about traveling around when Aunt Kat and Uncle Bob booked you.

"Yeah. We did that about six or seven years. We used to play in Junction City, Salina, Great Bend, Emporia, Lyons, and most of all them. Our main deal was in Junction City. Harmonica Chuck had to be there every weekend. We'd play at Fort Riley and do an early show and then come back and it would be jam-packed. Nobody but me and Earl, Johnel, and Henry Walker.

"We was doing 'Sweet Home Chicago,' 'Honky Tonk,' 'Green Onions,' a lot of Junior Parker, Little Walter, Slim Harpo, Johnny Lee Hooker. That was what was selling. You know, it got tough for me here in this town. Before I left here and hit the road, I'd tear a joint up. I'd start a fight. That's what a lot of people would say. 'Well, Chuck is all right but he make people tear up the place.' Now we could get off out on the road and people could handle it. But people in this town, something about it, they just couldn't handle the blues."

Because you were so strong?

"Yeah, strong. When I came back here off the road and started playing for Joe Garzelas, I broke my talent down so people would act right. When I got in business, then I had to break it down to a level. Once in a while, I could reach out there and really be myself."

You didn't want to wreck your place.

"I didn't want to wreck nobody else's place. And I been trying to this day, to come back to myself. I'm almost, but I'm not really there yet."

Aunt Kat and Uncle Bob treat you all right? Did you get enough money?

He laughs. "You ain't never get enough money, but I got my share when I stood up and argued with them. They fired me one time and they got another harmonica and guitar player. They carried him to Junction City and they was going to use Harmonica Chuck's name. They ended up giving all of the money back and there still was a fight. They told me, 'I don't have to beg you. I got a guy who blows harmonica better than you anyway.' She got up there and found out it wasn't all like that."

What is the main style of blues in Wichita?

"You take Willie Wright and them when they was playing—Charles Walker, Little Don [Dunn], Herbie, I'll put Berry in there. He's good anyway. Little Don, that joker back in his day, he was a cold, cold little man. And Herbie used to be a bad boy too. I can't think of Herbie's name [Welch?]. He's got some fingers off. There used to be some pretty hot bands around."

Did you ever think of where the influence came from?

"It was mostly just the down-south blues. That's where they really was coming from. Alonzo Mills and them, they played. I blowed with them. They blowed more brass, more jazz. I don't think Wichita is too much for jazz. When disco came out—that ruined a whole lot of things for talent. I tried it in the club. 'We didn't come down here to hear that stuff. We come down here to hear you.'"

Were you on your own then, or did you have a sideman?

"I had a bass, and second guitar. Mostly just me and Jerry. When Erick Robinson [see following interview] busted my new set of drums, that's when I got my automatic drummer and I carried it back."

What type of set-up did you have as a single?

"I had three amps. I went through all three of the amps and went through the juice box. It had speakers. You pull up outside, you thought it was a whole band in there. There wasn't nobody up there but me. This was in the late seventies and early eighties."

He talks about a performance circa 1991 at the Coyote Club in Wichita, put together by Wes Race.

"I played the session with—I can't think of this guy's name. He was from Arkansas. They had this white kid on violin. That son of a gun—you talk about burning that violin up. And that was sweet, because him and the harmonica went together good. People say: 'Chuck, you worked with them like you've been working with them a long time.' Like I say, it was mostly my kind of music and my style. Most of the songs they played, me and Johnel used to do."

Over the years at his club, Chuck gave many of Wichita's younger blues musicians their start. "They started off with the blues. They might have gone to something else, but they played the blues at the 904. What I'm proud of, I could talk to the public. I don't have no scars or bruises, and I didn't put any on anybody."

Does anybody in Wichita have the style you play?

"Not really. Some of them do them but they ain't got my style."

Anything you'd like to close with?

"I really have enjoyed this evening. And I'm really glad I'm about to become a member of KMUW [WSU radio station. Chuck misspoke; he meant the museum exhibit]. I'm real proud of you all and hope you all are as proud of me. I appreciate you taking up enough time with me. Only thing I can say is: I love you all, nationwide."

HARMONICA CHUCK WITH ERICK ROBINSON [1946–2009]

This interview took place in January 1997, during a Wichita State University anthropology class. At the time, Robinson and the author were playing in Harmonica Chuck and His Wildcats, part of the Kansas State Historical Society's Master Artist Program. Chuck was the Master Artist.

Question: Erick, you are currently with the Pentonics. What was your first group?

Erick Robinson: The first group I had was with Virgil Anderson and T. J. Demsey and it was called Erick's Men.

Q: You were the leader? That's why they called it Erick's Men?

ER: Yes. That's when I first started drumming.

Q: When did Chuck show up?

ER: He was later on down the line. We knew of Chuck because we played for a booking agency, Kat and Bob Smith. They would book us out at different places. T. J. and Virgil and I played in the north end section, mostly house parties. And we visited the 904 Club that Chuck owned.

Q: Did you have drums set up on stage, Chuck?

Harmonica Chuck: Yeah.

Q: Could anybody come in and drum, or did you have to hear them first?

HC: Well, anybody that could hold the beat could drum.

ER: Drummers was hard to find [*laughs*].

HC: A good one was.

Q: You came from Oklahoma, didn't you?

ER: Yeah, Pawhuska. And my family moved here to the Planeview area back in the forties. I was born in '46. Then we moved back to Pawhuska, and back here to Wichita. There was good employment opportunity. My grandfather worked on a job for construction, and they were buildin' McConnell Air Force Base. And most of those apartments out there in Planeview were built for McConnell people in the first place. Then they decided to let the public move in, and the workers. My grandfather was one of the workers and that's how we got out there on Roseberry Court.

Q: How many people were in the family?

ER: It was just my grandmother and grandfather, and I lived with them.

Q: Did you have a good schooling?

ER: Oh yeah. Will Rogers School was the first one I went to in Wichita. And then a place called Planeview Inn, out there on Roseberry, that's where I got my blues experience. I went in with my grandfather. During that time, the kids could go in with their parents.

Q: Chuck, did you ever go there?

HC: A few times [*laughs*]. I never played there. I hadn't started playing yet.

ER: They just had groups off and on, mostly a lot of guys like Hank Johnson—we called him Uncle Fiddler. He played on violin. Then they had another guy, Lonnie, he played banjo.

Q: That's old time. Where did Lonnie come from?

ER: Some of them were from Pawhuska. Uncle Fiddler was from down there. He played a violin at a young age and he was terrific. Boy, he could really play. And we'd set up on Roseberry out on the porch and everybody would get together and they'd sing and play the violin and play old tunes.

Q: What kind of old tunes?

ER: I imagine you never heard of it, called "Fanny Royal" [*laughs*]. One of these days I'll sing it for you.

Q: Was it like a country dance?

ER: Yeah, it was like a country swing dance. And they had several other songs that they sung then and one of them was "If You Don't Know, You Don't Know, You Just Don't Know." Well, the culture changed. I liked a lot of blues and my uncle had a set of drums. That's the first time I set up behind a set of drums playing. When he went in the service, he took his drums with him, or sold them or something and so I never played anymore after that. I used to enjoy just sittin' around and bangin' on them, actually.

Q: What year did you get your own set of drums?

ER: About '55 or '56. My grandmother bought them out of Montgomery Ward. You had to mail order. I think they cost ninety-nine dollars and they gave you a little bitty cymbal with it. She wanted me to play drums.

Q: Did you drive them crazy with practicing?

ER: Yeah, well, half the time they'd take them and lock them up in the closet and send me outdoors. It was kind of hectic.

Q: You must have had some talent, or they wouldn't have encouraged you.

ER: I used to do a lot of singing. We went to church all the time, and we sang in different choirs.

Q: Where was this?

ER: During that time, it was at Reverend Stanley's Baptist Church on North Water. During that time, the church was a red brick building by the jailhouse.

Q: Was it in the basement?

ER: Oh, that was the other church they had to go downstairs in the basement. I used to hate going down there. Every time you go to church, you figure you got to go down in the ground [*laughs*]. There weren't no windows and you couldn't see nothing. But Reverend Stanley's had a young choir and I participated in quite a bit of it.

Q: Did they have organ music or piano?

ER: Mostly organ. We started out with piano a long time ago and then they eventually got an organ. Organ would sound better anyway. I think they played a Hammond B-3.

Q: When did you start playing professionally?

ER: I got with Virgil Anderson and then I started with T. J. Demsey and we started playing a lot of parties.

Q: How old were you then?

ER: In my twenties. After that, I decided I wanted a group of my own and I went off and put together a group called Daniel and the Lions. And I worked with them for quite a bit. We played the Sheik's Tent, Hobbledehoy, Fun A Go-Go. The Fun A Go-Go was on South Broadway, on the east side, farther down from the Sheik's Tent. It was out by the T-Bone on 47th South.

Q: What kind of music did you play?

ER: We played a little bit of it all; a lot of rock 'n' roll. The only time we played blues was when we go down and hear Chuck. I'd take the band down there and play.

Q: Describe a typical evening in the 904.

ER: It'd be a lot of experience because Danny Smith wasn't too familiar with blues. We wanted to learn, so we went to the best place to learn. Chuck had the club and it was strictly blues. Anybody wanted to hear blues would go down to Chuck's.

Q: Was Harmonica Chuck playing with the Cavaliers?

ER: He didn't have the Cavaliers then. He had the Noisemakers. Let me tell you, one night I went down there and I took Danny with me. Chuck had an automatic drummer. I never will forget that.

Q: You don't like those, do you?

ER: Oh man, I hate them with a passion. It was going tic-d-tic-d-tic. And so Danny said, "What you going to do?" And I said, I'm going to fire this drummer. And he said, "The drummer?" And I said, yeah, this box he's got. So that weekend I came back and fired it and he hired me [*laughs*].

Q: Did you start playing at the 904 on weekends?

ER: Oh yeah. A lot of times I would come in and play, even though I had a group. I would always go back and play with Chuck. We kind of had a bond. It was kind of hard to describe. There was times when it was nobody but me and Chuck and we kept a packed house.

Q: You are both from Oklahoma. Do you find you may have had the same experiences in growing up there and migrating to Kansas?

ER: Oh, not necessarily because you come from Oklahoma. That's what people don't understand. You don't have to come from Oklahoma to feel the blues.

Q: There is a strong presence in Wichita of people from Oklahoma. Do you ever wonder why that is?

ER: Because the culture, the lifestyle down there is just different. When we look back at it now, we don't think it was really hard. But then we felt it was hard. Times was really rough. And blues came in specifically because it was something to ease the pressure. Like sometimes you had blues when you was sad. You played blues when you're happy. You lose your girlfriend, you play some blues. When you win her back from the fellow you lost her to, you play blues again. So, I think blues is just according to how you feel at the time. Everybody loves to play blues. I can play blues and be just as happy as I want to be and never think anything about it.

THE 904 CLUB

Q: How many people could fit into the 904 Club?

ER: The fire capacity wasn't that much and—

Q: The club didn't pay any attention to that, did it?

ER: Well, we never did bother with it. Oh man, it would get so crowded in there, and so much smoke, we'd have to open the front door to let it out the back! And there would be people going in and out like they was changing trains! It was just a riot, but we had some really nice times down there. And that way you would meet all kind of musicians you ever wanted to meet. That was the biggest thing. All the musicians knew about the 904 Club, because there's nothing like a home base. See, we didn't have no curfew for a long time. We'd come off of Murdock playing at different joints there, come down to 904, go back to Murdock, or out on the west side, and we played down on the north end. They had a big place called Big Mama's, out there by the Copa Ballroom and the old Flagler Garden Club. I used to live out there. Just about every time you turn around, you had little after-hours houses out there. People had lived there for years and them old houses kind of got shaky and the city finally decided they wanted to condemn them. Pay them off and let them move. They did the right thing. Those buildings were about to fall in on them. Man, the place we played in, you could get to jumping on the floor, and the whole building would start shaking [*laughs*]. I'm telling you, it was a riot.

Q: How late did you stay open, Chuck, at the 904 Club in the 1960s?

HC: We used to just stay open all night long. Things didn't get good until round about two-thirty or three o'clock in the morning. Through the week-nights, I'd open around seven or eight, somewhere like that. We had about four sets of people, different crowds. One crowd would come in around nine o'clock and stay 'til around ten-thirty or eleven, then break out to other places to get into. Then about eleven-thirty, it would fill up again. By one o'clock it would get empty; then about one-thirty it would fill up again and then you had them 'til about three or four in the morning.

Q: Did you collect a cover charge?

HC: Yeah, we used to run a cover charge. It wasn't but a quarter or fifty cents. Finally, I took the cover charge off the door and just let people come in free. And there was the same money. What I was collecting on the door, they was spending across the bar.

Q: How long did you have the 904 Club?

HC: I started playing there in '62, and I took it over in '64, and then I went to '85. When the guy first opened the place, I think I booked in there for ninety-five dollars and he made, I think, about five dollars on the door. So then I come to an agreement with him. I would play for the door and it was about a week or two, and you couldn't get in there. So then, I made like I wanted to quit.

ER: He wanted the door back, that's what it was. He wanted the door back [*laughs*].

HC: I didn't want him to pay me, because he wasn't going to pay as well as what we were making through the door. So, he took the back door off the deal [let people in free from the back] and then after we got it packed, people could come in and buy. So, I took a vacation and he hired Erick and T.J. When I came back, he fired them and hired me back, but he put the back door back on. That's when it was on Mosley [and 15th].

Q: The club's address was 904 E. 15th, before you moved to 9th, a little east of Grove. What kind of blues was at the club then, city blues or country blues?

ER: It was kind of a variety. T. J. and Virgil and I played low-down blues: Jimmy Reed, Howlin' Wolf, Jimmy Witherspoon. After we got with Chuck, Chuck played Jimmy Reed and Sonny Boy [Williamson] and stuff so it just spinned out. It wasn't country blues; some of it was kind of rocking blues. We just played it the way we felt it.

Q: How did you get your material, listen to records? There were no blues shows on Wichita radio then, were there?

ER: No. I learned my blues mostly from old-timers, the way they were singing and playing. And we used to have a lot of 78 blues records my grandfather kept.

HC: In Oklahoma, you could hear a lot of blues on the radio.

ER: You could get Stan's Record Shop and acquire really new stuff, because you could order blues records from the radio.

Q: You could hear them from Wichita late at night?

ER: Yeah, they came on about twelve-thirty or one o'clock every night. I think that's where they had Wolfman Jack. He played a lot of blues.

Q: You were still playing with Daniel and the Lions?

ER: Yeah. Then I ran into Jeff Husson. I had a cousin and I taught him how to drum, so I gave him Daniel and the Lions, and I went off with Jeff Husson and started playing. That's when I went to the Caravan Club. Jeff was from England.[1] He could play guitar. I learned a lot from him. I had a group then, Ronnie Ford, Big Jim Taylor on tenor or alto sax. We all played progressive jazz at the Latin Club. Ruth Searcy used to play with us and so did Iris Dean. They were pianists.

Q: Are they still around?

ER: No, I don't think I've seen the two anymore.

Q: Were you playing jazz or blues?

ER: Well, I like a little bit of it all. That's the only way at that time you could keep a job. I'd go with Chuck and play blues; I could go with Eddie

Taylor and Berry Harris and play a little rock 'n' roll, and a little of this and that. I had to be able to drum it all.

Q: Did drums hold up pretty well for you with all this playing? How often did you break a head?

[Laughter from ER and HC]

ER: I'll tell you something about that. I taught myself how to drum. I had a tendency—I'd get excited. I'd go two minutes on one side and it would break. So I'd turn it over and use the other side. I used to get so mad I couldn't control it. And I couldn't keep my drumsticks [from breaking]. At that time, they had to go out there and just chop me a piece of wood off something. Chuck went down to Jenkins Music Company to Chuck Blackham, the drum teacher. He say, "Chuck, tell you what you do. You take these metal drumsticks. You can't break them." So, Chuck come back with these drumsticks and say, "I think I can solve one problem." I said, well, all right. I tried them that night. We took intermission and I said, I got to have a little help here. They asked me "Where are your drumsticks?" I said, I left them up there on the bandstand, they're all tore up. I just sheared them off in half.

HC: Now he could take some wire, bailing wire, and them jokers would last a long time [*laughs*].

ER: Oh yeah, I can wire them up, unless they break up first. I went through so many foot pedals, man I'll tell you.

Q: I notice these days you use bungee cords to tie your drums to your stool.

ER: I have to. My drums have jumped all the way across the bandstand. I learned how to tie them up. It was about the time when I bought a new set, and we were at the 904 Club. I had put little old Christmas blinkers in my drums. Chuck says "Man, I have never seen nothin' like this." Everybody came out and seen these drums. One night, I got to playing so hard one of the bolts got loose and went up against the head. Then I had heads burnin' all out of the drums. I took the lights out of there.

Q: How much did you work with Aunt Kat and Uncle Bob?

ER: Oh, I worked with them quite a bit. Every time I turned around, they wanted to send me with a group. I went with Berry and them; I went with Franklin Mitchell; and sometimes with Chuck Wilkinson. We played roller rinks and different parks. I went to Junction City and Medicine Lodge.

Q: Were Aunt Kat and Uncle Bob fair to you?

ER: Oh yeah. They'd always keep you working, even though sometimes I had trouble with that money part. They tell you, "Hey, I'm going to pay you this, and you hush and don't tell the rest of them." It makes you shady.

Ruth Searcy with unidentified man, the L. K. Hughes Photograph Collection, Kenneth Spencer Research Library, University of Kansas Libraries, Lawrence, Kansas.

How many times have they done that on you? Overall average, it was all right. They had a club house over on Main Street. It didn't last too long. It was a place to practice. Right after that, I started the Musicians' Clubhouse on 13th and Hydraulic, a little behind there.

Q: So you were in on that with Don Dunn?

ER: Yeah. As long as I was there, two or three years, I didn't buy no cabaret license. Only thing I had was a chart and I had all the musicians around Wichita sign it. And then Bobby Stout [Wichita vice captain; Jerry Hahn Brotherhood had a song about him] told us as long as we participate with nobody but our musicians on that list, we were all right. Chuck would get through with the 904 and then come down there where I was, all night long.

Q: The police didn't bother you?

ER: They'd come in and talk to me and then leave. I kept it pretty quiet and didn't have any problems. But afterwards Don got a little greedy, so I decided to quit.

Q: What kind of music did you play there, live or recorded?

ER: We had musical instruments in there. Basically, everybody come and sat in and just played.

Q: Chuck, did you actually feel like getting out and playing after you closed the 904 Club for the night?

HC: Oh yeah. Shoot, I didn't even know what time was then.

ER: That's the time to party. We used to get through at the 904 and try to go find someplace to eat and party all night.

Q: Did you have many dealings with the Esquire Club?

ER: Sure. That's where the Smart Brothers played. When Smarts would have to play a gig out of town, I took my band out there. It was pretty nice.

Q: Were you ever in the Cavaliers?

ER: No, because Chuck had the Cavaliers way before then.

HC: That was way back when I first started. Me and my brother and Johnel, when we was traveling to Junction City, we was the Cavaliers.

Q: Which city in Kansas gave you the best reception, Chuck? And you too, Erick?

HC: Junction City was the best I got. I didn't miss a weekend in Junction City for about eight or nine years.

ER: Mine was in Dodge City. I used to take Miss Blues [Remona Hicks] out there. Her and Aunt Kat was related.

Q: Did you ever leave Wichita and try to get out there and do something?

ER: Oh yeah, I been different places: Tulsa, Oklahoma City. I went up in St. Joe, Missouri, and stayed up there. I sat in with a few groups. I knew some people up there. I had a job automatically when I got up there. I worked for a guy who owned two banks in Atchinson, Kansas, just mostly around his house and yard. They had a place in St. Joe called Bonkers, and they would let me sit in because I was from out of town. I did a lot of singin' up there but not too much drumming. They had another place, the Stardust or the Starlight. We played there several times. They played blues and a little rhythm and blues.

Q: What's the difference in drumming rhythm and blues, and blues?

ER: It's in the pattern and the tempo. I don't know how to describe it. R&B is kind of an up pitch. It keeps you alert. Rhythm is constantly changing. The blues give you a certain basic change. You got to have a lot of force behind it. That's why I tear up drum pedals and heads.

Q: Who are some of the good blues drummers you listen to?

ER: When I was comin' up, I would hear a lot of drummers play differently. After I had taught myself, my whole attitude changed. I didn't feel like I liked any drummers. I just stayed with my pattern. I would hear the music and would decide how I wanted to play it. I'll tell you one drummer I liked,

Gene Krupa. I wanted to play blues, a little rock, a little progressive jazz. I wanted to have guys familiar with a variety. That way you can play a little bit of it all, even country and western.

Q: These days you are playing some soul music.

ER: Anything we do was mostly in the Top Ten during certain years and the songs that kind of relate and just stick out. They have something to say.

Q: What do you listen to?

ER: Mostly I been going over some of the things we been doing and trying to upgrade our songs. When we do a show, I like for it to go like clockwork. I listen to new songs that I want to do.

Q: When you play a job, do you have a set list?

ER: Yeah. But we could play all day and all night and never stop playing or play a song twice.

Q: Are you playing every set the same?

ER: No. We got about eight or nine sets. We pick different songs we want to hear that night, Otis Redding, Sam Cooke, James Brown, Billie Holiday, Little Walter—anybody.

Q: How about you, Chuck? How do you come up with material?

HC: I never know what I'm going to do until I get up there.

ER: That's for sure [*laughs*].

Q: How many songs do you have in total?

HC: [*Laughs*] I don't know how many I have.

ER: Oh man, you probably have forgotten more than you ever sing.

HC: Some of them, I think about maybe once every three to four years.

ER: And somebody had to remind him of them.

HC: If you would remind me of it, it's right there.

Q: How did you learn songs when you first started playing, Chuck, off a record or from somebody performing?

HC: Off a record. I used to get a record [after listening] one time, but I don't learn them that fast now. And then, a lot of songs, I'd be in the cotton fields, or riding my horse, or bicycling and I'd just come up with something or put something together. And a lot of me and my partners, we had one horse watered to go to town. They had a car and the other one's car wasn't running. With each other, we'd make up a song better than me and my brother.

Q: So, you had cutting contests back then. How did that make you feel?

HC: There was always two on you, or more, and they want me to go first. But now [in performance] we all go first, and I have time to figure out what I'm doing [*laughs*].

Q: Now when you get up there, a song will come to you?

HC: It just comes to me, and I take right off with it. Now if you walk up to request one, if I done did it before, it might not be just right, but you won't know the difference.

Q: Do you ever write songs?

HC: I never did try to write any. I just take them and do what I wanted to do with them. Some of them fits in our show and some of them didn't.

Q: I have a few more questions and then maybe the class would have some that I missed. What about a style of blues in Wichita, Erick? Do you think there is a distinct Wichita sound?

ER: It's more or less distinct. Chuck had his style and that's distinct. I don't think we have anyone else who plays his style. We got different guys that played. It's the culture of the blues. It's a difference. I guess that's how come we all stuck together, because not too many of us can play it. It's hard to teach other people if they don't have any ambition to learn it.

Q: Did you have some lean years during the disco era?

ER: It didn't affect us too much. I'm thinking I had four, five, six, seven girls go-go dancing and everything.

Q: And you'd play drums behind them?

ER: Yeah, but the whole band would play swing music for them, that bubble gum snap, they used to call it, high tempo with just a push. But we still played blues. We'd be playing different gigs and I'd bring them and let them dance with Chuck.

Q: Did you ever work for Jack Van Gundy [nightclub manager]?

ER: That's who I worked for. He used to come to the house and eat chitlins [*laughs*]. Right down on Minnesota, yeah.

Q: I heard he made some people mad and they sent him to Kansas City.

ER: Yeah, it was kind of a rough deal what happened.

Q: You know about that story?

ER: I don't know for sure about that story, but I know a whole bunch more. I'll tell you, he was something else.

Q: He really had connections, right?

ER: Oh yeah, a bunch of connections. That's why he connected on out of here. I forget now who he sold out to when he left from here, because he had to get rid of all them clubs, the Sheik's Tent, the Hobbledehoy.

Q: So, Chuck's club was the house of the blues?

ER: Yeah, they wanted the blues at the 904. Chuck was the culture of the blues. Far as I was concerned, it was the only place down there to play blues. Berry [Harris] has his style of blues. He's talking about an upbeat on it; that's the way he plays his blues. Don Dunn plays a progressive style

Harmonica Chuck as a young man, Kansas African American Museum,
Wichita, Kansas.

of blues. I knew Don when he got married out in Planeview. His wife had
came from there, had family members there.

Q: The Black neighborhood in Planeview was a thriving community?

ER: Oh man, it was real nice out there. It would remind you of an old
country town, because you could leave your doors open twenty-four hours.
It was in the county. Joyland [amusement park] was over there on the other
side of Hillside [Street]. They were just building part of that. You never knew
it was in Wichita; it was just Planeview, Kansas.

HC: It was an outlet. You could leave here and go out to Planeview. And
it looks like you done been out of town when you come back here.

Q: What else beside the Planeview Inn was there?

ER: There was a pool hall, barber shop, and the whole works. Had a little
store down there at the end.

Q: Did most of the people work at the aircraft factories?

ER: A lot of them worked for that. My grandmother worked out at the Domestic Laundry down on Douglas. After my grandfather got laid off the construction out there, he went to the Domestic Laundry.

Q: Did anyone play instruments in your family besides your uncle?

ER: My uncle played drums and grandfather played harmonica. He'd always blow it a little bit. That was all. I never really heard him play too much, other than with Hank Johnson and the guys sittin' out on the porch late at night. You can imagine everybody sitting there and listening to the music all night long.

Q: Does anybody have any questions?

Student: Why did your grandmother want you to play the drums?

ER: Ah, I don't know. She's ninety-five years old, still living. I think after she heard me play—and it took me a long time to learn—she decided that that was probably my best instrument. I tried guitar and bass, and I had a horn.

Q: How many people did you have working for you in the club, Chuck?

HC: At one time, I had three waitresses, a bartender, two ladies on the door, and about seven in my band.

ER: We were part-time assistants, you know. We came off the bandstand sometimes [*laughs*].

HC: One thing I can say, they sure watched Chuck's back.

Q: You could cause some fights yourself, Chuck, when you were playing your music. That's what I heard.

HC: Yeah. It's true.

ER: You got to imagine these guys, sitting there thinking. They just like a time bomb waiting to go off. They already know when they go out there that they are mad at the old lady or whatever. And you get to hearing them blues with "Oh, baby, why did you leave me?" Then you see this guy over here standing in the corner with her, he's the first one you want to kill.

HC: This one night, this lady had on this pretty red dress. I didn't know her. I kept seeing her standing over there by the jukebox, and Lord, I'm up there blowing. Finally, after a while, there she was, up on the bandstand. I see her man get up and looking up there. I tried to turn my back to keep away from her. Now, Erick and them wouldn't help me that night. After a while he snatched her off of the bandstand. They come from out there in front [of the club] and said, "Chuck, they fighting out there." I said, where? "Right out there." I said, whereabouts? "Can't you see them fighting out there?" I wasn't going out there. Then after they got through there, they hugged up and kissed, come back in and sat down and had a good time [*laughs*].

ER: Oh no. Never walk out that door.

Q: You had your club during the '67 riots, didn't you?

HC: Yeah.

Q: Did the police bother you then or did they stay away from that area?

HC: No, they didn't really bother me. It was the National Guard, because it was them that I knowed from McConnell [Air Force Base]. So, you're going home, and they'd just done been in the club that day. They don't know you. When the curfew come on at 10:00, they can shut every light off in this town, all but the lights in your house. There was a few running around out there, still racing their motors and popping their pipes. But boy, when they shut this joker down, you couldn't hear nothing.

Q: That lasted two or three days, didn't it?

HC: Yeah. You couldn't even travel through this town. People couldn't go to work out to Boeing. Something had to break then.

Q: Do you think the blues is good for people, or do you think it holds them back?

HC: I think blues is good for people.

ER: I don't see how it holds them back. I think blues is going to be here, and I think it is a wonderful thing. Even though I play a variety, them blues is here to stay. Harmonica Chuck kept the blues alive. Even when we'd go play parties and different balls, it would always come right back down to the same thing, the blues. And we'd go back down there with Chuck and close up with him.

Q: When did King B's Club open?

ER: That was in the nineties.

HC: He come along after I sold the 904.

Q: Was that location a club all the time that you were running the 904?

HC: It was a beer tavern, the Rocket [2323 E. 9th].

Q: Ninth was one of the main streets where you heard blues back in the fifties and sixties?

ER: Murdock, too. Murdock was full of joints all up and down there then.

HC: And then 9th Street from Mead all down and plumb on over to Grove was nothing but blues clubs.

ER: You got to realize there was a lot of after-hours houses to party in.

HC: And there used to be a lot of cafes, like Miss Smart's, and Steve's Chicken. And there's Dunbar's, she was on Murdock. Any time of night you could go somewhere and get something to eat.

ER: You could go behind the Washington Street Hotel and get something to eat in the alley at the after-hours cafe.

Q: Did they charge you to go in an after-hours house?

ER: No, just walk in. They'd sell you liquor, food.

Q: Without a license?

ER: Well, yeah. How else you going to build the people up? They made a lot of nickels and dimes in those places during that time. Everybody came to those places; that's where the blues was being played.

HC: When the curfews came on at two o'clock—then they put it to three o'clock—all the clubs had to close. No sooner than the clubs closed, everybody was headed out to after-hours houses. And then they partied there all night.

Q: Did they pay the musicians, or just take donations?

ER: They'd have them pass the hat. Good Lord, we made a lot of money that way.

Q: Where did they park, just out in the street?

ER: Everywhere. Anywhere you can.

Q: Where was one of the most popular after-hours houses?

ER: Happy houses? You could go on Washington St. in Wichita. And then you could go on Roseberry, Munger Lane in Planeview.

HC: But you take like Miss Dunbar's. She stayed open all during the day and overnight.

ER: If you sold food, you could stay open anytime automatically.

HC: And she just sold like maybe beer.

ER: Yeah, or half-pints.

Q: Are you guys getting dry and hungry talking?

ER: I've had fun thinking about all the stuff we're trying to remember. I bet we done forgotten more than we remembered.

Q: What's the future of the blues?

ER: It's going to always be there. It's not always going to be number one with everyone, but it's going to play its part. It's not going nowhere. It's been surviving all these years.

HC: The blues will always be around.

Q: Did any younger drummers come up to you and ask for lessons?

ER: Yes. When I was playing the Elks' down there with Berry and them, Bill Lynch was a car dealer. And his son was about eight years old, Bill Lynch Jr. Bill had me teach him how to play because he felt that he wanted his son to be a musician and play drums. He paid me to teach him two days a week. Now he's one of the baddest drummers around today. Been playing in California, and Denver.

Q: Anybody come up to you these days?

ER: I have a few guys come up and ask me, but not too much.

Q: How about you Chuck? Do people ever come up and want to learn your stuff?

HC: Yeah, I have them come around a lot of times and they want to tell me how to do it. And they tell me "Well, this is the way you do it." What that is, is they want me to show them; they don't want to admit it. But I don't have as many kids now as I used to, who wanted me to teach them harmonica. Harmonica is an instrument that you just can't hardly teach because it's too much inside of your mouth. I've had some, and I used to have them get in the mirror and hit different notes. Just take the harp down and look at the positions that my tongue be in sometimes and I say, goodness gracious.

S: I'm curious about the Black club scene. Is there a group of clubs that people go to, or did it die in the eighties?

HC: Well in the sixties, it was a big family. And along in the eighties it died down. But now it seems to be coming back.

ER: The only difference, you don't have these spots out in our neighborhood anymore. They be moving everything south, like Old Town, and they have tore down all these other buildings. So we have to go down there and play, if we're going to play at all.

Q: What are some major Black clubs in town?

ER: I don't think there is any more clubs down this way no more. They just died out in this neighborhood. There was so much ruckus and problems anyway. I tell you, when the 904 quit, we just lost all interest in playing anyway. And most people wanted to play the jukebox.

HC: Now, you take like the 904 Club back in '61 and up through the seventies, everybody was there. Even broke the race barriers. There was just as many white, Mexicans, Indians. That was the place. I mean, from all out of Blackwell [Oklahoma], Junction City, Salina, it was just a place that people loved to come.

Q: No one took the 904 over after you got out of it?

HC: No.

S: What clubs do you guys go to and what bands do you listen to in Wichita?

HC: Just wherever we find here that a band is playing.

ER: I go and listen to Don Dunn sometimes. I play with him if he call me up and want me to drum for him. Or Little Jesse [Anderson] and them. We used to play years ago at Dearmore's, Stagedoor Inn. [Mike] Finnigan² and them was out there all the time. They used to come down to the Latin Club and play with me and Ronnie Ford. That was right there at 21st, between Piatt and Minnesota. They tore it down and put a lot back there. Gene and Laura Pryor owned that. Yeah, it was pretty nice. We had some pretty nice groups going through here and some fine musicians around here. That is one of the reasons I wished we could have kept the Musicians Clubhouse in good standings. Because see, everywhere else you went, they'd always have a club where a musician could go anytime day or night. A lot of musicians get out there on that road and run into a whole lot of problems. The gig you get through playing, the man don't have all the money and you're up somewhere and can't get back home. So, by having that Musicians Clubhouse, I thought that would be the best thing Wichita had. You'd be surprised how many musicians would sign the ledger and would be willing to put in dues to keep it open.

Q: Have you still got that ledger?

ER: Yeah, I think I got it. I been packing it around for a long time.

Q: Did you have a scrapbook of your write-ups and pictures?

ER: The only thing ever I kept was my records of track and field and stuff like that.

Q: You better hang on to stuff like Chuck does.

ER: He's probably got his first firecracker even [*laughs*]. I've always been one of them guys, I just pull up stakes and go on.

Q: I think we better let you guys close. This has been a treat for me and a treat for the class, I would assume. Because, it's the real thing.

ER: Well, this is a wonderful class. They didn't ask a lot of questions [*laughs*], that I had to remember.

ALBERT TUCKER (1928–2007)

Guitar, vocal

"I was born in Purcell, Oklahoma, in the year of 1928, a little old town down from Oklahoma City. I have a family of six. I was the middle boy. My daddy, he played a little, and I had a uncle who played a little guitar. I just picked it up. Taught myself.

"My father did public work for a while. And after, he moved on the farm in the year of 1938. After mother passed, I stayed on the farm for twelve years. After twelve years, I was twenty-one years old and I said this is no place for me. In the meantime, during the time on the farm, I got carried off on music.

"I met a guy named Buster King in a little town called Boswell. He just a farm worker and he had a banjo in a sack. I was very inquisitive about what was in the sack. Later, he got the banjo out of the sack and began to play. That's what made me crazy about the blues. That was the first I ever heard anybody playing the blues on a banjo. He played 'West Texas Blues' and he sung it. That just put me out on the road.

"Then the next few days, I made me a banjo and I tried to play it. That was in 1941, and ever since then I been crazy about music. We moved to Paris, Texas. I got more interested in blues then as I grew up, and in 1943 I finally bought me a guitar, a Harmony arch-top. I give $3.50 for it. It was used, good and used, too. My dad had to tune it with wire pliers."

When you were in Texas, what kind of music did you listen to?

"Just blues. After moving to Texas, I kind of got away from it because I didn't go to town, to the joints and things. After I grew up, I begin to get around pretty close to town. Then I begin to hear a little more of the blues. The more I heard it, the more I wanted to play it. I heard a piece of blues on a record by Tom McClennan, 'Bottle Up and Go.' And that's when I got crazy about it.

"In them days, we didn't have a record player. Had Victrolas. Crank it up. But we didn't have one, we was unfortune."

What kind of work were you doing around Paris?

"Farm work. Choppin' cotton. I never did play for anyone, just for my own use. I'd hear a piece and I'd put it in my vocabulary, and during my working hours I would sing it, hum it. I like to hear all three of these: T-Bone Walker, Sonny Jackson, and Johnny Lee Hooker."

T-Bone Walker was pretty modern back then, wasn't he?

"Yeah, he was. He's out of Dallas."

Did you ever see him play?

"Oh, I heard him play. I never did actually go in. It was too crowded. I went to the club where he was playing at, and I'd sit out in the car.

"I first came to Wichita in 1953. I left Amarillo, I and my first wife, Earline. I was doing steel work then. Later we went back to Oklahoma, and we departed, and seven years later I came back to Wichita. I got acquainted with Mary, my wife now. And her and I got married and been married for thirty-four years now.

"First time I was in Wichita, I worked at Cessna Aircraft. But I was working kitchen work, and I was trying to work my way into the plant and into the factory. There weren't too many African Americans working in those plants, not near about as many as there is now. My wife left and went back to Oklahoma, and I left and went back where she was at."

She didn't like it up here?

"No, she didn't. It was a pretty friendly community back in 1953, but her family, close relatives were all back down in Idabel, Oklahoma."

Why did you pick Wichita when you came up here the first time?

"I used to hear my dad talk about Kansas City. Kansas City was my aim."

Albert Tucker, photo by Arthur Kenyon.

What was he doing up in Kansas City?

"That's when he was young and single man. He just travelin' through, you know? He's born back in 1800s. So that was way back in the 1900s, way before I was born.

"But I got to Wichita and that's as far as I got. I always wanted to go to Kansas City, and see what Kansas City was like. I got a older sister live here in Wichita. After she came, well, all of us brothers came here, the whole family.

"We decided to not probably get no further apart now, as we done grow old. When I came back here the last time, I was thirty-three years old."

Why did you come back?

"Well biggest portion of the family was here. I was just going to roam around, and then I finally decided to get married. And after getting married, I said it's time for me to settle down. I thought one of these days I might live to retire. And that's what I had in mind. So I begin to work. I'd work at anything, just so long as I could make a dollar.

"Then the very last, I went out to Beech Aircraft and hired in as a painter. I was a spray painter after fifteen years, and retired on the twenty-fifth of December 1991.

"I laid the guitar down for four or five years. I still kept it in mind, but I just didn't do no playing. Unless I went somewhere else and I seen somebody else playing, and I'd let them know that they wasn't the only one who could play a guitar."

What clubs did you go to?

"Any I thought of. I used to go to the 904. Harmonica Chuck let me get up there and play once in a while, one or two songs. I wouldn't break up the band, but during the intermission I would tease the guitar a little. I just used a guitar up there. I didn't have a guitar when I came back to Wichita. I came back in '61; my first guitar I bought was in about '68.

"After then, I kept a guitar pretty good around. The last one I got, is electric. Got an amplifier with that one, and I been had it ever since. For a long time, I couldn't keep it out of pawn. Every time I turned around, I pawned it, pawned it, pawned it, pawned it. [Berry] Harris told me, he said:

"'Where your guitar?'

"'In pawn.'

"'Where's the amp?'

"'In pawn.'

"'Did you pawn both of them on the same ticket?'

"'Yeah.'

"'Listen, if you're going to pawn them, pawn them on a separate ticket. If you want to get your guitar, you can get the guitar, you don't need the amp. You can hook up with somebody else if you going to play.'

"After I went back to church, First Church of God in Christ, I took it to the church and left it. That's where it's at now. I play there practically every Sunday.

"I didn't belong to no church in Oklahoma and Texas. My wife was in the church here, and she enticed me by her being in church and all her people was in the church. I'm telling you they are very respectable people! I said, well, I don't want to break no reputation. Even if I did drink and gamble, I didn't want to tear her reputation down. She wanted to go to church; I didn't keep her from going to church. I'd go to church with her.

"And then after we started raising a family, I couldn't think of a better thing than trying to stay somewhere near the church. I ain't always been in the church, but I decided I quit doing a lot of things such as gambling and drinking, and feel good behind it."

What was the best blues club in Wichita in the fifties and sixties? You mentioned the 904 Club. Were there any others?

"Well you know, that was about the only one. They brought in different bands to play. I didn't hang around them clubs too much."

Would you go down to the 904 every Friday and Saturday?

"I didn't do it every weekend, because I did a lot of gamblin'. I'd rather be sittin' and playing cards than to be sittin' up in the club. I'd just get me a bottle of my own and drink and gamble. We didn't have no music when we were gambling. Just paying attention to them cards."

Did you have some good winnings back then?

"Once in a while I'd pull down pretty good and then I'd lose quite a bit."

You still listen to the blues.

"It doesn't really bother me, blues. I just listen at music. I'm a music man. I play a lot of spiritual. I don't play no blues in church."

How did you meet Berry Harris?

"He lived in a little town called Stringtown. Young lad, left home, I had some kinfolks lived in Stringtown and so I ran into Berry. Berry had a guitar. He was trying to learn how to play when I was trying to learn. He'd strum on it awhile, and I'd strum on it awhile. Neither one of us right then wasn't making too much progress. But before we departed, he could make a tune that I couldn't make, and I could make one that he couldn't make."

What kind of blues did you hear in Wichita, in the clubs or when people had records in their homes?

"I never really paid no attention. But everybody tells me, I play a rarer type of music than nobody. They say: 'I ain't never heard nobody play like you play. You play like way down home blues.'"

Did you ever work with a harmonica player, or with different guitar players, violin, or anything like that?

"No, I never play with nobody."

Where did you buy your records in this town?

"They had a record shop right there on Cleveland [Street]."

What kind of blues did your father play?

"He wasn't a blues man, he played in the church too. But he was just sittin' around the house and didn't have nothing, and he just pickin'. And that's when I know what blues does to you. It puts your mind on to wander sometime."

Does it help? Do you think blues are good or bad?

"Oh blues is good. I don't know how come, but one thing—I'll say this much—if you got something on your mind, it'll help level it out. I could have something on my mind real drastic you know, and I be off to myself, and I just keep on singing. After a while whatever it is, it seems like it's lifted."

Is that true for church music too?

"Well yeah, spiritual is. Now the song 'Walk with Me Lord,' that helps me more than anything in the world. When I had my guitar here at home, I'd play that and then I'd play 'When the Saints Go Marching In.'"

Do you play "When the Saints Go Marching In" in church?

"Oh yeah."

It seems like there was a lot of music in Oklahoma when you and Berry were learning to play. Was there more music down there than there was up in Wichita?

"Well, at that time, neither one of us didn't know anything about Kansas. We hadn't even been to Kansas."

But if you could compare Oklahoma, Texas, and Wichita, which had the most music?

"Texas and Oklahoma. We had a lot of places in West Texas, and when I say West Texas, it was flat. And they did them wild in West Texas and East Texas and Oklahoma. And quite a bit in Arkansas, too. The music came from the South. The way the Black people picked it up, they worked on them plantation farms and things and when they'd come in Saturday noon, they didn't have nothing to do. They pick up the guitar and maybe think about some girl, and play 'Baby Please Don't Go.' That's a song that definitely came out of the South. You never hear nothing like that up in this part of the country, unless somebody play it like me."

Do you think the blues has been good to you or has it hindered you?

"I'll say it like this: it didn't hinder me because, it ain't nothin' I ever done that I can't quit. I used to say that I couldn't quit drinking. And I smoked for twenty-two years, and anybody would talk to me inside of them twenty-two years, tell me about, you ought to quit smokin'. Huh uh, I can't quit. One night I just decided to quit, and I been quit thirty. Therefore, I know anything a man want to accomplish in life, might he then can accomplish."

Did any younger musicians come around and listen to you and try to learn your songs and the way you play?

"Yeah. They say, 'Where did you learn that at?' I say, well I just picked it up from a kid. I never did plan to make a living doing this. If I had, I could've got good, if I'd have just set my head when I started."

So people don't really come over here and visit you and listen to you play the guitar?

"They just hear me in church."

Are there any younger musicians and guitar players who try to play like you do in church?

"No. We had one guy, but he played a different style."

Blues is popular again. A lot of musicians have been playing it and trying to learn the old style.

"I know it."

Do you think that will last, and do you welcome them to try to learn your kind of blues?

"Yeah, I welcome them to do it. Because that's going to be it. The blues going to stay. I got a nephew here, Earl Starks. I started him out to playing a guitar. He chose to play rock 'n' roll. I told him, rock 'n' roll is going to fade away. You won't hear nothing but the blues."

Is there anything you'd like to say that we haven't talked about?

"No, no more than say I enjoyed this. It was quite surprising to me. What really surprised me: my granddaughter and I is sitting out on the porch. I saw you drive up and when you drove up and got out with that [equipment], I took my eye off of you. I didn't think nothing else. Then when you come walking, I said, now where is he going with all this crap? And by that time, you called my name.

"Let me phrase it like this, when God sent the Savior into the world, the Jews wasn't expectin' the Savior to come like he did. They wouldn't accept him. But ours was different. When Berry Harris told me about you and give me the number and everything, and told me to call you, I called you. If anybody told me you wasn't a Black guy, I would have told him, he was a liar.

"I was lookin' for a Black man. Of course, you know, I don't have no trouble with colors. I love everybody. My wife finally said:

"'Is he a Black guy?'

"I said, yes, he's Black. But I tell you, if anybody would have told me that you was white, I'd have said, oh no, no, no, no. You don't know who I'm talking about."

Chapter Seven

THE 1950S OKLAHOMA INFLUENCE

Jesse Anderson, Donald Dunn, Berry Harris, Charles Walker, Remona Hicks

This chapter chronicles those drawn to Wichita's expanding economy in the 1950s. This group is representative of the style performed in the city at the time of the interviews: Oklahoma and Chicago urban blues and rhythm and blues, tending toward sophistication within the strictures of the form.

JESSE ANDERSON (1940–2014)

Saxophone, guitar, vocal

"I was born in a little town forty-two miles from Ft. Smith in Paris, Arkansas August 21, 1940, down there in what they call the Gray Rock community. That's down in the bottom. I'm an only child. My mother's Mabel Anderson, and my dad he's deceased now, was Jesse Anderson. My name is Octiver Jesse Anderson.

"We came to Wichita in 1954 from Muskogee, Oklahoma."

So you moved from Arkansas to Muskogee.

"Actually from Muskogee to Tulsa, and then to Wichita."

What did your father do that made you move around?

"In the earlier years after he come from the service, he worked in the hotel business in Muskogee as a waiter, hotel man. He was sort of a hustler really, to put it bluntly, but I'm tellin' it like it is. Back then, during that time, a man had to survive the way he could and take care of the family. But I never went without, anything that I know of, as a kid. My aunt and uncle they in Arkansas, they all sung the blues. And I was around it, I guess all my life. I use to get the old Victrola and I could tell the records I wanted just by the labels. They had a different identity to them, like they had Bluebird Records.

They had a little blue bird on it. Then they had the Sun records, which Junior Parker was the first artist on Sun Records of blues. Sun Records was actually a country label, but the guy [Sam Phillips] wanted to go in a different direction, so he got Junior Parker. The next thing he had Elvis, and then after that he was in the highlight and the high dollar.

"But anyway, my aunt and them all sung the blues. I was listenin' to Smokey Hogg I guess when I was four or five years old. Cats like Smokey Hogg and Memphis Minnie, and Big Boy Crudup, and all those guys. Then one night later on, we use to get a station out of Memphis where we could hear B.B. [King].

"B.B. used to be a disc jockey on WDIA and we'd pick him up on that old battery radio. And then we'd get a chance to hear cats like Gatemouth Brown, Long Gone Sonny Thompson."

You were in the city of Ft. Smith, weren't you?

"I came to Ft. Smith later on, I guess maybe when I was eight or nine, and I lived with my aunt there. We didn't play the blues in her house."

Was she religious?

"Yeah. But I used to turn the radio on and listen to them other boys, Hank Williams and all, as I went to a different area that I guess you could consider more sophisticated than where I was born at. I started hearin' other types of music and got interested in it.

"When I got in Tulsa, the teacher that got me into talent shows, her name was Mrs. Hodges. We was practicin' a song, a Valentine's song and I'll never forget it as long as I live.

> "I Have Bought a Valentine
> Pink and Lacy and Blue and
> It's the One That I Like the Best
> And I'll Give It to You.

"I was a little chubby guy when I got to Tulsa. Tulsa was a city and kind of hard city. I was sort of a little different you know, because I got this little defect on my eye, you know what I'm sayin'? So, you know kids, they use to laugh and poke, but kids will do that anyway, regardless of what you look like. Anyway, we was in her music class, and she give us all the words to this song, and she was rehearsing it one day, I never will forget.

"We were singin' it, and she walked over and she was listenin' and then she got over to my little ol' chair, and I thought I had done somethin' wrong. She says:

"'Don't stop singin', don't stop, don't stop.'

Jesse Anderson, photo by Arthur Kenyon.

"So I went on and sung and she had me to come up in front of the class. I went up front of the class, and after that, I was in every talent show that school had. She promoted me. I knew I had talent before I came there, but she showed me that I could do something. Because up and until that point, I just thought that everybody could sing. I thought it was natural because I was around everybody that did.

"I never will forget the first song that I took the house was with, it was called 'Chattanooga Shoe Shine Boy.' And like, wow, after that, every time the school had a program, I was on it. Then we left Tulsa and came to Wichita."

How old were you when you got up there and sang the "Valentine"? What grade was that?

"Probably first or second, because we had the little bitty chairs, man. I might have been a smidgen older than that, maybe six or seven. Because see, they let school out down in the country for choppin' cotton and stuff like that. It wasn't like it is now, where kids is enrolling at five, four you know."

What did you think about Wichita?

"To tell you the truth, it really seemed like the end of the world. I'm not knocking Wichita, but you see Tulsa at that time had so much to offer Black youth. That's all I knew; it was my environment. But, we had kite seasons, we had marble shootin' seasons. When that season rolled around, every kid had two, three hundred marbles in his pocket, stuck in his hat. We had yo-yo seasons, and yo-yo competition. We had bicycle races and bicycle competition that was sponsored by the Tulsa Police Department. We had a lot of things that was fun things. But when I came here, it was like, you're going to be my friend, you can't be his friend.

"I enrolled in the old L'Ouverture School. And that's the way it was, and I wasn't used to that. In Tulsa, I belonged to the Cub Scouts and everything like that, so you see, when I came here, I was heartbroken. To come here and well I guess at twelve, thirteen, fourteen years old, there was guys that were on parole. Going to the Boys Home, Boy's Farm, and that kind of stuff. A lot of people say Tulsa's wild but Tulsa loved their children.

"I remember my mom and dad couldn't rent a place to live here very easy, because they didn't want kids. They didn't like people that were from Oklahoma and Arkansas. I'm not talkin' about your people, I'm talkin' about my people."

Why did your family come up here?

"This was the promised land. Dad was going to get a job at Boeing. Mom was going to perhaps get a job at Boeing's because my mama's brother, he came up here and his wife and they had hooked up at Boeing's. A lot of people from Arkansas used to come up here and do construction work, work in the summertime and go back home to Arkansas in the winter and be with their family. They came, and I was a child; I had no choice, so I came.

"I managed to slide through the bad boys and I went to a Monday night talent show here at the Dunbar Theatre. I never will forget that. And on that show, one of the groups that was a beautiful group was the Jones Brothers, one name Lindsay and one name Curtis. Their father was a minister and they sung gospel. They was good.

"So I went that one Monday night, and I'd heard of the talent show and they said, 'Anybody want to be on the talent show, be here next Monday night, $25 first prize, and you don't have to pay to get into the movie.' So $25 back then, that was good money, when you could buy a loaf of bread for a nickel, neckbones was maybe twelve cents a pound, three pound of hamburger for a dollar. It was almost as much as my daddy made on his daily job.

"I was probably hittin' into fifteen, but I hadn't been here too long. I wasn't over fifteen. I went home and I told my mom, and see my mom, she could learn them lyrics real quick, see? And then she would sing it to me, and then I would get it from her. You hear what I'm saying?"

Has she got a good voice too?

"Yeah, yeah. And so this thing, 'Walkin' My Baby Back Home,' was popular by Johnnie Ray. Well one thing I say is, what I had learned from Mrs. Hodges, I learned how to do my homework. In other words, you know what you up against, and then you know what you need to beat the competition. So, what I did was, I went there and I heard the Brother Jones group and some other people. And they and the other people on the show was doing tunes like Fats Domino and Lloyd Price.

"So I says, uh huh, I got to come up with something unique, something that they are hearing every day on the Wichita top radio. So, that's what I did. I really don't know how that I knew all of these things, but I located a girl around here, Betty Shorter, that played piano. And went down to Jenkins music store and bought the sheet music and took it by her house. And brother, we rocked the house with that tune. They was throwing money on the stage, just right and left. And I wouldn't pick the money up. You know, I wouldn't pick the money up. I don't know where I got that from, I guess in my heart I thought, stars don't do this. I was just a kid, you know. But so the stage manager, he'd come out with the broom, and would be sweepin' money up and puttin' it in a bag.

"I come off the stage and they'd load my little suitcoat. I'd be leanin' to the side. I won so many talent shows until the people started thinkin' it was rigged. They still think it was rigged. Then that kind of went out. I think he sold the Dunbar Theatre to somebody and then some lady dismissed the talent show—all the people that was involved there. A lot of those guys like Little Willie; he was a tap-dancer out of New York, see.

"Wichita had known hits [makers] before, like when they wanted to rest the top guys out in the world, they'd come here. In other words, you know maybe kick the habit, or get away from a ex-wife or somethin'. So, you ran into a lot of people that had been out there. Little Willie had been out there in the vaudeville for years. He could tap up a storm. He was as bad or was as good as, I'd say, Sammy Davis."

What was his last name?

"Don't make me lie. But that was his stage name, Little Willie. He was a tapper, hoofer and he was a good emcee.

"There was a guy—we had to move into another place that mama and them couldn't move me with them, so I stayed with this guy's parents and him. His name was Ivy Tugger and he was taking saxophone lessons from Mr. Walton Morgan. He had a saxophone there at his house and he would be tootin' his little lessons and stuff.

"One day I say, 'Man, how do you do that?' So, he took the mouthpiece and washed it out and showed me. Just in a matter of seconds, I was playing whole tones, half tones. So, then after we had gotten a place where the whole family could live, see, I started buggin' my mother for a saxophone. Her and dad, they finally got me a little ol' C-melody. Which I didn't know whether it was a tenor. But anyway, I was able to find sounds, anything I could hear on the radio, I could find it on the horn and started makin' patterns and stuff.

"I went to Mr. Morgan and was gettin' him to get me some lessons. So he said:

"'What are you doing with this C-melody?'

"He kind of broke my spirit. Because my mother ain't no lazy—she had washed dishes, and stuff like that, and strained for that C. There was no one purer than her. Her and my dad was separated. And those don't come cheap. I think she paid $35 or $50 for that little ol' C-melody horn. I'll show you the spirit and the power of determination.

"When Mr. Morgan said that, see I had done learned through life that, sometime a push can be a shove. So, I went home and for a couple of days that worried me, and it hurt me. There ain't nothin' in the world like mama. This was during the summertime though, because school was out. I'd been going by Jenkins lookin' at them new horns, off and on settin' in the window."

People have mentioned Jenkins Music. Was there any other music store that was as good back then?

"There was another music store down on Douglas, Calavan, I believe. But Jenkins was in the Board of Education system. They did horns for the schools. Uhlik's and them was down there by where the River's Edge is now. But they were guitar people. Of course, Lester Wiley, they were guitar people.

"But anyway, this particular day, the Lord told me, He said go down there. Mama had gone to work. I got up, I believe I walked down there. I was standin' there lookin' up at that horn locked up in the case. Over there was a little white-haired lady, snow white. Nice lookin' lady in her sixties. And she said:

"'Young man, are you going to buy that horn?'

"I said, 'Well, I don't know. I ain't got no money.'

"'Do you want to try it?'

"'Yes, ma'am, I'll try it.'

"'Let me get the key.'

When she went to get the key, there was another guy and lady over in the sheet music department wantin' to get some sheet music. So she came back and unlocked the case.

"'You know how to put it together?'

"'Yes, ma'am.'

"'I'm going to go over here and help them and then I'll be back.'

"I took the horn out of the case and I put the neck strap on, put the mouthpiece on, the reed. I was down. Because as I started learning, I started readin' all the *Down Beat* magazines and anything that had to deal with musicians. I was off into it. They had music listenin' rooms back then that you go into, a little like telephone booths. So, I went in there and did my little warm-up. And I hit this thing 'Night Train' by Jimmy Forrest, and the people in the store, they'd come at the door like a kangaroo, neck start stretchin'. Pretty soon they were comin' around to the little window booth and I hit a few more passages and executed a few things.

"So, she says, 'Young man, you need that horn.'

"'I don't know. My mama ain't got no credit. She just washes dishes at a little ol' place.'

"'You wait right here.'

"I'm going to tell you what that lady did, man. That lady went upstairs and she came back.

"'Young man, I'm doing somethin' for you I ain't never done with nobody. I signed for you to get this horn. You going to pay?'

"'Yes, ma'am, I'll pay.'

"I think the payment was about twenty dollars a month and I paid her. That's when me and Jerry Childers started playing together. I had it for over a year, it was paid for. It was a Constellation. Then some guys, they stole it but I got it back. I kept that horn almost to the final end of my career. I didn't care what them other guys out there had, them Selmers, and them Bueschers.

"Somehow me and Jerry Childers hooked up with a guy, Adolf Thurman and another guy named Donald Franklin, a guitar player. Thurman was on piano and vocals."

Were you still a teenager in school?

"I was going to school but I gotta quit school 'round seventeen, though. Dropped out of East High.

"We opened up a club for Polk Jordan [Gene Metcalf's uncle], the Oklahoma Quarter Club down there on 9th and Mead. It's a machine shop down there now."

What did it mean?

"Quarter, like twenty-five cents. I think when it opened up, they'd charge a quarter to go in. Then later on, it went up to fifty cents, then it got on up to a dollar or two."

And you could play in there even though you were a teenager?

"Well yeah. I had sense enough to check with the union. A youngster can play in a club, if he's supervised by older adults and not served no drinks. I wasn't drinkin' then. I was strictly a music lover. We banded together. Jerry was playing drums then. We used to go by his house and practice. Then we ran into Bo Jones, and Bo Jones come into the picture. He was a blues singer and a piano player, sort of on a Fats Domino kick. Matter of fact, he kind of looked like Fats Domino. He was a good, good piano and blues singer. Then you had this boy Carl out of El Dorado. He passed away. Saxophone player. Then Sam Franklin, he was here. And the House Rockers and the Floaters."

Did you play with these different groups?

"Yeah, because see in that era, things weren't closed down. Almost all the cats knew all the songs. I don't care if you went from Maine to Spain, they played something that you knowed, and you knowed something that they played. You could go from here to New York and you could walk in to a set, and say do you know 'Honky Tonk' by Bill Doggett, and they knew it. You could say do you know 'Hand Clappin'' by Illinois Jacquet and they knew it. You could go to Mississippi, and them boys there would know it. You understand what I'm sayin'? So, it was just like a great big party all of the time playing back then."

Were you still living at home then?

"I was still livin' at home. I'd go out on the weekends and come home. And then I'd go to school. But I quit school because I was really makin' more money. It became a money thing."

You were doing pretty well then, weren't you?

"Oh yeah. I was makin' close to $150–$200 playing two or three nights back then. Then we had blues guitar players, Raymond Boston, Larry Johnson. Then we had Willie Wright and the Sparklers. I cut my first record with them for King Records. We was released on the Federal label. They was out of Muskogee, but they merged into here and set up. They still live here, and had an auntie here, Mrs. Smith, Kathryn Smith. They use to call her Aunt Kat and Uncle Bob. They did some bookings, they had the bookings sewn up. Them boys was her nephews; they was the first group, but I was their second group."

What did you call yourselves back then?

"Little Jesse and the Blues Toppers, and then I was Little Jesse and the Groovemasters."

Where did you record?

"In Cincinnati, King Records, 1540 Brewster."

What year was this?

"That was probably in '59 or '60, somewhere along in there, yeah."

Who signed the deal?

"I wasn't twenty-one, and so I think Carl and his brother signed the deal with King Record Company."

When you recorded as Little Jessie and the Blues Toppers, was that with King too?

"Well, I never did use the Blues Toppers. I just used them locally around here. What they did at King, first they started us out like, say Little Willie Wright and the Sparklers, vocal Jesse Anderson. They did our first couple of records like that, and then on the last record that was released with King, it was just Jesse Anderson."

♪ ♪ ♪

In an interview for the Wichita Blues Society newsletter, Anderson relates a more involved depiction. In 1960, he went with the Wright brothers to Chicago to try to record. This was with Carl on bass, Willie on drums, Gordon Simms organ, Herbie Welch guitar, Bob McVey[1] trumpet, Eddie Caddel saxophone, Sammy Lynch vocals, Anderson sax and vocals. Anderson's mother gave him ten dollars, a sack of potatoes, a skillet, pork and beans, and some onions.

They got lost in a "Mormon town somewhere in Missouri. The people were pretty nice and helped us out get back on the road. Then we blew a transmission seal and started putting ten-cent [waste] motor oil in the transmission and we had a flat tire with no spare." They went to a farmer's house and he had a mounted tire that fit. When they arrived in Chicago, they tried to get a gig at the Rock and Roll Club without any luck. They went to a flop house across the street and the manager let them stay the night at no charge.

The next day, they went to Chess Records, and Bob McVey approached Ralph Bass, A&R man. He said that if they could get set up within an hour they could audition. "Man, we had to carry all of our equipment upstairs." They played songs mostly written by Sammy Lynch. After a few songs, Bass said, "I have the best blues cats in the world here, and you cats come in wanting to play blues. We are looking for something new and fresh. You have anything?" Jesse told him that he had some songs but they had not rehearsed them. So, Jesse played and sang his songs a cappella. Bass liked it. He left and came back with Leonard Chess. After listening, Leonard gave the nod. The only problem: he just wanted Jesse, not the rest of the band. They said they were going to go on to Cincinnati. However, as Jesse was only twenty years old, Bass told him he would need parental consent for the contract.

Jesse knew it would take at least a week or two to get the paperwork signed by his mother, so he went with the band to see if they could get some paying gigs in Chicago. They went to Pepper's Lounge, owned by Johnny Pepper, but the doorman wouldn't let them in. Johnny Pepper came out, heard their story and said they could play that night. The reason behind this was Detroit Junior and St. Louis Mac had a fight the previous night over a woman, during which the front window of the club had been broken out and all the customers had been run off.

When they came back the next night, Pepper had knocked out one of the walls, expanding the club quite a bit. The band began their show but were interrupted by two representatives of the musicians union who inquired as to their union membership. Jesse thought Detroit Junior or St. Louis Mac had likely contacted them. Johnny Pepper tried to bribe the representatives, but no luck. They had to pack up. Another man, Bobby Valentine, who used to play with Sonny "Long Gone" Thompson, took them to another club, Ceramax. They set up and started to play once again, but the same union men arrived and started cursing and knocked their amps over. Giving up, the band took the highway to Cincinnati.

They spent the first night in Cincinnati in the park, cooking up the potatoes and onions from Jesse's mother. The next day, they went to King Records, got an audition and a contract with Syd Nathan, the owner. Jesse described him as "cold-blooded. We went to see him in a large office with this huge horseshoe desk. It was like standing across the street from him." They ended up recording some of Jesse's songs, and the band changed their name to the Sparklers, a name registered by King. Jesse was still too young to sign the contract. "The only thing I got was a shared room, a double cheeseburger, fries, milkshake, piece of pie, and one long-distance phone call."

They stayed in Cincinnati for two days, then drove back to Wichita. Later, Sonny Thompson contacted Jesse to come to Kankakee, Illinois, about seventy miles outside of Chicago, to join a group from Georgia sponsored by John Walton, brother of Sam Walton [founder of Walmart]. Sam named their band the Wallettes. They played thirty-one nights backing up Little Esther Phillips, and fourteen nights backing Brook Benton. Jesse worked his way back into Chicago, unhindered by the union. Over the next decade, Jesse played all over the country, performing in the same venue or part of the backing band for Syl Johnson, Earl Hooker, Luther Allison, Muddy Waters, Howlin' Wolf, Sonny Boy Williamson, Little Milton, Bobby Bland, Little Joe Hinton, Clarence Carter, Shirley and the Shirelles, Big Mama Thornton, Big Joe Turner, Etta James, Buddy Guy, Junior Wells, Paul Butterfield, AC Reed, James Cotton, B.B. King. Jesse cowrote and recorded songs with Detroit Junior, he also backed John Lee Hooker at Pepper's Lounge, and played a gig at the Apollo Theater with Clarence Carter and the Shirelles. Buddy Guy, Bobby Bland, Albert Collins recorded some of his compositions.[2]

"I still get royalty checks from a lot of these things here. And then I got some tunes that I'd written with other people. So I still get stuff in from that and, but I never got anything from King. I never even got a statement from them."

You were nineteen or twenty. You were cutting a record. How did that make you feel?

"It made me feel okay. When we came back, well, the records and things, it meant more to them than it really did to me. In other words, they got really popularity struck, and for a while they didn't want to do nothing. So, I pulled out by myself."

Sonny Thompson hired you?

"Right, I played with him and then he recorded me under his direction-ship. Then I hooked up with another guy, then I went back, because Sonny's office in Chicago was right across the street from Chess Records. Then I started leadin' guys over to Chess on a personal level, you see. Then I met this cat, Gene Barge. He was a saxophone player. He use to be the top man with Chuck Willard and he also was the man on that thing, 'Dancin' with Daddy G' ['Quarter to Three'].

"Well, Gene is Daddy G. He started recording me out of the Chess budget. Then it just kind of sprang off from there. Once in Chicago, you play with some of everybody, Muddy Waters, Buddy Guy."

So you just played sax and then you came in for a session and did your vocals too?

"Yeah, all my records is vocal. They didn't want me to play sax, because back then they wasn't interested in groups. They was interested in single art-ists. For the simple reason is, and I can see why, when we were at Cincinnati, it took us almost twenty-one hours man to record five tunes. Like I tried to tell a lot these guys around here, nightclub musicians is not necessarily good studio musicians. Because it's things that you do in the studio that you don't do in a nightclub. And things that you do in a nightclub, you definitely wouldn't do in a studio.

"See, you make it hard for an engineer. You take an experienced singer out of the nightclub, he grabbin' the mike and runnin' in and runnin' out. When you start trying to edit it, and master that man, you liable to spend eight hours. Well, you spend eight hours at a $150 an hour for a man that try to get a mix, so they didn't do that. All my sessions were with cats like Phillip Upchurch, and Donny Hathaway, Maurice White. I used polished people.

"The first recording I did was an unpolished, that was with those boys, Willie Wright and the Aces. But after that, I strictly recorded with polished musicians. I only use other musicians on the road."

Did Chess treat you fairly?

"I say he treated me fair for the simple reason is, back then if you could go in and do a session, pick up your $1,200, $1,500. Come around, if you have a bad Monday down the road and you need $500 and make rent payment or something, you could go in there and get it. Yeah, they treated you fair. Because that was the way they operated. They operated like that with Muddy, and Little Walter. You get it if you was a good beggar. It's still happenin' now.

"But a record always have been for a blues man, and a rhythm and blues— it's the son of the blues—have always been the advertiser. Somethin' to work the chitlin' circuit on. It never has been a thing so much as sittin' back enjoyin' your long royalty checks. I won't call a record company now. Albert Collins didn't have a record out until this man come along and recorded it and started promotin' him, so Albert made money on his public appearances.

"Like I say, so far as I'm concerned, Chess and them were good to me. I could go in when one of my kids were born, and I needed $1,200, $1,500. I might have to hang around all day to get it, but I'd get it."

Where were you living then?

"I was in Chicago from perhaps '60 on up until probably maybe '70, '71. Just tourin' around the country, playing everywhere, Mississippi, Arkansas, Texas, Oklahoma, just everywhere. You know that was just it, that was the circuit. If I wasn't out there on my own, I give those guys a call, I'd hook up with somebody and do a stretch with them. I played with cats like Earl Hooker, great blues man; matter of fact, he taught Ike Turner how to play guitar. Pinetop Perkins, he's still around. Oh man, my head is just so full of people. I can't even bring them out—like they just in there jumpin' up and down."

Did you do more blues or rhythm and blues in those days?

"Well now, here's the catch. The sale of a record determined what it was. If it sold 100,000, it was a blues record, I don't care what it was. If it went 400,000, it was a rhythm and blues. It's still like that today. That's why you got blues rappers out there and then you got contemporary rappers, but they rappin' the same thing. But there's a market that ain't buyin' that blues rapper record that's buying the contemporary rapper's record. So, they ain't hit that margin. Everything was blues until it sold a certain amount of records.

"You had some definitions that blues was what you slow-danced on, rhythm and blues was what you danced on. It's not the public. It ain't the disc jockey. It's the record sales. Because if any one of these old records was released right now, and it went ten million, it would not be a blues. They would change and these would be contemporary blues, pop blues.

"I left Chicago in, uh, 'bout '73, then I went to California, to Oakland, Frisco. I had relatives out there, but I hooked up with Jimmy McCracklin out there and worked with Jimmy for a while."

What were you doing then, just vocals?

"Just vocals then. We'd do three sets a night. We'd kick off about nine o'clock till about two."

Was it fairly good money?

"I didn't have a family then. It was good money for a single man. But I still had to work on the side. I was operating a little old hotel down at Richmond. I was kind of on my own time. I stayed out in California 'bout a couple of years and then I came back home here. I worked around here for the first couple two or three years when I came back but, it just took too much out of me, man. I mean, trying to pull people that don't really know what it's like to be out there in the big water. It's strenuous.

"So, I said, I'd better back up before I get myself a heart attack. Because when you done played with these people, if you don't cooperate with these people, it really makes it hard to go back to square one. Sometimes you say, if I can't get back to at least where I left from, then I just bow out gracefully."

You were gone a long time, about fifteen years or so. Concerning the Wichita music scene, was there any comparison between when you left in '60 and when you came back in '74 or '75?

"No. Because you got the same people that were playing the same thing when I left here when I was seventeen years old, and makin' the same mistakes they made then."

You think there hasn't been much evolution in the music here?

"Well, on a broader scale, yes. But if you talkin' about the racial end of acceptance, the white people here always love the blues. You know they always have. And they are a gracious, loving group of people. They love what's good, or what they think is good. I played in two or three white clubs here, back when I was sixteen, seventeen years old, and there was standing room only on the weekends. Like that old Rock Castle [37th N. and Broadway] out there, standin' room only on the weekends, man. Used to be a place called the Tic Toc Lounge. Played out there."

Let's talk about that Curtis Mayfield composition "Mighty, Mighty."

"I did that, just a band track, ain't no vocals on that. That's one of the technicalities that they use to do back in the old days. Other words, if you do a session, then the company had the right to pick something that they wanted to put on the other side. Because the other side gets a free ride. So, they could take one of their songs, that they got absolute 100 percent copyright on, and put it on there. Because both records—whatever one side get, the other side gets."

What about "I've Got a Problem" on the Thomas label, a Jesse Anderson and Gene Barge composition?[3] This is probably one of your biggest hits, isn't it?

"Yep, up to now. The other, 'Let Me Back In,' was right up underneath it."

When did "Let Me Back In" come out?

"It came out 'bout four months after 'I've Got a Problem.' It's kind of an answer song. Now those would be what you would call rhythm and blues."

When did "True Love Express," on Cadet, that's a Chess subsidiary, come out?

"That one come out probably around '68, '69."

Has Chess reissued any of these?

"Not that I know of yet."

From Out of Sight records we have "Oh Wow Man," Jesse Anderson. What year was this 45 put out? It's backed with "Women's Liberation" so it must be the seventies.

"Yeah, it was in the seventies. Gene Barge Productions. Barge worked with me quite a while. He became my producer after Sonny Thompson. He wouldn't sign me up directly with the company because he felt that when the company got a hold of you, then they controlled you. So he would just do things and pay for the sessions and lease the sessions and presumed got the money. But he was good to me, too. Because that's a gamble.

"The one thing I say about the new generation, these new boys, I don't necessarily approve of the way some of them are gettin' their money, and producin' theirselves, but they are doing it whole hog. You know, Ice Cube, and those cats. They gettin' them a bankroll and going in the studio and payin' for everything and doing it theyselves."

Do you like any of that new stuff? Who do you listen to these days?

"Everybody that I always listen to. I haven't changed my taste. The new stuff, really, I don't know what they singin' until they curse on that rap music, those are the only words that I understand."

Who are your current influences?

"Oh, I listen to Stevie Ray Vaughan, Lynyrd Skynyrd, Albert Collins, Buddy Guy. I listen to everybody that's upgraded the blues or brought it up another level."

How about Robert Cray?

"Well Robert, he's great, but I'd rather go to the well than to go to the faucet. He's like going to the faucet."

You work a day job now.

"Yeah, and it ain't nothin' wrong with it, builds character. It helped me. When I was an entertainer, I was strictly entertainer. I had attitude, character, charisma, strictly that. When I left the stage, I left the people and I went into my own world as you would say, but now workin' a job, I've learned a different, a real true love for people. Not that I never loved people, but I loved the simpleness in people. And so work builds character and I started buildin'. I mean even bein' fifty-five years old, I'm still building something within myself."

Your mother still works.

"Yes, she's a physical therapist. She went on and got her training. She's been in that 'bout twenty years now."

She must be pretty strong.

"I imagine she is, yeah. She handles them people. Yeah, because that's what it takes."

I'll ask about your church.

"I'm a member of Victorious Cross, Church of God in Christ, 1837 North Ash."

Do you sing in church at all?

"Congregational. We got a beautiful young group. The minister got three sons, one play drums, one play organ, and one play keyboard, piano. And I do congregational singin'. I lead sometimes from the deacon's seat. I enjoy that aspect. Other words, I like bringin' the church together in spiritual deliverance of the music. I like to be there pushing. I enjoy that. You can do that in the Church of God in Christ. Some churches, you can't really get loose, but you see Church of God in Christ, which are down in Arkansas, we used to call it the Holy Ghost Church. That's my traditional church heritage. When I was little in Arkansas, that was where everything happened at, the church.

"You would go there to rock, I mean the musicians and the tambourine players and the drummers and the trombone. Like church rocked, so our church up on Ash rocks! Rocks with the Holy Spirit!"

Did you attend services when you were away from home, like in Chicago?

"No, truthfully I didn't. I should have, but I didn't."

Do you belong to any organizations or lodges?

"No, I don't."

Do you have any hobbies like woodworking or gardening?

"Not now, but I did. I live in an apartment now. But I did gardenin' for a while as a profession, and landscaping. That's a hobby, but since I been on this guitar, it's like my all-day study. I hear it in my head at work. Like it's occupying almost all my free time."

You said you had to get up at five o'clock the other day to go to work after having played until two in the morning.

"It was really good for me to do that because it's sort of like gettin' back in shape. It was good to see if the old body could tolerate that. It wasn't bad, matter of fact, that Tuesday went by real quick. I thought I'd maybe be draggin' but no I didn't drag. So, it went by beautiful and I work for some nice people. It's a small company, but I like the way they treat me, and I like the way they treat the other employees."

You touched on your definition of the blues or at least your distinction between blues and rhythm and blues. But if somebody asked you what is the blues, can you define it?

"I can more or less tell you what it's not, than to tell you actually what it is. The blues is not the condition of mankind; blues just interpreted the conditions. At one point in our history, I'm sure you probably know, blues didn't even have a name. It came about, and some people don't really like to bring it into a perspective, and I hope that people is educated with enough love in their heart to hear the truth when they hear it.

"The blues was called the blues because of the peoples that played it. It didn't really define the music. It defined the people that played it. Before they called it blues, they had several other names that they refer it to as, darky music, Black music. Blues is just a title for that beautiful music."

How can you explain the long life of it?

"The long life of it, you see, originated out of different people's culture. First, let's go right here and then we'll go right here and then maybe it will help me say what I say. Music, from the beginning of time, was always played to the gods. That's what the first musician ever played. You can go back to David, if you choose, but it was played to the gods. Every nation of people. When the Africans came from Africa to the States, the rhythms and things that they were playing was music to their gods. Music, so far back as you go, wasn't played to sway a woman, it wasn't played to make you get up and dance. It was a petition. Blues is only a petition, like: 'They call it stormy Monday, Lord have mercy, Lord have mercy on me.' That's a prayer. Heaven, please send me someone to love, understanding, and peace of mind.

"'If it's not askin' too much, please send me someone to love.' Percy Mayfield. That's a petition. A prayer is a petition for results or an answer. So that's why blues keep livin' on, because it's a spiritual influence."

Sounds like you tried to put that into your compositions.

"Well, we did and we do. You can't get around it. It's not somethin' that just happened."

What about the main style of blues in Wichita?

"In essence, Wichita has no sound. It don't have a West Memphis sound like you can tell if a guitar player is out of West Memphis. You can tell if the cat's out of Texas. You can tell if the cat's out of Los Angeles. But Wichita in general, by being in the Midwest, it hasn't emerged with a sound. And it needs to emerge with a sound.

"I had a little studio once and I was trying to work on a sound that could be produced from out of Wichita, with Wichita talent. This was around '77, '78. I had a little production company and things. In this city, it's a lack of trust here. Greatly. In Chicago, if a guy come to you and say he wanted to do something for you, you would take a chance and say, 'Well, I'm going to see.' I set up operations here with people and spent my money for advertising and et cetera. Nobody was doing nothin', and they still ain't doing nothin'. But they have a lack of trust. Not so much they couldn't trust me, it was better like they couldn't trust theirselves. I say:

"'Tell me guys, where you want to be booked tonight?'

"'Well, I don't know.'

"'What do you want, three hundred, four hundred?'

"'I don't know.'

"'I'm going to guarantee you, and if I can make anything over that.'

"But they couldn't trust themselves to come up with a figure. It's like, 'What if I say five hundred, he might make nine hundred, and that's too much for him.' So, this is what makes it so hard to get a sound out of this city."

What kind of blues do you mostly hear in Wichita?

"You hear a lot of West Texas blues here, from south of Douglas [main north-south dividing street, meaning majority culture]. I'll put it like that. And I say that to glorify those young guys out there, that's playing their acts. There sittin' and listenin' to Stevie Ray Vaughan and really listenin to Albert Collins, and really listenin' to Buddy Guy.

"Now the guys north of Douglas is playing, they playing, they playing. No aim, see? And without aim, are you ever going to hit your target? You can't.

"A lot of the music that you hear now was back in the fifties. Like the style Stevie Ray Vaughan is famous for now, that style is partly from Gatemouth Brown and Albert King. It's still all connected to me and I'm old enough to know where it come from. I appreciate it that they keepin' it alive. They're doing that.

"I'm fortunate enough to have met Albert when I was a youngster and could have played with him. And I used to tell guitar players throughout areas in Chicago how well I love Albert's style. They use to laugh at me. They, the so-called good guitar players, said:

"'He ain't playing on nothin' but two strings.'

"I said, the man got somethin', he got somethin'. You better watch him. And sure enough, the time proceeded, man. Albert is one of the most copied guitar players around. And a lot of those guys that use to talk about Albert, ain't nobody playing their style."

Has the blues been good to you?

"Yes, it's been good to me in this aspect that, it's been a platform for me to sail on."

If a youngster wanted to get into some kind of music, what kind of music would you send him to?

"First, I would have to know how he heard things, because blues is a lot of what you hear, and what you interpret. But I definitely would recommend that he learn some of the basics of his instrument. If he's going to be a guitar player, learn the fretboard. If you going to be a saxophone player, learn the fingerin', learn your keys. If you're going to be a piano player, learn your notes."

When did you take up guitar?

"I picked up guitar approximately three, maybe four years ago. I'm making progress. I'm pleased. For one thing is that, you get some people say when you get old, fifty, you're dead, you can't learn anything. The blues have helped me prove to them that they were wrong. Yeah, the blues have been good to me. It's been my pacifier. It's been a comforter. And it's been a friend. It ain't never really been violent to me and as maybe some guide. Never made me a drunk. It never made me a drug addict. Whatever happened to me, happened after I was out of music. It wasn't the music that drove me in no detrimental direction."

How is your blues style different from other blues that people can hear in Wichita today?

"That's a difficult question but I want to take a stab at it. My blues style developed all the way back from Mrs. Hodges in Tulsa. And she embedded in me professionalism, and Miss Catherine Jeeter, the music teacher here, embedded me into working my diaphragm how to pull notes from up out of my gut, how to work the mass up in my head for sound and tones. I think my blues that I deliver is more rounded. It shows that I have worked my voice. I have worked; I'm not just opening my mouth and saying something. I always believed that a singer, whatever singer you hear, he's doing the best that he can do. And if I can sing a record that say that Albert Collins put out, then I'm going to try to sing it better. Not just to be able to get it just like him, but I'm going to try to do it better. Because I think that he's doing his best.

"Even Bo Diddley, when he did his thing, that was the best Bo Diddley could do. So, if I can do it better, uplift it to a higher degree and still it's

Bo Diddley, it's Jesse. So, I think that sort of what separates the chaff from the wheat."

Are you still writing music?

"I got some ideas and things. I haven't done a lot of writing because I don't see no foreseeable thing right now to do no recordings. My experience was that, as fast as the sound of music changes, if you write something and you ain't got it out, man, ninety days from now, you got to rewrite again and upgrade it. The market changes so fast. Record companies, they're not recording blues as much. They're releasing a lot of blues. They've gathered up all the available old blues artists that's left alive. But as far as new blues, nobody's doing anything for new blues, because we go back to that money market thing.

"You got disc jockeys out there, 'Heh man, I'm not going to play that on my show, man.' They never play anything by Albert Collins, B.B. It's strictly the boom-d-boom-boom-boom. I haven't sat down really just to pen anything down and say, well, this is it and I'm going into the studio, because I don't see no foreseeable thing. Nobody wants to take chances. Costs in the studio now is almost ten times what it was when I was recordin'. When I was recordin' you couldn't hardly do a session under $2,500. Now it's almost $15,000. And it would be more because don't nobody want to record just no one or two. They ain't doing no 45, so they at least want eight to sixteen songs.

"When you go in and try to do eight to sixteen songs, you lookin' at right at $50,000. That's where it's at. Hopefully I maybe get to scufflin' back out here again and come up with me a little thing and put all the records that I got into a CD or some cassettes and promote them, and get me a bankroll, and work blues off my own label. It can be done. That's the hope for it right now.

"With the right people pullin' together, you really could get a sound, man, out of Wichita. That was my idea. I had took my mother's house and converted the basement into padded walls and made me a isolation booth and one thing and another like that. I had really set it up. Maybe I was too far in advance. People had a tendency to think, if you're going to live out of the big city, 'Ah, he's slick; he done learned something.'

"I did learn something. What I had learned, I wanted to pass it on. They been runnin' out there at that studio out there, over there during their little session, and the engineer out there's puttin' the sound on them that he wants on them and all of that. I know what the blues have to have.

"I have took artists in and directed sessions, and told the engineer how I wanted it balanced. Then when they come out, they listen to it and they all look excited because it's the first time they ever heard theirself on a tape and then two or three days later then they set back and wished 100,000 times what they could've did. That's money wasted. I had my studio set up to practice and then get ready when you go to the studio. You walk in, you set up, you warm up, and then you record."

You could still do a project like that.

"Where we going to get a studio, where we going to get equipment? That equipment is high."

Do you have any final last words?

"Long live the blues."

DONALD DUNN (1939–)

Guitar, vocal

"I was born in Sallisaw, Oklahoma, 1939. I had four brothers and sisters. Sallisaw was very small. Everyone is almost related. I was there about five years, then we moved to Muskogee. I had relatives in Muskogee. My father was mostly self-employed at the time. Wasn't so many jobs available.

"Wasn't too many musicians in my family but we listened to a lot of music. Mostly on the phonograph, because there wasn't too much ethnic music on the radio. Sometime one record we'd play for maybe two hours, if we really liked the song.

"In junior high, I played trumpet in the school marching band. I got my first guitar when I was twelve. My aunt gave it to me so I could learn to play gospel songs.

"I guess I tried to sing, but my mother didn't think I could sing that well. Eventually I developed singing. I really got back in guitar my senior year. I had some friends who were playing the blues, Guitar Slim, B.B., T-Bone Walker. We heard them in taverns or juke joints, they had records there, and then we would order records from Stan's Music Company. There was also a Black record shop in Muskogee."

What did you do for spending money?

"When I was younger, Oklahoma was a dry state. But they had bootleggers, and they would need bottles to pour their moonshine in. So, I'd offer bottles and sell them. And a couple of occasions I would pick cotton, and that is a job. Then, in eleventh grade, I started taking barbering. On the weekend, they'd see me walkin' up and down the street with my kit, going to the neighbors' and friends' house, cuttin' their hair. Then I had a few gigs playing with Ivory Starr, a real good piano player.

"He was playing standards like 'Satin Doll.' His son was in the same class with me, so he would just take us and pay us about four dollars on Friday, and six dollars on Saturday. We played at a hotel in Okmulgee. It was a Caucasian bar. I think they could serve beer.

"When I was seventeen, we got a little band together in high school, they would call it a Hy-Y show [YMCA], actually a talent show. That was the first I actually played in an organized little band.

"I finished high school I remember on a Friday and that Sunday evening, I was en route to Minneapolis. I had a brother live up there, working at a sandblasting place. He was a few years older than I was, married and had some kids. He figured maybe I'd have a better opportunity to do things. I was up there about a year. I'd ordered a couple of albums by B.B. King and learned to play those songs almost note for note in seclusion. I never did get on stage up there. I still had my barber tools, so that's how I made money.

"I left Minneapolis, supposed to be taking a vacation, going back down with another brother in Muskogee. He had just been a prisoner of war of the Korean conflict and he was getting a lot of money and everything but he was drinking a lot. He was older than I was, but I was supposed to be there to help him watch his money and stuff like that. We rode the bus down there, and we was going to stay a couple of weeks. It was home, so we stayed there for a while.

"I felt a lot more mature and I had more confidence in myself. Eventually, the money run out. I was a fair pool shooter so I used to try to hustle pool. I got a little job at the pool hall, rackin' balls. I'd almost quit playing.

"Some of the fellows that was in this Hy-Y show kept their band together, playing in Wichita. They heard that I was back in Muskogee. So they told these other musicians about a guitar player and one night, someone knocked on the door. Said they needed a guitar player. It took me about fifteen minutes to make up my mind.

"They was playing for these Aunt Kat and Uncle Bob. I never really had a real job at this time, and I'm about nineteen years old. This was Little Jesse Anderson and the Blues Toppers. Jesse knew my friends, but I didn't know him.

"My sister had bought me a three-quarter-size Rickenbacker, Black and white. I loved that. It was solid body with the double cutaway. I took that to Minneapolis with me. She thought that I had potentiality. She put out a lot of cash.

"Our main house gig was at the Sportsman. But after I got up there, we was playing all around Kansas through Aunt Kat and Uncle Bob. They gave a lot of musicians opportunities, but they were business people, so they made money too. They would go and rent the halls in the cities that wouldn't have too much entertainment.

Donald Dunn, photo by Arthur Kenyon.

"They lived in a nice little house on about the 1100 block on North Minnesota. A lot of people stayed in that little house. I never did stay there. When I come up here, I moved in with Jesse Anderson."

When you played around Kansas, what were some of the receptions you got?

"The best I'd say was Junction City. It was a fast city. It was an army town and it was just crowded. I stayed with Jesse's band maybe a year. The group broke up, then I got hung up with Gilmar Walters at the Sportsman. They was kind of like a jazz group, Helen Carey playing piano. At that time, it wasn't a [group] name."

Describe a typical night at the Sportsman in 1960.

"Normally we'd play Friday, Saturday, Sunday. Ninth Street was pretty popular then. There'd be people, fish market and all that next door. So we would always have traffic. People came out early. About eight o'clock, people would be out on the streets ready to go. We would start playing sometimes about eight-thirty, nine o'clock.

"We'd play four sets. Jack Ponds [owner] would want us to take breaks. We would sometime be playing, he would send the waitress up there with the tray of liquor so we could kind of slow things down. His theory was, if everybody was dancin', he wasn't makin' any money.

"The Sportsman was pretty good size. You could get two hundred people in there. The Sportsman was next to the nicest Black club in Wichita, the

Esquire Club. The Smart Brothers bought the Sportsman and turned it into the Smart's Palace."

What type of music did you play?

"With this group, we kind of mixed it up. Later on when people start comin' in, we'd get more on the blues side. We never did rehearse. On stage we'd wear sweaters. With Little Jesse, we had little uniforms. We all would go by the store and buy the same-colored shirt. We wouldn't hardly wear suits too much. Like the name of the club, it was nice, but kind of sports-dress-like. You couldn't just come in there, any kind of way. You had to have a nice sweater on and pants."

Were there bouncers?

"No, just the people that ran the club. And if I remember correctly, I don't think they was charging on the door. You could buy liquor, okay, but it was still dry. You could buy half pints and pour them in a cup."

Did you ever know anything about any organized criminal element that the club owner had to pay off?

"No, I don't think too much of that happened. People had a lot of respect for Jack Ponds. Not too much violence there. But some places, yeah. There was a lot of fist fightin' and stuff. One of the roughest place where I played was the Jack and Jill, on Murdock [two blocks south of 9th]. You go down on Murdock, you can wear what you want. There wasn't no rules, not really. You know, the last man left standing was the rules. And it stayed open all night.

"The Esquire was real nice, you had food. Of course, like a lot of the places then, on in the back room, they had a little crap table, but it was organized. A few times I would go back there. You get a nice little rush when you see those dice roll across the table and you see everybody with the money in their hand.

"At the Sportsman, the blues was primarily stuff by Bobby Bland. That's what people like. Now the Esquire, they had the other blues, and most of the standards."

What happened to your career after the Sportsman and playing with Ms. Carey?

"Little Jesse left and went with this other band to Topeka. So I go to Topeka to play with Jesse and Bo Jones and Floyd Graham. Bo Jones didn't need to be amplified. He make the piano shake. He was from around where Berry lived. And Floyd was from Oklahoma.

"I liked Topeka. We played mostly at a white club, the Rainbow Club. And the money was pretty good, close to twenty dollars a night. We played there about a year, Floyd Graham and the band. I'm sure Floyd was gettin' more money. Back in those days, musicians expected that because we had leaders."

Looks like a lot of musicians migrated from Oklahoma to Kansas. Do you ever wonder why that happened?

"Because you could get a job here. And if one person going, just kind of followed a tradition. I got married in Topeka and come back to Wichita. Then I found an experience working little jobs. For a long time, I supported myself and my wife just by playing in a lot of white places, Dearmore's, Seneca Lounge, the Flame. It was about '65. See at this time, I'm just a musician for hire. Then I formed my first group, King Dunn and the Royal Subjects. We got a steady gig at the Esquire Club, every weekend for a year and a half.

"We played what was popular at the time, Sam and Dave, everything on the radio, all the Black numbers. I think that soul was about the most gratifying music, that pleased everyone. After the Esquire, I went to the Starlight Club [2418 E. 9th]. It was a little smaller, but it still pretty good sized."

Did you ever use a female vocalist?

"I've used a few, but not steady. There wasn't too many lady singers around Wichita. We played at the Starlight about a year. It had kind of a general crowd. Wasn't elites there but it was a hip place. The music was getting real soulful now. Back in those days, you had to practice, because you had to play what people was currently listening to."

So, you left the blues behind?

"Not entirely, because B.B. King and Bobby Bland was still pretty popular. My bass player left town and went to California and was playing with Johnny Otis. I was working out to Boeing, and tried to get a leave of absence, but I couldn't, so I quit to go play with Johnny Otis. That was about in '67. I was there about five or six months.

"He played every week. Then every weekend, we play two gigs, on Friday night and Saturday. Making decent money, but it still wasn't really enough to take care of myself out there, and I had a family back here too."

Did you record at all back then with Otis?

"No, I didn't. He was talking about recording me, but he wanted to record me under his show, really not as myself. It would just be Johnny Otis featuring Donald Dunn and at the time I didn't want it like that. I really didn't like workin' with him, to tell the truth. I guess I was out there, at the height of my ambition.

"But on the gig, it was all Johnny Otis and I wasn't a bandleader. I just played what they played. He would give you one number a night, and I had all this other stuff that I wanted to do. I had never really been restricted like that, because most of the groups I played with, they really needed me to put the thing together. I wish I had been more mentally prepared for it, but I wasn't.

"I came back to Wichita and the Starlight Club needed a band. This saxophone player was in town, Johnny Johnson; real good. So I got Johnny Johnson, Jay Miles, and Little Robin Murr over there playing drums.

"We had a little reputation. I felt good about myself, because I knew I had experienced something a lot of them hadn't. The pastures weren't quite as green as I imagined, but opportunity was there."

Describe what kind of music you were doing toward the end of the sixties, into the seventies.

"Mostly Motown stuff. Still done some blues. Always have and always will do B.B. King. I would just book my own deals because I knew I could make more money. I would go get my own job then go get the band. Johnny Otis taught me a lesson. So I was being a hard bandleader then. My biggest problem was I would get two jobs at the same time. I would cancel the one I got first if the other one would pay more.

"Well, disco came around, I'd gone off into the business for myself then. I had what you call a Musician's Club [mentioned by Erick Robinson]. Wichita police called it a speakeasy. Also, by this time I had a barbershop on 21st and Piatt.

"The club was on 13th and Hydraulic. My kids were growing up now and I needed a place to practice, so I really just got this building for that purpose. But after the musicians didn't really support me, I turned it into an after-hours club, which was real good. A couple times the police would come in, take my whiskey and beer. But overall, they didn't mess with me too much, because I was keepin' the people off of the street.

"The club was really something. All of the clubs would close and they would come down there. It would be capacitated. I was charging a dollar on the door and usually I'd make about $135 to $140 on the door. I had a DJ, because when I first opened for the musicians, they didn't support it. I ran this from '72 till about '78. I wasn't playing at all.

"Now I'm trying to get the old fire going again. It's hard. Really, I prefer to do a single over a group. It might be harder and a little more pressure, but I have a lot more control."

How about a church affiliation?

"I wouldn't say I belonged to a church. In Muskogee, I went to St. Mark's. Then I went to Lutheran Church a little. Actually, my family is Baptist. I'm spiritually inclined, but far as my religious virtues, I guess I just haven't really found any that called me say, 'Come on in.'"

What is your definition of the blues?

"I could say what my definition of the blues are, maybe repressed or spontaneous feelings. I think the blues is just really a inner expression."

What kind of blues style does Wichita have?

"It's really hard to characterize. I could say it kind of has its own, but I think it's like any other. I think all blues are a little different. Probably blues in New York be different, because their environment is a little different."

So, you don't think Wichita has a separate blues style?

"I think Wichita may be not quite as bluesy as Mississippi or somewhere like that, because conditions and environment was different. Wichita blues are not quite as traditional; they're a little more progressive."

BERRY HARRIS (1929–2020)

Guitar, vocal

"I was born in 1929 in Atoka County, north of Stringtown. I went to an all-Black one-room school through the third grade. I was about eleven when we moved to Boggy Bend. That was a real nice school. It was a large Black community.

"I'm from a farming community. We had the Katy railroad and everyone that didn't farm worked on the railroad. My dad was a farmer. He always liked to work for his self. We rented a twenty-acre farm we paid two dollars a year for. We were poor with money but we had everything else, places to stay, food to eat. We had a lot of love from our mothers and our fathers and the family and the community.

"Later on when we moved to around Stringtown, my mother had divorced and married another man. The war started. The economy was good during the war. My mother worked at McAlester ammo depot and my stepdad went in the army.

"The music thing started when my grandmother and my grandfather moved to where we were living at. Grandpa bought a battery-operated radio, and we used to go to his house and listen to the *Grand Ole Opry* every Saturday night. That was all he was going to listen to on Saturday night.

"I got to pecking around on guitar. Then we move on to Boggy Bend and this man, U. L. Washington, run a good-time house. On the weekends they would drink whiskey and home brew and play poker games. All these other old men played guitar. I didn't have no special interest in music. I guess I got a music education after I went in the army. I didn't play in the army; I just plinked around.

"I was in Osaka, Japan, 1949 until '52. I came out of the service and moved to McAlester. A band came through there named Gene Franklin and the

House Rockers and I went on the road with them. We got way off down in Texas and they discovered I couldn't play. I was too far from home so they had to keep me down there until they got back to Oklahoma, or pay my way back. Then Benny Johnson came through from Muskogee and I played with Benny and I began to learn how to play chord progression, jazz, but I didn't put nothing into being no musician. There wasn't no future in it. I was always disencouraged from being a musician from my father. His father was a minister. He'd seen too many people go down. And the theory was then that everybody you seen with a guitar was lazy. All they was going to do was pick on that old guitar, drink whiskey, and chase women. Then I came to Wichita.

"This friend of mine, Jerry Burns, who played piano, he came to Oklahoma and got me and Sam Franklin and Floyd Grim, a drummer, and a saxophone player. They came there and said, 'You want to go to Wichita, play in a band?'

"I said yeah. I think it paid about thirty-five dollars a night, room and board. That was a lot of money to a twenty-six-year-old man that was driving a cab in Muskogee. I played old Flagler Garden out there, which was Rhythm City at this time. The music I was playing back in Muskogee, in a twelve-piece orchestra, was 'Satin Doll,' and the clubs I was playing in here, they didn't want that kind of music. They wanted the [Hank Ballard and the] Midnighters and 'Work with Me, Annie.' The music taste was different here."

Did they like blues in Muskogee?

"Yeah, but a different form of blues, not so much like the old traditional sort of blues like John Lee Hooker. The reason why I think Muskogee flourished is because Manual High was a Black school and they always had good musicians: Jay McShann, Claude 'Fiddler' Williams. I knew Claude Williams. I didn't really know Jay McShann.

"I started playing with Gilmar Walters at the Esquire, me and a friend of mine named Bo Jones. We played with Gilmar until Gilmar got sick and then I started to play Gilmar's gigs. I know all the musicians that been around here. Not many old musicians left. Some of the musicians I never played with, like Walton Morgan and Shirley Green—the ones that were playing jazz. But we all known each other; at least we had a good relationship. That's one thing that older musicians have, younger musicians don't have.

"You were always welcome. You couldn't get in a club and not play. A musician should never have to pay to hear another local musician in nobody's club. Club owners know more about musicians than anybody in the world. They know what it takes for us to survive, what we should be playing, everything. They also know how to stand and beg you, when there's an empty house, to come play in their joint. They don't know how to pay you when

Berry Harris, photo by Arthur Kenyon.

you get a crowd. Once you build up this crowd for them, then he's going to hire everybody except you. I have to look at the Black clubs, because that's where I spent most of my time."

How about a union? Would that help?

"Union don't work in this town because this is a right-to-work state. You got too many hungry musicians out here. They just want to be heard. Well, I can't compete with that. They're killing themselves and me along with them.

"We got a union here, but Black folks never been welcome into it. And they have never done nothing for the Black musician, and they won't do nothing for us now. But one thing that has been wrong up here with us, as musicians, we fail to have stood together with each other and tried to help each other.

"All these guys that have been so good haven't done nothing. They all still here. I never had a desire to go no place. I never considered myself a good guitar player. Everybody told me I wasn't. All the good musicians shunned me, like I had the plague—all of them. Now today, these same people they grin and talk to me and they forgot how they've treated me. I haven't forgot it and I want them to know I ain't forgot. I don't throw it in their face.

"I never got a chance to play with the so called 'elite' musicians. I played with all the damn drunks. Erick Robinson would be so drunk he'd kick his drums clear out into the middle of the floor before the night was over. Drunk a whole gallon of whiskey.

"I had to go down to the white part of town and play before someone might recognize that I might be a decent musician, even though I can't play nothing but blues. But that's not the point. The point is being able to maintain and hold a little dignity and be a respectable person.

"Once people understand that you're doing the best you can do, that's all that's expected out of a man. The reason I'm not a better musician than I am, I never got the chance to play with the good musicians."

Finally you're getting some recognition. How does it feel?

"It feels very good. There is one man in this town who deserves more credit than any man, and that's Harold Cary. Harold was the first musician to play on the radio show here, and one of the best piano players in town. He can play in one key and play anything you want to hear.

"In the sixties we had a lot of good jazz musicians here. We had Henry Powell, and we had Cerrcy Arnold. And we had Helen Lewis, piano player, and her husband James, tenor player. Silvester Mathis. Fred Ponds, trumpet player.

"Albert Collins and Frankie Lee came here with Little Milton. Jerry Jones was running the Starlight. Albert Collins stayed here for about a year and a half and Frankie Lee stayed here for about two and a half years, in the middle of the sixties, playing at the Starlight."

Did you spend time with Collins?

"Oh yeah, all the time. Every weekend we sat around talk, drink, have a good time with each other. Freddie King used to come to town and he'd hang out with me a lot."

Did you pick up some influence from them?

"No. I never could imitate nobody. I'm struggling to play that little bit that I can play."

Do you think Albert Collins and Little Milton had an effect on Wichita's blues style?

"Bobby Bland and Little Milton. That's all you could hear. Because you know what makes them so good is that good vocal. But you see, this is another thing what the people got to realize is, when Albert Collins come here, this was just beginning to turn into a guitar town. This always been a saxophone town. When Hammond organ come out, B-3 and saxophone town."

Who were some good organists who played here?

"Ready Freddie used to come here. About the best organ player that really hung around here would be Gordon Simms and Jerry Childers. There ain't any more around here, unless you go to church. Then you can find a jillion of them.

"This never been a hard-core blues town. Not out there on the streets where I been. You want to know why? 'I don't want to hear that. I heard that all my life.' I say the same thing. What is it about it I don't want to hear? What is it I don't want to be reminded of? Why have we done a lot of things that we have done? To be accepted. The more you elevate yourself to a high status, don't you expect to be rewarded with acceptance?

"That's the reason why our kids don't know anything about this heritage. Because we weren't playing that in the house. We were playing something else. The songs the young white kids are hearing today are old hat to us. We don't want to hear it. We're lookin' for something better. I play up-to-date R&B and blues, but modern blues. Not John Lee Hooker. I got very little Muddy Waters. I got plenty of B.B. King, and Booker T. and the M.G.'s, Jimmy McGriff and Jimmy Smith. Whoever was playing this up-tempo feel-good music. You can't feel good, someone picking on some old guitar and singing out of tune, changing key when you want to."

You retired from aircraft work in 1992. How do you like that?

"This is the only time in my life that I ever been free since I was a child."

You play keyboard, too.

"Slightly. I used to be the keyboard player in the band when me and Little Eddie Taylor was playing together. Eddie died here not long ago. I play harmonica, and a bunch of homemade instruments that I don't ever drag out—you know, spoons and buckets. The kids used to make them instruments when they was growing up."

What's your definition of the blues?

"I really can't answer that. I don't understand that word blues because, somebody put a label on this and say, 'Well, this is the blues over here.' But when you get down to the whole theory of the thing, everything we play comes from this music. I prefer to call it just music, opposed to the blues and jazz and this, that, and the other.

"I don't believe that the slaves were singing blues. I don't think the man that got off the boat was singing no blues. They was singing for deliverance, the same thing the Hebrew children of Egypt was singing about. The blues is not the first thing. It's just a label."

So there is no definition of the blues?

"No definition of no blues; it's all music. So, we just got a label on every-thing. They say, 'Oh, the blues coming back.' Hell, they never been nowhere.

Then folks say, 'Well, you know white folks don't have no blues.' What you think he got when his stuff is wrong, when he ain't got no money? What was Hank Williams singing about? What was Bob Wills singing about? And what are they singing about today?"

Do you think there is a distinct Wichita style of blues?

"No, because we're playing everyone else's music. Another thing what folks don't realize, musicians that come from this area is better musicians than you find in Chicago or California. You know why? If you live in Chicago you can play blues all you want. That's all you have to play. If you live in California, you don't have to play but one style of music. But if you play music in the Midwest, you got to be able to play other folks' stuff, jazz, R&B. You got to please a wider variety. You got some people there that will sit you down and say, 'I don't want to hear that.' They going to ask you for something else.

"You got to have a vision. If your vision is thirty dollars a night and that's what you come up with, that's what you deserve. If you're playing on 9th Street, or you're playing in Old Town, you're making thirty-five, forty dollars a night per man. At the country club, seventy-five, a hundred dollars a night per man. But you got to play what they want to hear. We may get away with bein' a blues band at a country club now, because the blues are real popular. Everybody wants blues. You can believe twenty years ago you had to play 'Stardust' and you had to play what the ol' white man there with the money been hearing when he was a kid.

"In the future, I would hope that the musicians in this town would be better recognized, and I would also hope that they would be better to each other and stop bein' envious and stop bein' stars. There ain't no stars. You can write all the articles you want to write about me but I still need that piano player, and that bass player, and that drummer, and that second guitar player to help me be what I'm doing. I can play all night by myself but nobody going to dance to it. And after a while they get tired of hearing it.

"You're no better than the man that stands next to you on the bandstand. I don't care how much you can play, if that man next to you is not capable of playing with you, you got to come down to his level. Sometimes you're better off to have a man that you have to come to his level.

"I'd rather have a man that I have to come to his level that's sober and out here trying to do something. If you can't be making a whole lot of money, you ought to be leavin' something here for the people, so they can look back and see that you made a contribution to society."

♪♪♪

Berry Harris talked about musicians he has worked with in Wichita. The interview took place in 1997 at the African American Museum.

IRA MORTON "BO" JONES

Berry Harris: We called him Bo. Piano player and a vocalist. And a big whiskey drinker and a good friend. I met Bo here in Wichita but he's from Rentiesville, Oklahoma, where we have the blues festival [Dusk to Dawn Festival].

Question: What year did you meet Bo?

BH: Nineteen fifty-nine. We were both playing around here in Wichita.

Q: Who did he play with at that time?

BH: I really don't know who he was playing with at that time. But later on, we played together out to the Esquire Club [3400 N. Broadway] with Gilmar Walters.

Q: Did Bo play with you up in Topeka?

BH: No. I know he played some with Donald Dunn. He played with everybody. Aunt Kat booked him and they went to Topeka and played. But I don't really remember. I was going out of town too much. Me and Bo, we went down to Oklahoma City and played in the Johnnie Harris Band, David Carr on the saxophone. We played in Oklahoma City a lot, down on Second Street. Second Street was just about gone to the dumps when we got there. We first started playing for George Foreman on 4th Street in Oklahoma City.

Q: On the weekends you would drive down there?

BH: Yeah. I drove to Oklahoma City every weekend for two years. And finally Bo moved down there and stayed. He fell in love with my cousin. He came back here and stayed awhile and then he went to Kansas City, where he died of cancer somewhere in the seventies, I think. I would say that Bo was just about my age. He was born about 1930.

Q: What kind of piano style did he play?

BH: Boogie-woogie.

Q: So he used his left hand a lot.

BH: Yeah, boogie-woogie, blues piano. Where we had that blues festival over at D. C. [Miner]'s in Rentiesville; well, D. C.'s grandmother used to run that place. And Bo used to be in there playing. Seems like Bo told me that he used to go in there and drink chock, which is Indian beer, and dance and get people to give him money. He could really dance. I think his mother, Irene, was a dancer. He weighed about 300 pounds, but he could get up on his feet like he weighed about 125–30 pounds. He was a lot of fun to be around, a real nice guy.

Q: Did you haul around a piano with you when you played with him?

BH: No. We'd find him a piano in the places where we'd go. Some places had a pretty nice piano.

Q: Like the Esquire Club—was that a good piano?

BH: Oh, Esquire had good instruments.

Q: Did he ever play electric piano with you?

BH: No, no. Electric pianos were just coming in when Bo left here and went to Kansas City.

Q: Did you go and see him in Kansas City after he moved up there?

BH: Oh yeah, I went up there. He drove a cab and played for a church in Kansas City.

Q: By then he had switched to performing in church?

BH: No. He always played in church but [*laughs*] he was on both sides of the fence. He played church and the streets too because he liked to drink. He liked a good party. So he was always out in the streets.

Q: That's unique, isn't it? Not too many people would play blues and play in church.

BH: Well, I think a lot of people did do that. Those that found it to be all right done it. I didn't, because I didn't find it to be all right. But Bo played for a Baptist church in Kansas City.

DAVID CARR

BH: Big David Carr was not around here very much. He was in and out of here because he played with me a lot. He's a good saxophone player, a good singer.

Q: How big was he?

BH: Six foot two or three or six inches. Two hundred pounds easy.

Q: So you guys had your own bouncers in the band?

BH: Yeah, [*laughs*], we could have. David Carr and I met playing with Gene Franklin and the House Rockers. I used to drive to Oklahoma City on Friday evenings, and Dave and I would start playing in the club there on 23rd Street from twelve o'clock to six o'clock in the morning. Dave left the band and moved to Denver and got married and he had about three children. His wife died and he moved back down to Oklahoma City. Then when I got to going back down in Oklahoma City playing, I ran into him and we started playing together.

Q: Were you both in the musician's union?

BH: No! No union. Union didn't do nothing for Black musicians. Before I came here they had a Black union, but it had dissolved. David was a nice friend, good musician. He got a son that plays drums and one that plays alto saxophone, both in Dallas. I'd say David was born in 1930–31, somewhere in there.

Q: What did he die of?

BH: Heart attack. He had played that night and came home. He had a garden outside his house and his wife found him dead the next day in the garden.

GERALD "JERRY" BURNS

BH: He was the uncle of Karla Burns [Broadway performer]. This is the reason I'm here in Wichita. Gerald Burns and Levy Langover, of Langover Trailer Rentals, came to Oklahoma and got me, Sam Franklin, and Floyd Grim; drummer, saxophone player, and me, guitar player. I was living in Muscogee, playing with Benny Johnson. We played at old Flagler Garden, which was named Rhythm City. At that time, it was me, Jerry Burns playing piano, Floyd on drums, Wily Joe Taylor playing guitar, Good Rocking James Best on bass, Sam Franklin on tenor saxophone. Then, we had a singing group. That was Sammy Lynch Faggitt. Sammy Faggitt is what we knew him as. Lynch we learned later. Claude, James Day, Trotter. Four of them. I can't think of everybody's name right now.

Q: That was a pretty big ensemble you had.

BH: We had a band and floor show. We done all the [Hank Ballard and the] Midnighters things. Like "Work with Me Annie" and then "Annie Had a Baby."

Q: Rhythm City was that big, that they could have a floor show?

BH: Oh yeah. That was a big club. It would hold about four or five hundred people. We had a bandstand big enough to do a floor show with a five or six piece band.

Q: Where was this picture of Jerry Burns taken?

BH: It was taken down here at his mother and father's house on Indiana. And the way I know that is because I recognize this piano. It was sitting in Mr. and Mrs. Burns house. Jerry must have been born somewhere around 1928, 1929.

Q: What style of piano did he play?

BH: Jerry Burns could sound like Erroll Garner one minute; he could sound like George Shearing the next. He could sound like whoever he wanted to sound like. He could play blues, play jazz. He played organ. Now, Gordon

Simms played organ with Willy Wright and the Sparklers when they first came here. Gordon was just starting to play. Jerry Burns run the Sportsman [Lounge on 9th Street] at that time. Gordon used to go get Jerry in the morning and buy a fifth of vodka and they'd lock up in that Sportsman down there all day long and drink vodka and Jerry would teach him how to play organ. So Aunt Kat, Kathryn Smith, was my booking agent and she stayed over on Minnesota or Minneapolis, one of the two. She had an organ in her house. We used to go over there every day, because Jerry stopped in and played organ.

Q: Could he read music?

BH: It's what I been told, but I never seen him read none. He said he could, which you know how that goes.

Q: When did he pass away?

BH: Ten or fifteen years ago.

SAMMY LYNCH

BH: Sammy was in the vocal group at Rhythm City when I met him. Sammy got a son here named Gaylon. He was a self-taught drummer and later on he sang with Willy Wright and the VIPs. Sammy died in federal prison. We just had his funeral a couple of years ago.

Q: He got in some trouble?

BH: Yeah, trouble followed him.

Q: Did he have trouble when he was playing with you?

BH: No, no.

EDDIE TAYLOR

BH: Eddie Taylor was a graduate of Douglass High School in Oklahoma City. He had trophies for saxophone and trumpet in the high school band before he was a guitar player. When he came out of the navy, he started playing guitar with the Bill Parker Band. Eddie lived in Wichita for twenty-five years approximately. He and I played together in the Elks' Lounge when we used to talk about opening up the Elks' and we didn't have no people. The band was Eddie Taylor, Erick Robinson, David Brewer, and myself. We made three dollars per man on Friday, four dollars per man on Saturday, and two dollars per man on Sunday. That was our guaranty.

Q: This must have been when you first came to town.

BH: Oh, no, no. I'd been here a long time.

Q: How is it you were playing for so little money?

BH: Because we weren't playing anyplace else. This was an opportunity to play. So J. K. Smith opened the Elks' up and we started playing for him. This is when we went down on Murdock and got the female impersonators to dance. We began to get a crowd, so we went up to Citizens Funeral Home and rented a casket. We stood that casket up out there in the back in the Elks' and when the floor show started, we had all these female impersonators out there dancing. They turned out all the lights except one light right there behind the bar that said "Elks'" and they shot a smoke bomb in there; all that green and yellow smoke. And about that time, they roll that casket out of the back. They had this other female impersonator in that casket and he got out and did a dance and got back in the casket and we rolled him back out. That's how we built the crowd at the Elks' Lounge. So, you need to understand bands built that crowd.

Q: About what year was that?

BH: Oh, this was in the sixties. I just can't go back and pinpoint it. I pretty much can tell where I was at time to time, because I worked on the missile base from 1960 to 1962. Went to work in Iowa and then I came back here and went to work at Beech in 1963.

Q: How long did you play at the Elks'?

BH: We played there seven and a half years. We ended up with me and Eddie Taylor, Richard, John, and Leroy Smart, the Smart Brothers. Richard played bass, John played tenor saxophone, Leroy played trumpet, and Robert Morgan was our drummer. That's when we started going to Topeka playing the Potentate Balls. I went to Topeka for twenty-eight years in a row. And then, for twenty-six years I played for the Pleasuremere Club. The man responsible for that was Mr. Hardy; Elks' out of Topeka, Kansas.

KATHRYN SMITH

BH: Her husband was Robert Smith. They were known as Uncle Bob and Aunt Kat. She died not long ago. He's still alive. He's preaching. See, they kind of raised Reverend Franklin Mitchell. Ah, what can I say about Aunt Kat? We been all over the state of Kansas, me and Aunt Kat. We had good times. We bought Aunt Kat three or four station wagons [*laughs*]. But we went places. We played in Junction City down on 9th Street in whore alley. I hated Junction City because all it was was prostitution back then and you couldn't find places to stay. You couldn't get motels like you could just now. Now this is 1960 when we first started going up there, when I first got hooked up with Aunt Kat.

Q: How did you meet her?

BH: I don't know how I met Aunt Kat. But she was involved with all the musicians at that time. Anybody that was playing was playing for Aunt Kat.

Q: What kind of a set-up did she have with you? Was it a fifty-fifty split or sixty-forty?

BH: Who knows? Whatever she promised, you know; fifteen dollars, twenty dollars. Nobody knew what she was getting. The only thing that we knew was what little we was getting.

Q: But she got you work?

BH: Oh, we worked all over Kansas: Junction City, Hutchinson, Lyons, Great Bend, Dodge City, Independence, Ark City, Pittsburg, Parsons.

Q: And you traveled by station wagon?

BH: And a car.

Q: Did you have Miss Blues [Remona Hicks] with you at that time?

BH: Miss Blues was singing with Franklin Mitchell. Franklin and Raymond Boston had a band; and, it seems like, Calvin Scales. All these guys usually hung out together and played together. Miss Blues didn't sing with me until down at the Elks', when Tom Holmes was the Exalted Ruler.

GILMAR WALTERS

BH: Everybody in Wichita that know Gilmar know him by the name of Goodbutter.

Q: Why?

BH: I don't know. Maybe because he played good bass or maybe because he talked a lot of stuff. Dr. Ronnie Walters is one of his children. And he was the husband of Maxine Walters who still lives here. And he got other children here, Jerry and Marsha. I can't recall everybody's name. Gilmar Walters played with the Syncopators Band before I got here. This band, the Syncopators, was Walton Morgan, Shirley Green, T. J. Simms, Don Govan, and I can't think of who else. Gilmar was with the 9th and 10th Cavalry, Buffalo Soldiers. He was retired from the air force reserve out here at McConnell Air Force Base. He had served in the army and the air force.

Q: Kind of like Perry Reed.

BH: Yeah. Well, him and Perry Reed and George Johnson, the helicopter pilot, they was all in the military together. I never met Perry until about three or four years ago but Gilmar used to tell me about Perry because Perry won the Hiedt Trophy on the talent show. That's what gave him all the recognition. Only thing I can say about Gilmar, and really know what I am talking about, is he and I were good friends.

Q: How did you meet him?

BH: Oh, by being a musician. Just get in the club and, you know, he was there playing, like the Esquire Club. Gilmar Walters, Helen Lewis, Big Sam, Drumski (Elvis Forrest) the drummer: there is so many of these fellows here that I could get into naming, just from club to club. Jerry Hahn used to come in there and listen to us. We taught all them guitar players how to play, like Pat McJimsey.

Q: How about Clif Major? Did he ever come out?

BH: Nah. We never seen Clif Major in this section of town. But, Jerry Wood, Rene Aaron who plays harmonica, Rick Meyer, they all been over here. The older ones, you know, Dempsey Wright, Luther McDonald; these are the white musicians. There are so many more that I can't even name them, and there are so many more musicians that are gone that we haven't even mentioned like Cerrcy Arnold, and Toran, played piano. But, see, Harold Cary, Gilmar, and a white drummer, Chuck Blackham, played for twenty years at the Candle Club on Woodlawn. They set endurance records. That's about all I can tell you about Mr. Gilmar Walters other than this was my buddy. When I was one of the very first people in Northeast Wichita to have cable TV, Gilmar and I spent a lot of time together. We watched boxing and he was at my house about five, six nights a week. I seen him when he was in good health and I seen him when he got in bad health and I seen him when he began to halfway recover and when he got sick and died.

Q: What did he die of?

BH: I don't know. I don't know what the complications were. All I know is he went to the hospital for a check-up and he knew ever since then he was sick. And I wouldn't want to get into saying what he died of because I wouldn't want his family mad at me. I'll let them tell you.

THE JIVE FIVE

BH: The Jive Five had numerous personnel over the years. There was Stanley who was the bass player. Ah, he's still here not doing nothing. Eddie Gaines was from Enid, Oklahoma. He was our drummer. Woodrow Cooper, the organ player, he's still here. We call him Fly. Lee Williams is currently the leader of the Just Us Band. And of course Herbie Welch, one of the best guitar players come through here and let us get away from him.

In 1969, we were still playing around the Elks' and the Esquire and up there on 17th Street, and we had other clubs to play.

Q: What kind of music did you play?

BH: The same thing we playing now, R&B. We play a little funk.

Q: What other Black bands were in town playing in the early seventies or late sixties, and what were they playing?

BH: We was all playing blues. But we weren't playing Johnny Lee Hooker and Muddy Waters style blues. We were playing B.B. King, Bobby Bland. The Smart Brothers were here, and Fred Williams had a band, and four or five little singing groups. We had plenty of local groups, but we had some good floor shows come through here.

Q: Did they have their own musicians?

BH: No, we were the band. They was just the vocal group. We had to learn their material.

Q: How did you do that, just by ear?

BH: Yeah, listen to it. Of course, we knew the same songs that they knew. There wasn't no problem.

Q: Did they dance too?

BH: Yeah, they was a working show. The Esquire always had good shows. Richard Cooke and Mr. Irving Harris run the Esquire and they always had good shows. They had women dancers and they had musicians and they had ventriloquists; all kind of good shows came into the Esquire.

Q: These were all African American performers?

BH: Yeah, yeah. Most of them came out of Kansas City and Chicago. A few came out of Oklahoma City and Tulsa.

Q: How did you get jobs back then? Did you have to hustle for them or did somebody call?

BH: You didn't go out and look for no jobs. People call you. But you knew if you went to work in a man's club, you were going to play there until he got tired of you or you quit. It wasn't like it is now.

Q: Were there more clubs to play in, or fewer musicians?

BH: About the musician status: it's about the same, just fewer clubs.

Q: You mentioned all these white musicians learning from the African Americans: Jerry Wood, Jerry Hahn, Pat McJimsey. Do you suppose that was unique to Wichita?

BH: Oh no, it's always been going on like that. I was in Tulsa before I came here in the fifties. I remember the Flamingo—and you can verify this with Sam Franklin and any of those people. You go in Saturday night at six o'clock and may not come out until nine o'clock Sunday morning. Be in there all night, unless you just want to walk outdoors. I heard these Black bands playing and then you have Bob Wills and the Texas Playboys come in there when they'd get off, without fiddles, and with saxophones and French horns, playing all night long. A lot of white musicians would get off their jobs at one, two o'clock and they'd come on Greenwood Street and be there until daylight. But you see, [in Wichita] I played from eight o'clock to twelve o'clock at the Tick Tock Lounge and then pack up and go to the Bomber Club and play from one o'clock to daylight. I was playing with Kid Thomas, harmonica player and a drummer called Tricky Marvin out of Chicago.

Q: Did Thomas and Marvin go on to record?

BH: You know, Kid Thomas got killed in California. He ran over a girl out there and they said that he was drunk. But Thomas didn't drink. And they finally discovered he was on medication. Then they freed him and when he got out, so what I been told, he came out of the courthouse and the girl's father killed him there on the courthouse steps. Because he couldn't accept the fact that Thomas wasn't drunk, that he was sick.

Q: You have some good memories.

BH: I am glad to be a part of this history of Wichita. We glad to be a part of history. This is something that need to be done for any Black person in this town that has done anything besides went to jail. Because they can remember us for all our bad things, but they can never remember us for our good things. These are so easily forgotten. But when we mess up, and get locked up, they can remember us forever. You know, I had no idea in my life that I was doing nothing for the community. I had never looked at it that way. But I never make no money playing this music, you know. I've done this for the love of what I like to do, and the people. It's because if it wasn't for the people, it wouldn't be no point in playing. Even though I could have done this for a living, but I chose to take care of Loretta [wife] and the kids.

CHARLES WALKER (1939–2010)

Vocal

"I was born in Muskogee, Oklahoma, 1939. I knew of Berry from down there, but I really got acquainted with him when we came up here. There was so many from Oklahoma up here. I came up here in '58 or '59.

"My mother used to do house cleaning to take care of two boys. My father and my mother wasn't together. I was in Muskogee from birth till I graduated from Manual Training High School. And the day that I walked across the stage, we had a van waiting to come to Wichita. We'd been comin' up durin'

spring break, or then sometime on the weekend. We'd come out and play at
Flagler, through Uncle Bob, and Aunt Kat. His nephew, Bob McVey, went
to school with us. He was the trumpet man."

What did you think of Wichita when you first got here?

"Anytime that you are in a city that appreciates you, then it's going to make
you like that city. So, we fell in love with the city. At that time, we were Willie Wright and the Aces. We changed it to Willie Wright and the Sparklers
later on. We were tourin' down south with Joe Tex and Jackie Wilson, and
the Vibrations.

"I think the management that got the tour for us just thought maybe
that the Aces was too old and they wanted to pep it up with the Sparklers.
They had all those gigs booked; we went along with it. We played behind
Joe Tex and I would open the show up singing. This was before he really got
nationally known. He was known real well down South. We went to Arkansas, Georgia, Alabama, Mississippi, Florida, and then we came back up the
East Coast. Most of it was one-nighters. Mixed clubs, Black, white colleges.

"All of us was from Muskogee. Willie and Carl Wright, his brother, lived
probably two blocks from me."

Why do you think Muskogee was such a musical town?

"I don't know. It may have been because of fellows like Berry Harris.
He was pretty popular down there before he left, and I think we just kind
of picked up instruments and started peckin' on them. I was singing in a
spiritual quartet. And at that time, I had a pretty good voice. Carl used to
play the piano. Gordon Simms played organ. It was two brothers and all the
rest of us was just classmates. We had a pretty good size group at that time.
Through twenty years playing together, it was always about five of us that
stuck together. But some additions would come in, like Jesse Anderson.

"The place we rehearsed the most was a community center. The people
heard us and they liked us and gave us a key and let us rehearse there. And
a lot of times after football games, basketball games, we would come and
play music and the high school would come in and we would have a ball."

So it was a Black community center?

"Yeah. Back in those days, it was pretty much segregated down in Muskogee. The community was behind young people playing."

When you got to Wichita, did you have to get a job?

"No; didn't any of us work. I took care of a family of four in the clubs here
for about fifteen years. Of course, the wives worked during through day. We
worked with Uncle Bob and Aunt Kat all the time we were in school, and a
couple of years after we got up here. But most of the time we were just playing
from club to club like the Esquire. We played there I think four years and

Charles Walker, photo by Arthur Kenyon.

the Sportsman, we played there for about five years. And then the Starlight Club down on 9th Street, we played there for about three years."

This would be early sixties?

"Yeah, up through I would say probably the early seventies."

How did your music evolve from your arrival to the early sixties?

"More of a variety, because when we first started, most of our stuff was R&B. And then we had to venture into some pop, and I've even sang country. Wilson Pickett, Lloyd Price, B.B. King, Bobby Bland, mostly all of the top ten. If you wasn't playing what the people was acquainted with, you wasn't where it was at."

Was there a tradition of music in your family back home?

"I think I'm probably the first one in my family, and probably the last, to be involved in music as deep as I was."

Did you ever get a chance to record or do any demos?

"After I quit singin' in the clubs, I had a friend that wanted me to help him write a song and we wrote the song. And he said, 'I want to connect you with a friend of mine in Chicago.' I cut a couple of songs off of that. Got booked with 20th Century Fox, and they released a song, 'Undivided Man.'"

You used session musicians in Chicago?

"Yeah. They were Johnny-on-the-spot. Couple of practices, man, and they were hittin' it. It was kind of a R&B ballad."

Do you have any copies?

"I sure don't. I hate that I don't. At the time, it wasn't that much of biggy to keep one, because 20th Century was really hot on it and they thought that they were really going to put some money behind it. We supposedly split the composer rights. We did split but some kind of way, the money got kind of tied, and wasn't any made really."

So you were a professional musician in Wichita for at least fifteen years? That would take you up to 1973 or '74.

"That's about right. When disco started showin' up we did some few disco tunes."

Did you quit the band, and it went on, or did the band break up?

"I quit the band and they played two or three years after I quit and then I think they all joined church and started playing."

Which church were you in Oklahoma, and are you active in church now?

"Old Agency Baptist Church. Right now, I'm really not that active. I joined Tabernacle Baptist Church and I sang in the choir there for a number of years, but I haven't been attendin' regular enough."

Can you talk about the difference between the Esquire Club and the Sportsman?

"Ninety percent of the crowd stayed with us, from the Sportsman to the Esquire. The Esquire was a lot larger in space. I'd like to think it was a little nicer. But the Sportsman was more of a fun type club. At the Sportsman, if you didn't have shoes, shirt, that type thing, they wouldn't let you in, but mostly anything—as long as you covered—would go at the Sportsman. The Esquire was more of a tie and suit type thing."

Describe a typical gig at the Sportsman and the Esquire.

"We played the Sportsman the late fifties. I think it was the mid-sixties when we started playing at the Esquire. When we played at the Sportsman, you may go in that place at ten o'clock and when you come out, the sun was comin' up. We didn't have any curfew. We had a ball. And when we played at the Esquire, it was basically the same atmosphere. It was wide open during those days, because back then, you could buy beer but it was a bottle club. Either one of those [Sportsman and the Esquire], you had to bring your own bottle.

"Our starting time was eleven o'clock. I used to go out to the Stagedoor Inn to visit with Mike Finnigan and I think they started at nine. I'd sing until twelve, and then Mike would come down and sit in, because we'd play until three in the morning. Mike would tear the place up. If you come in as a stranger and you were really doing something, then the crowd would have to get behind you, because you were new blood."

How much of your show was blues?

"I would say probably 40 percent of it was straight blues. Soul actually became 75 percent of our program. And we'd play one set of jazz."

What did you dress like on stage?

"I use to try to sew. And I'd sew me up a outfit, kind of real sparkly and that type thing. But most of the time, when we were playing at the Esquire, we had maybe jackets, and pants alike. When we were tourin' we had pretty flashy stuff on. When we wanted to get new uniforms, we kind of pool into the kitty and do that type thing. In the fifteen years that we played, we had maybe five costumes. Most of the time, at the Starlight and the Sportsman, we'd kind of dress casual. But we always tried to look pretty good because the girls was lookin' good."

Was there ever any violence when you were on stage?

"Yeah, but most of the time, it was mainly fights. Every once in a while, a guy would get his life taken. I've seen guys fight and get up and shake hands. You don't see that nowadays. Out to Flagler, we just had finished playing, and a guy came in and lost his life out there. I guess they threw him out or something, and I heard him say:

"'That's all right; I'll be back.'

"And just as we were ending up, he came in with a gun and started shootin' over the counter at the bartender. And the bartender got back in the kitchen and shot him as he jumped over the bar."

You were a teenager then?

"Oh yeah. Scared me to death. People scattered, man, and I crawled back in the men's rest room. When they stopped firing, I eased out. Yeah, that shook me up."

What about when trouble would break out, what would the band do?

"You don't stop playing because once you stop, then all the attention is on the scuffle. So you tried to keep playing to keep the attention on you so the bouncers or whatever could get to it and break it up."

Do you think music influenced violence, or do you think the music calmed the crowd?

"I think the music probably calmed the crowd more than it would stir up the ruckus. I think it kept it in perspective more by us playing, because a lot of times by us being on the stage, we could see it, but some parts of the club would not even know that it had happened."

How many people do you think would be in the Sportsman on a good Saturday night?

"The fire code was about two hundred, I believe. It was pretty good size place. I've seen people just butt-to-butt, back-to-back. We played Wednesday to Sunday. It wasn't open the other nights."

Did you have a contract?

"Just a verbal handshake. Jack Ponds was a pretty fair guy. When you pack a place five nights a week, usually you don't have any problem."

Who else played with you in the Sparklers?

"Eddie Cadell. He was our sax player for longer than any sax player we've had. Fred Ballard played with us. Trumpet. Very good. I loved singin' behind those guys."

How did you pick material? Was it by democratic vote?

"Well, if a guy like Fred would hear something that he liked, he would practice it and bring it to the group. If one of us wanted to do it, we'd practice it and do it. We had good rapport."

When you got out of music, what sort of business did you get into?

"Retail sales and then I went to Boeing and I finished up my work career at Boeing."

Was that a big change, or were you ready to put on a suit and go out and get up in the morning?

"Yeah, I was. At first we had no problems. I mean musicians worked together fine, but then after a while, you had the younger guys comin' up and they would come in and underbid the gigs until it was no money for a fellow to make a living. And when you go to a club at eleven o'clock and then maybe six when you get out, there's no other time for you to go to a straight gig. Another thing, we was splittin' the money right down the middle. Then they started workin' this thing where the vocalist wouldn't get paid as much. That's when I kind of bowed out of it. We got along a lot better, and things worked real nice, when all of us was gettin' an equal amount."

What does it take to please a crowd in Wichita?

"I would say, you got to be funky for one thing. The people in Wichita feel what you feel. If you don't feel it, they can't get into it. My thing was slow stuff most of the time, and this Bobby Bland type stuff and ballads."

When you were singing, what kind of money did you make?

"When we were at the Sportsman, I think we were doing about $300 a week. And then, at the Esquire, we were doing about $350–$375 a week [apiece]. Back in those days, that was good."

What style of blues did Wichita like?

"Mostly it was B.B. King, Bobby Blue Bland. I think when we first start comin' up here, it was Fats Domino."

Did you ever see groups when they came through Wichita?

"Bobby Bland and B.B. King. I'd always try to make their set at the Cotillion."

Do you think Wichita has its own music sound or do you think it just copies other regions?

"I think Wichita has just a tremendous amount of talent and it hasn't been tapped. And I think most of the guys that's got good talent is basically doing their own thing. And I think for a producer to come in here, that really had something going on, he could pull a lot of good stuff out of Wichita."

How did you get Wichita audiences motivated?

"It's tough because, for Black people, they don't have a lot of things going on. So you take a place like Chicago and Los Angeles, and those places, you got things to do each and every night. The Wichita people has trained themselves to just kind of live more of a subdued life because there's nothing happening—just every great once in a while."

Would you recommend that a younger person today get into music?

"Oh, I would say definitely, if he's got a desire to be one of the best. Do it. Music is more competitive now than it has ever been."

Did you ever have youngsters who wanted you to give them help learning how to sing?

"Oh, yes. I never did give voice lessons, but it was quite a few young fellows that would come out and listen to me sing. Sometimes I'd let them come up and sing while I was doing my sets. A lot of those young fellows, I didn't even know their names. I just knew they could sing."

REMONA HICKS (MISS BLUES) (1936–1996)

Vocal

"I was born in Pawnee, Oklahoma, 1936. My mother took in ironing and washing, different jobs, housekeeping and everything. Then she had a truck farm. It was a lot of acres. She sold greens, green beans, watermelons and corn. Then on hog-killin' day, they sold meat to stores. My mother had a lot of pigs, hogs, cows, and chickens.

"I had two sisters and I still got two brothers. Both of my sisters is deceased. We helped our mother. We chopped cotton, cut sugarcane, worked in the garden and helped ourselves to vegetables. We shook pecans and sold them to grocery stores.

"My mother was a guitar player. And she was also a church lady, and we was raised up in the Holiness Church. I was a leader of a lot of choirs. I started out in the church and when I moved from Oklahoma to Wichita, that's when I started singin' the blues.

"When we lived in Silver City, everybody had a one-room school. Mother cooked hot lunch for the schools. I had a pretty good childhood life. I did but it was in the olden days. Back in them days, you could take a quarter and eat a whole full-course meal, but now you can't do that.

"I got to the ninth grade. Mother had to keep us out of school a lot. When it got real cold weather, we wasn't able to walk to school because we lived so far. They'd give us so many weeks out of school for the winter, and time to work our farms.

"They had dinners in the country. They spread the tables and stuff and four or five different churches get together. I was in a singin' contest, when I was eleven. I won a certificate and a gold Bible. And I won a trip to Arkansas to sing in one of the big churches."

Did your mother encourage you to sing?

"She encouraged all of us. We all three sung together. She also played guitar like she didn't play it at church; have her friends over and they'd throw parties and she'd play guitar for them. Them old timin' blues, like 'O Lordy Lord,' and 'Worried Life' blues, and 'Workin' On a Railroad.' She wouldn't sing nothin' like when I come to Wichita. I was singin' up-to-date songs. My mother died when she was forty. I was livin' in Wichita, but I went home to the funeral.

"We moved from the country to Bartlesville. My stepfather, he worked the property and they let us live there for him keepin' up his property. I didn't know my real father. I went to a girls home, Taft, Oklahoma,[4] when I was thirteen and I stayed there till I was eighteen, but I sang with different groups and I sung my way out of there."

For good behavior?

"Yeah. And I was off into the church real good."

So you got out of the girl's home and decided you'd come to Wichita. How did you decide that?

"I had a aunt stay up here, and one of my sisters was here. I moved up here so I stayed with her, but then I got pregnant with my son."

What did you think of Wichita?

"I liked it because I was singin' in every club in this town almost."

When you were eighteen, they let you come in and sing?

"Because they knew I could sing. I went to the club one night and I just got here. I think it was the Bunny Club. It was way back. The band was playing and I asked, could I set in. They heard my voice and then different bands started to get me to sing with them. And then I hooked up with the Jive Tones.

"Then I started singin' with Willie Wright and the Aces. They was good. They gave me a lot of help with my voice. I needed the strength. I been singin' in churches and things, so I needed to get out there [to project]. And different bands pushed me. I took Tina Turner's place one night at Flagler Garden. Because she couldn't sing, couldn't talk. And then I sang a couple gigs with Joe Simon here at the Club International, up here on 21st Street."

That was in the seventies or eighties, wasn't it?

"Yeah. I also sang with B.B. King in Manhattan, Kansas."

What was Tina Turner doing in Wichita?

"They booked her here. And she had laryngitis. And Dick Smart—I was playing with him at the time—said, 'I know a singer that sound just like her.'

"I sung all her songs. I was paid $500 to do it. I was so pregnant and I didn't want to, but I did. I made that money. Then I sung against Koko Taylor down at the Century II. That's been about ten, eleven years ago. But they said we look like twins.

"I used to be there. I used to sing. Franklin Mitchell's the one I started with. And Raymond Boston."

Do you ever go to Pastor Mitchell's church?

"No, because I haven't been able to get around too good. But I go to the hospital, have an operation or something and he's right there. Him and Berry, I'm kind of their big sister."

You were pretty popular in the club scene.

"Everybody in this town, I can be walking down the street and they'll stop me and talk to me. My kids used to ask me all the time, 'Mama, do we ever get where we going, because every time we get out, people stop you and start talking.'"

What was your stage name back then?

"Miss Blues. I got the name from Dinah Washington. Because she died, and she was the only Miss Blues and I asked B.B. King, could I used her name. He said she was already deceased, so I always used her name."

Where did you ask B.B. King?

"I sang with him in Tulsa and Muskogee. We played in the same town with him. Me and Berry and them would go to his club through our intermissions and we'd sit in with him."

Remona Hicks, photo by Arthur Kenyon.

What kind of music did they like back in the fifties in Wichita?

"Oh they like blues. I'm only Miss Blues; I don't sing none of this rappin' and all that stuff. Yeah, Lord, I make them fight. I was good. I used to pattern most of my songs after Bobby Bland, B.B. King, and Johnnie Taylor. I don't never sing no women songs, if I can help it. Because I have a low voice and I can't sing background anyways.

"I met Berry when I moved to Wichita. I turned eighteen, I was just gettin' so I could go to the clubs. Back in them days, you didn't have to have no ID and all that, and you just walked into the club. They wasn't fightin' and gang bangin' then. And I heard Berry and them playing one night and I set in with his band. He liked me."

You weren't shy back then, were you?

"No. I'm not now either. Berry wrote a lot of songs for me. He helped me with a lot of my music, my timing and everything. Him and Franklin, they taught me a lot."

What was the band you stayed with the most?

"I worked with the Jive Tones for 'bout ten, eleven years. Raymond Boss was the guitar player, Franklin Mitchell was the bass player, Troy Banks was the organ player, and Adolph Thurman was our drummer. He played piano and drums. Then we got Ted Baskin out of Chicago. He came to Wichita and wanted to play with somebody. He started being our drummer and Adolph went to piano."

What clubs did you play in?

"The Oklahoma Quarter Club, the Elks on 9th Street, American Legion. I sang there. I sang out to Flagler and the Esquire Club. I sung at the Holiday Inn, the Century II; I sang in a lot of them. Because we had a pretty good manager. She booked us quite a lot of places. Kathryn Smith. That was my sister. Everybody called her Aunt Kat and Uncle Bob.

"I was way down on, well, the tracks one day [after arriving in Wichita] and I was standin' up by the jukebox and I was singing. Franklin heard me and went back and told Aunt Kat. See, they didn't know Aunt Kat was my sister. I'm going to tell you the exact words he said: 'I want you to go down on the tracks down there and get that great big old Black woman, because she can really sing.'

"Aunt Kat said, 'What's she look like?'

"And when he was telling, Kat said, 'That's my sister.'

"She came straight on down there and got me. I moved in with Aunt Kat. After I had my oldest daughter, we always stayed with Aunt Kat and Uncle Bob. And she really gave me a start. She was our bookin' agent."

Your sister did a lot of good for this town.

"Yes she did. I came to stay with some friends of mine because I just got out the girls training school and then I was doing a little running around. So I moved in with her. Then she started me to singing. She told me, as pretty as my voice was, I needed to be doing something with it, besides singing with the jukebox."

They had musicians staying with them?

"No, I was the only one that stayed with them. But they booked a lot of dances, you know. And we played for the door, they'd get 60 [percent], we'd get 40 [percent]. We done that a lot, just to get started. We had to pay for our uniforms and everything. If we rent a building and get a dance, we'd get it all. And we did that a lot."

How much did a job pay back then?

"They always paid me separate than they paid the band. I got mine whether the band got paid or not because I was the one drawing the crowd. Aunt Kat booked us everywhere. We went to Nebraska, Little Rock, down in Mississippi. We had a station wagon with a picture of the band and me singing on the side."

That was the Jive Tones?

"With Miss Blues Hicks. That's right. We traveled together. We'd get a U-Haul. That's how they took their instruments."

How did you handle the road?

"There wasn't no problem with stage fright or anything. Because I was raised up in the church and I had to sing against a lot of people."

What attracted you to singing the blues?

"I don't know. From a kid on up, we used to go to these joints and slip in. Back in them days, they didn't play nothing but the blues. And I just liked that type of music."

What about during the sixties?

"I moved to Junction City, because we did a lot of playing in Junction City. That was our stable home, that's where I raised my kids at. I played with two or three different bands up there."

Did you do any other kind of work?

"No. That's how I raised my kids. I got three girls and one boy. The club owners was giving more money than the welfare was giving me. Because we'd do two jobs a night sometimes, four hours a job. Sometimes I'd be so hoarse I couldn't hardly talk, but I'd suck me a lemon and I'd go on to that other job."

Did they have a pretty good sound systems back then?

"I had my own PA system. I had a Mercury mike because I blew a lot of microphones out. That's what I'm saying, that's why when I sing, I have to step back off the mike, because I got strong lungs."

Where did you get musical equipment?

"Aunt Kat did most of that because after she once get the instruments for us, we'd pay for them. Anything happen to them, she'd go get them for us. But then we had rules. If we be late for band practice, they'd dock us. Be late for a job, you'd get docked."

Your own sister would dock you?

"Yes, she'd dock me. I remember a lot of times I didn't get paid. They'd dock me, and take my whole pay."

How many musicians were in the union?

"I don't know if any of them was ever in the union. You know, I think they just played. Because no union ever bothered us. B.B. King said, 'Don't ever play a instrument, because once you walk up and you play your instrument they can fine you a lot of money.' So, I never touched an instrument.

"I moved back to Wichita and then I stayed here for a long time and then I went to Detroit in the early seventies. I got married and I had got a job up there. We stayed there two and a half years. Then I missed Kansas and I come back home and got right back into the music."

Where did your husband work?

"I forget, because he's dead now. It been a long time ago."

How did you like Detroit?

"I liked it but it was fast. I went to Motown about two or three times, went to cut me a record, but then I got scared after I got there. Because I'd never did it before."

Did you cut a demo or anything?

"No. Herbie Welch that played with Willie Wright wrote a song for me and I could've put it on records but I never did. I just sang it in the clubs."

Did you hear any good blues up in Detroit? John Lee Hooker?

"I don't sing no songs like that. My mama used to sing songs by him. Otis Redding, I like him. Gladys Knight, I like her. Now these musicians they got nowadays, I don't know nothin' about them."

Where else did you perform in Wichita?

"I sang at the Blue Light on [1119 E.] Murdock, and then I sung at the Elks' [Lounge] when it was on [1003 E.] 9th Street."

Did they have a lot of trouble back then?

"It used to be pretty nice. That club used to be so packed. We used to draw some good crowds. Everywhere we went, we did.

"I never see no gun, but I see a lot of fights. People that run the club, they'd break it up and sometime the police come in and they'd break it up. But the Esquire, that was a nice club. They had another club on the west side. I can't think of the name. It was right off of Main Street, where the new courthouse is. But they tore all that down and made buildings."

When you came back, did disco cut into your music?

"It bothered a lot of musicians. It didn't bother me because a lot of people would leave all their records and they'd come hear me. I always worked with a band. I sung a lot of gigs in Kansas City. When we left Kat, we started bookin' our dances. Uncle Bob and Aunt Kat used to run, I think it was the Bunny Club a long time ago. And then I used to sing at the AmVets Club.

"When the band play one set, then they'd call me. I do 'bout four or five songs. Then I go back and change clothes, and then I'd come back out and I'd do another set, and I'd close the club up. I'd talk to the people and tell them to come back tomorrow night and all: I don't know where you going, but you're gettin' the hell out of here.

"We did a lot of country and western tunes. Me and Berry. We'd get these bookings at these white clubs and they like these country western.

Berry could really sing that. He taught me some too and I used to do them with him. And he done tell nasty jokes."

Any other lady blues singers in Wichita?

"Hazel Hopkins was out when I was. But I don't know where Hazel live."

Was she a good friend of yours?

"Yeah, all the musicians was good friends. And then I had another singer, her name was Carolyn Bell. She was good too. We'd stand in for each other. Musicians supposed to stick together like that."

What is the blues to you?

"The blues to me is something that I grew up with and something that I like to do, something I can do very well. It's just like a job to me. It's been good to me. I raised my kids off of it, because welfare wasn't doing nothing, honey.

"My kids went everywhere I went. Like if I'm going to Great Bend [100 miles away] tonight, I'd be back tomorrow. I'd get my sister or somebody to keep them. Now if I'm going be gone for a month or something, then I'd take my kids with me. If I'm going to stay for a long time, I get me a house. The kids never lived at a hotel. I would leave them at my sister's until I would find a place."

It was a little harder to be a woman in the blues world then, wasn't it?

"No. To me, I loved it. Because they treated me more like a big sister. All of the musicians, they do that right now. 'Bout me being sick; all of them come over and they throw me a party. We talk about music and stuff that we used to do and how much fun we had together. It's just like I'm still out there. I been sick for 'bout ten years, because I had open-heart surgery. I did some singing since I've had my surgery, but not like I was."

Did you have a lot of rehearsals?

"Oh yeah, I like rehearsals. But they got boring, because we had to go every night until we get a song down pat. We get it down to where we can play it and sound better than the record. We learned new songs every week."

Do you think that helped you?

"Yeah it did. That's why everybody liked me."

How much money did you spend on your dresses?

"My gowns and stuff, the band all chipped in, because they wore, maybe like red shirts and black pants, white shirts."

Did you have it made, or could you go buy it?

"No, I go buy it. Make sure they get them at a store where everybody get them alike."

What kind of blues style does Wichita have?

"I don't think they have one. Because all of them listen to different types. You go here, and hear one type of music, and you go to another club, you hear something different."

Would you encourage the young generation to get into music?

"If that's what they want to do, I would. Because it's really not a bad job. But you can make it what you want. I stayed in there a long time. After I got my timing and got my songs—it'd take me a day, I'd know a song."

What makes a good singer?

"You have to be alert. You have to know your business. You can't be hot-headed. You have to listen to what the people is sayin.'"

Chapter Eight

THE 1960S

Joe Lotson, Ray Valentine, Barbara Kerr

In this chapter, two of the musicians, Lotson and Kerr, are the youngest musicians interviewed, and show the benefits of the national integration movement. These two found positions in mixed groups. Valentine performed with Berry Harris in the 9th Street Blues Band at the time of his interview. Though he didn't come to Wichita until the 1960s, he is included.

During the 1960s, Wichita continued the expansion of the 1950s. The city had 4.6 percent unemployment in 1960. The trend of African American migration continued as well, and by 1990 the city held 34,000 Blacks, 11.3 percent of the total.

JOE LOTSON (1945–)

Drums

"I was born in Tulsa, Oklahoma, in 1945. I'm an only child. Bandleader Ernie Fields's son was my principal in elementary school. I stayed in Tulsa until '56, moved to Wichita, stayed a year, then went to California for a year. Then I went to Tucumcari, New Mexico. My mother stayed here. I kind of traveled with my grandmother. In New Mexico was where I started to play drums. I beat on pots, pans, chairs, and everything till I got me a drum.

"My mother sang, but that's about all the heritage that we have in music. She was just a jazz fanatic, from the big band era, and I was raised on it. In Oklahoma, you start out as a kid and learn to play a musical instrument in elementary school. I started trying to play the saxophone. I just never really developed a like for it. Then when I played the piano, I did fairly well with that. But with moving around, I couldn't keep a good teacher.

"I got my first set of drums when I was in the tenth grade. My mother paid seventy-five dollars; they were a used set. I played a couple of years in school band."

How did your mother end up in Wichita?

"She came here in probably 1954 for a better job. We didn't have any family at the time in Wichita. I stayed with my grandmother in Oklahoma and eventually I moved up here with her. Wichita was okay. I guess this is one of the first places that I came to an integrated school. And there was a difference, an adjustment that I had to make. Once I started playing music, I just kind of let that dominate. I went to Wichita East. I would say it probably took me a year before I adjusted."

What sort of jobs did your mother have?

"She worked in a cleaners. She did sewing, and alterations on the side. She had wanted to be a tailor. When she got out of high school, she left and went to New York. And that's where I came about. When I moved to Wichita, I started taking lessons from Chuck Blackham, and then he referred me to Harold Cary. That was my first professional gig. I had to be sixteen. We played at the Petroleum Club downtown on the ninth floor. Gilmar Walters was playing bass. That's what hooked me into playing music professionally because they paid me seventy-five dollars and that was more money than I'd ever seen in my life. I couldn't sit out in the audience. They had a table set up for us.

"Harold and Gilmar came out of the same era. The bass was always something that if you got a good bass player, he's going to inspire the drummer. And you know you're the timekeeper. I think I probably did about three gigs with the Harold Cary Trio.

"I graduated from East High and went to Wichita State for a couple years. Then I took off with a band called the Renegades. They was basically an all-white band. There was two Blacks. We did a James Brown routine. We played 125 nights throughout the Kansas, Nebraska, Colorado, Texas, Arizona. I was making $350 a week. But that was probably one of the most tiresome jobs that I've ever had, because we played the same songs every night.

"Prior to that, I played with a group called the Elegants, rhythm and blues group. After that, I formed my own group, Joe Lotson and the Jades, with Robert Hardaway and Jerry Jackson. We did a rhythm and blues thing, and a little bit of James Brown. This was the end of '62, '63, '64 while I was going out to Wichita State.

"Basically, we did a lot of getting the gigs on our own, because that was the way we kind of insured that we were going to at least get paid. We

Joe Lotson, photo by Arthur Kenyon.

played at the old Dunbar Theatre. They had stopped showing movies and turned it more into a place for teenagers to hang out. We played at St. Peter Clayvern, private parties, anywhere we could. Because at the time, just to get to be heard, that was more important than getting paid."

What about band attire?

"Used to be night clubs had a dress code. And they wanted the bands to be as presentable as the people that patronized the club. We felt more comfortable in suits and ties at that time, because that gave us more of a professional look. Then as disco came about, everybody got more relaxed and wear whatever they feel. I think the relaxing of dress codes tended to create problems in nightclubs simply because when you're dressed up, you tend not to want to get into confrontations.

"I was raised in the church, Baptist. When I came here, I was active up at Tabernacle [Baptist Church] probably until I got out of high school, and then I kind of got away from it."

Any other interests?

"I'm a member of the McAdams golf club, a Black organization, that has been around [a long time]. It started out as the McKinley Golf Club, a three-hole golf course back in 1930. Eventually it became a nine-hole sand green course. African Americans were excluded from public courses. Club members back during that time were instrumental in breaking the color line and getting to play on public courses.

"In 1946 there was a member who was a very fair-skinned Black guy with straight hair that could pass for white. He and three other guys went out to Sims Park [Wichita public course]. While they hid behind the trees, he went up and paid the green fees.

"When he came back, the other three guys came out and they got on the first tee. Some of the white patrons out there contacted the pro, who called the police. The park commissioner at the time said, 'Well hell, if you sold them the tickets, let them play.'"

Do you think that your ability to make music helped at all in the integrating forces that were at work in Wichita?

"I think music has, over the years, helped to get some people closer, simply because somebody of all cultures will like certain kinds of music. So, it has helped to bridge some of the problems and allowed us to gain acceptance. The roots of music go back to slavery, especially in blues. I think that all music was derived from the blues—jazz, rhythm and blues, rock. It all came from singing on the plantations. You have musicians that technically are good. But in order for them to learn to play music the way it is intended to be played, with feeling, they have to go where you can learn that. And basically, that has been within the Black community because that's where music was played by feel.

"That's the one thing about musicians, we didn't care what color you were. As long as you could play your axe. You know you can get high off of music, higher, than you can any form of dope, alcohol. It's a mental state that allows each one in the group to know what the other is getting ready to do."

You played occasionally with Mike Finnigan.

"Mike was a hell of a piano player! I thought he was a much better piano player than he was an organist. But when Mike and the Serfs were playing at Dearmore's, he would finish up there at twelve o'clock and then come down to the Aladdin Club and play. He, and Freddie Smith, and Carlton McWilliams, Lake Anderson, and Larry Faucette would also come and sit in."

Jimi Hendrix used Finnigan, Smith, and Faucette as session musicians on his third album, *Electric Ladyland*, 1968.

"There were times that we would have jam sessions after the club closed and we wouldn't leave till 9:00 the next morning. The Aladdin was located on

21st and Piatt. I think it was the Imperial Club, prior to it being the Aladdin. And that's when Ruth Searcy and Chuck Blackham played there.

"I played with Jerry Childers at King B's when it was the Twelve Horsemen. I also played across the street at the Starlight. It was big, two hundred people. I played with Sammy Faggitt [Lynch]. We had two drummers. Eddie Cadell played [saxophone], a guy by the name of James Carr played bass. This was like early sixties.

"I think the Esquire was probably the place to go at the time. We would go to the Esquire and we would stay at the Esquire till about three, maybe four in the morning. We would leave there, and then we'd go to the Starlight, which would stay open until nine o'clock the next day. I worked out at Lear Jet at the time. There were many days I went in sleepy because I had stayed up all night long."

Were employment possibilities pretty good in Wichita in the sixties?

"Outside of aircraft, I don't think so. I worked in aircraft for about five years. I taught art for four years for the Wichita Neighborhood Art Centers, kind of a Model Cities–funded program. We were able to help kids. This was after the riots[1] and the government gave out all these programs supposedly to help minorities. The money didn't channel down to provide the kind of assistance that was really needed. Most of it was eaten up in administrative costs.

"I worked for a construction association for four years as a loan and bonds manager, and I helped minority contractors put bonding packages and loan packages together. This was still another funded program by the government. I became a contractor for about eleven years. Then I went to work for the City of Wichita. Been there five years."

When did your musical career come to an end?

"About two years ago. It got to be a job. The club owners didn't want to pay you what you were worth. Basically, they were talking forty dollars, maybe fifty dollars for a gig. I felt that I should make at least twice of what I would make on a regular job per hour."

What were some of the bands you played in?

"I played with the Johnny Johnson Quintet, Rudy Love, Chris 'Skip' Taylor, a pianist, the Gaye Brewer Band, and with Jerry Childers off and on from the sixties to present. I played with Clarence King,[2] sax player, Charles Walker, Regents Band, Fred Williams, and Don Dunn.

"I thought I could really play, then I met Homer Osborne. I was probably seventeen years old, Ruth Searcy sent me to him. So I went over to his house, and he says: 'Young man, sit down and show me what you can do.' I'm thinking, here's a blind guy don't know what he's talking about. I sat down and I played a little riff.

"'Is that the best you can do?'

"So, I sat there and I recall myself really doing somethin'. Then he got on the drums and went around there with no eyes much better than I could with both of mine. 'Let me tell you something—you think you can play? You can play a little bit, but don't you ever think that you can't learn something from everybody. Don't ever stop learning.'

"That was a good lesson to me. I took that lesson in and used that throughout life."

How much jazz did Wichita audiences want to hear?

"It was limited. People around Wichita wanted rhythm and blues, something that they could move their feet to. Once you got into a club, you could intermix jazz and blues for about the first two sets until people consumed some of that alcohol. After that, they wanted to dance. Wichita has never really been a musical town, unlike Kansas City or Tulsa, where musicians were accepted as musicians. I think now there's more acceptance for just an all-blues band. You can play jazz but I think they want more of a commercial jazz, something that they can recognize, that has a strong back beat to it."

Is there a Wichita blues style?

"I don't think there's been a Wichita blues per se. I think there has been a mixture that came from other places that was acceptable here. I don't think that the audiences or the people that went to night clubs were ear-mindful of what blues really was, or where the roots of music came from. They just wanted to hear a sound that they could relate to. They were passive people that accepted what was given to them, and not demanding music. There was things that I've played or things that I've heard other groups playing in this town that you could not go to Kansas City or Chicago and get away with.

"There are a lot of young musicians in Oklahoma in general that are great. They still have live entertainment there. And they come up from the old school, so they learn. You go out and you listen at a guy and you finally get up enough nerve to go up and say, 'Can I set in?' You know, the old guy's kind of keepin' his eye on you. And then you know if you kind of do okay, he accepts you. Then he starts sharing with you things that you should know about music. And I think that Wichita did not do that. The guys would share some things with you, but not in the same light that you would get it in a musical town.

"I used to go and watch Chuck Rucker with the Smart Brothers hours upon hours. Charles Beans was one of the guys that I helped. He stayed down the street from me on Lorraine when I was coming up. He was one of the kids that used to come out while we rehearsed in the backyard and listened. He has from time to time said, 'Hey man, thanks for some of the stuff you showed me.'

"I think that I passed some things on to people that were under me, and there were things that were passed on to me from people that were older. But I just don't feel that the exchange was the way it is done in cities like New York, or Chicago, where musicians really share. We were musicians that had to have jobs in order to survive. There is a distinct difference when you do it for a living to feed your families, as opposed to doing it because you want to do it."

What makes a good blues drummer?

"One, timing; the other, a good solid back beat, a good heavy foot. Using a cymbal, you don't really pay any attention to it or hear it. Even though you're using it, you know, it's not as predominant as if you were playing jazz, where you always hear it."

Were you ever around any serious violence at a gig?

"Sure. We were playing at St. Peter Clayvern on Indiana and 11th Street for a high school somethin', and we were playing the theme from *Batman*. Two girls got to fighting, and somebody pushed somebody else—you know how the crowds circles around a fight—and pretty soon the whole building was in an uproar. Luckily none of them came up on the stage. But there have been several instances where we've played and fights have broken out. But during that time, there were fistfights, and probably all of the people that were involved are friends again today. It's unlike the kind of thing that goes on where somebody's trying to kill somebody else basically over nothing."

Do you think music is a good thing for people to make a career, or avocation?

"I think everyone, from the time that they're in the second, third grade in elementary, should be exposed to it. It's something that you can keep with you the rest of your life. I think that a person should be exposed to all kinds of music, because it allows you to understand other cultures."

RAY VALENTINE (1928–2014)

Piano

"I was born in Washington, DC, in 1928 and lived there until I was about twenty-one. I joined the US Air Force. I went quite a few places overseas. My regular job was servicing aircraft with fuel. And I would play music after hours, sometimes with the Air Force Band. I played at the officers' club, popular music. And when I played with the Air Force Band also jazz, blues. I started out playing classical music at the Washington Junior College of Music. I had to learn blues on my own. They wouldn't allow us to play blues in the college.

"So, I had to go into the clubs and learn from different people I ran into and to get an idea. I was playing in a little group, tenor sax and drums, bass, piano, and electric guitar. Blues was popular then—Charlie Parker, also B.B. King. This was the late forties. The first club we ever played was called the Cotton Club. The majority of the audience was Black, but you see a mixed crowd every now and then.

"My father was an electrician for the government, and my mother worked at the Navy Yard in DC. I had quite a few brothers and sisters [eleven], but along the way most of them were deceased. So, it's only two of us left now."

Was there a tradition of music in your family?

"No, there wasn't too much of a tradition. The way that I came on to music was through my buddies. We were all in high school, and they went to this music school studying piano. One lived right across the street from me, so every evening I'd hear him on the piano. That got me interested, so I joined the music college. That was interrupted by the Korean War, more or less.

"In 1952, I decided to make the air force a career. I ran into a lot of people in the music world from the different cities that I was stationed in. Paris had excellent blues. There was a club called Sagele and I met a guy named Jacque Butler, a trumpet player and he used to hold jam sessions there on Sunday evenings."

All this time you were playing popular ballads and maybe a little jazz and blues?

"Yes, always there was some blues there. My most interesting tour was actually in Nashville, Tennessee. I met Jimi Hendrix through his manager, Billy Cox. We were good friends and after Jimi Hendrix got out of the service, Billy Cox called me on the base, and told me he had a friend for me to meet. They got a band together. Four or five pieces. I played for him for about six months. Then all of a sudden he disappeared."

What did you guys call yourselves when he was playing with you in Nashville?

"Just Jimi Hendrix Group, or something. It was just a regular blues club. We had a pretty nice crowd, a mixed crowd in Nashville. When I played with him, he was playing just strictly blues. But he'd throw one of his pieces in there every once in a while."

What did you think about him?

"I thought he was very good. And he was very nice to get along with. I met him after he got discharged. He was in the Airborne in Ft. Campbell,

Ray Valentine, photo by Arthur Kenyon.

Kentucky. His whole world was wrapped up in music. We'd go to the club and rehearse about two nights a week. Then there would be some acts coming in, singers, and we would have to rehearse with them for weekend shows and stuff like that. I had an electric piano, a Wurlitzer.

"I got stationed in Wichita in 1968. The first thing I did was look for some clubs. I went to the Inn Crowd on Mosley one Sunday night and met Jerry Childers and Don Dunn.

"They let me sit in and we got along fine, just fine. Later on about a month or two, I met some other people, Tommy Gray; let me see, we call him John Henry, but his name is Henry Harvey Tisdale. We had a little trio, piano, drums, and bass, and we played at Bill's Le Gourmet, jazz, and mixed blues. I got the Ray Valentine Trio together in '72 after I got out [of the service]."

What church were you raised in back in Washington?

"Second Baptist Church. I sang in the choir. Now I go to New Covenant on 17th and Green. It's what they call C.O.G.I.C. Church. I go there some-times and play."

You're currently with Berry, doing a little soul and funk in the 9th Street Band, but most of your material is blues, isn't it?

"Most of it, yeah. Everywhere we go, people respond to it. I love playing the blues. I think blues is more or less an inner feeling of each person and it seems to soothe a person to a certain extent. I think it soothes the people listening also. It soothes me."

You came to Wichita and hooked up with some players. What did you think about the Wichita blues?

"Well, I think that it's just as good as anywhere else. It's the feeling that you put into it. I'd say that it was very good quality."

What style of blues were they playing at the Inn Crowd?

"I think it was mostly urban, sort of B.B. King. In 1968 when I came here, Mike Finnigan and the Serfs were the top group here. They had a good band."

Does Wichita have its own style of blues, or did they just borrow a style from somewhere else?

"It's a mixture of both. I think they have their own unique style of blues. The different chord structures have changed. It's more variety now than it was then."

How did you learn to play the blues?

"When I first started, I'd go to clubs and sit in, and I'd learn from different other piano players. One was John Malachi. He used to play for Sarah Vaughan.[3] He told me that he liked the way that I played and to come around and he'd give me some pointers and stuff. It happened quite a lot. In every city that I went to, if I met some celebrity musicians, they give you a hand. They try to help you, especially in Nashville."

Who were your main influences on your piano style?

"Horace Silver, Dave Brubeck, Oscar Peterson, and Hampton Hawes."

If you could play whatever you wanted to, what would you be playing?

"I'd be playing jazz and maybe a little commercial, like the up-to-date songs that they play on the radio."

Do you think that blues is good for the people to play, or would you recommend a different kind of music?

"I'd recommend them to play blues. Blues is the most impressive because it has feelings. It has a lot of elation and it's more or less inspirational too, I think. It's gettin' a rebirth. There's hardly a movie that you see that there isn't a blues tune in it."

Do younger musicians come up to you and ask you to show them some stuff on the piano?

"Yeah. The younger generation seem to be real interested in the blues."

Do you think that music would help today's youth if kids got interested in music?

"Well, if they had some place to go to learn just strictly blues, it would help. It's not easy."

BARBARA KERR (1941–)

Violin

"I was born on the 1300 block of Ohio Street, 1941. There were three of us originally, and an adopted brother. He was the baby. My dad was a shoe builder, a cobbler over on 9th right by the Dunbar Theatre. He did that until I was two years, and then he gave up on it because it was pretty difficult being a businessman during that period. He remained a cobbler and made a pair of cowboy boots for Hopalong Cassidy. I thought that was pretty slick. We moved to Riverside after that, and that's where I grew up, on 1825 Payne.

"I was born on a Sunday afternoon upstairs in a carriage house. Dr. Jeter—his wife was one of the Wichita's first Black schoolteachers—told my mom I was going to be born at 1:45, which would give him time to get out of church, but I cheated and came at 1:30. Those ol' country doctors."

Did you take music lessons?

"I took piano for a little while. I was too impatient to learn how to read the notes. I started playing the violin in the fifth grade, taking from Walton Morgan. I lived a block away from Woodland School, but schools were segregated then, and so they bussed us to L'Ouverture, 13th and Mosley. That was a very difficult time in my life, because I was being put in a foreign environment, really. All my friends were over in Riverside. There was our family and the Bradfords, two families of Black kids in Riverside.

"I remember they had a meeting at our house to see if they felt I could integrate at Woodland [Elementary] and not feel bad about it. I was the first Black to go to Woodland. It was great. I was at school with kids I played games with. I knew all these kids, so I didn't notice anything wrong. I felt like getting sent to L'Ouverture was wrong. Because I talked funny, I played funny games, and listened to country music. They didn't know where I was comin' from.

"The first time I heard the 'n' word—my girlfriend lived two doors from me, a little redhead with freckles. We were riding our bicycles across the 18th Street Bridge out of our neighborhood boundary, and these little kids came out and they were just yelling that 'n' word. I thought, boy, what a nasty word. Winnie's got freckles and she's kind of a dorky kid. They've got to be talkin' about her. We went back home and I was calling her the 'n' word and my mom heard me.

"'Where did you hear that, Barbara?'

"I told her.

"'No, honey. I hate to tell you, but they were talkin' about you.'

"Then I was the only Black in John Marshall [Intermediate]. Of course, I didn't realize I was really Black, because I was with my friends. You know there was no color barrier."

Did you have any newspaper coverage then?

"No. They were concerned that I would have a kind of social trauma behind it, I guess. I had more trouble going to L'Ouverture. L'Ouverture was real down-home people. That's a terrible to way say it, but there's a lot of things that I just didn't understand in the Black society then, because we were so separated."

What about your music? Mr. Morgan started you out with the violin. Did you continue at Woodland?

"Right. I started the whole public school thing, and when I got into the eighth grade, my older sister introduced me to Mary Katherine McClanahan, who was one of Wichita's finer young violinists. And I started taking lessons from her. She got killed when I was in the ninth grade. She went down to Texas for a big music camp and they had a wreck. Had she still been alive, I would never have played the fiddle, I would have just been truly a classical violinist, because that was the track that I was going on."

Your church was the Calvary Baptist Church on North Water?

"Yep. I was a birth row baby. I guess they call them cradle rollers, somethin' like that. The only church I've ever gone to was Calvary. When I was older, I was the director of the junior choir. My sister Doris played the organ. It was a great choir. They worked real good for me. By then, I was at WSU.

"In high school, right after Mary Katherine [died], I decided that I didn't want to play anymore. I was really upset about it. I played the viola all through college, three years, in the university orchestra. I went to San Francisco in '62. I'd spent a lot of time in Wichita, and it was time to get away. I was a folk singer when I first went to San Francisco. I played [Wichita] coffee houses, I & Thou, B.C.'s. Folk singing became one of those things. If you had a guitar, you sat around and you sang. I quit for ten years when I had my daughters. I've two daughters.

"I lived in the Haight-Ashbury. I had a houseboat in Sausalito. I lived in Marin County, Mill Valley, just the whole Bay Area. I was a real San Francisco hippie. My daughter's name is Earth. I did some communal living. Made pretty good money singing. I played some of the Odetta-style folk blues, but I had really put myself away from the blues. Identifying with blues at that time was not the Black person that I thought I had grown up to be. I had

Barbara Kerr, photo by Arthur Kenyon.

one aunt that used to listen to blues all the time. But to my mother, blues was truly the working class.

"We didn't have blues in the house at all. Now that I've gotten grown, I realize that I knew the blues long time ago. Because I've had a lot of doors slammed in my face. I have opened a lot of doors, too. I cannot complain. I was doing things that I didn't realize was pioneering, just because I was in that space.

"Right after Earth was born, I had a friend that told me he wanted me to meet a friend of his. We went over to see his friend who was sitting at the dinner table eating. He was a very gracious man and we started playing together and he was quite impressed and told me that he felt like I could do a lot. And this man was Taj Mahal.

"So, he's really the person that kind of gave me that OK; yeah, you can do it, you can improvise. You don't have to read music; you can do it both ways. I came back to Wichita in '72 and met these kids, Nan Geary and Andy Markley. We formed this progressive folk rock group, Equinox. I realized I needed the higher sound, so I started playing the violin. Then I joined up with Prairie Swing. We played country swing."

They were all white?

"Yeah, yeah. Cowboy blues. In '80, I went to the Hank Thompson Country Music School in Claremore, Oklahoma. I decided that if I was going to play the fiddle, I was going to learn from the best. I got a chance to play about eight concerts with Leon McCullough, and all the living Texas Playboys at that time.

"I've taken that fiddle of mine and I've been in places in the South and in North Dakota and Montana where I know they've never seen a Black face. And being a woman playing a fiddle, it opened up conversations, and it opened up doors. I was in Hattiesburg, Mississippi, playing country with a band called Just Us out of Louisiana. And there's this man that kept comin'. For the first week, he'd sit in the back of the bar, and just watch us. Finally, I decided, if this man's going to share this, I'm going to go introduce myself so I can find out who he is.

"Well come to find, he was the grand wizard of Hattiesburg, Mississippi. He wouldn't call me Black; he called me his little Indian fiddle player. But just the idea that this man—and everybody knew who he was—was acknowledging my presence as a musician and a person. Before I left, I finally started teasing him and telling him that I wanted him to get some pastel sheets in his Klan. What a thing to be able to laugh about. I mean, that could be the very thing to make him realize his beliefs were wrong.

"Music is truly that universal language that opens up a lot of doors. The fiddle is one of those instruments that everybody has had a grandfather or an uncle that's played. And if you play that instrument, they immediately transcend all barriers and you become that person that they loved that played that fiddle. It's like they could remember being at that person's knee and being fascinated."

Back in the fifties, did you go listen to any blues?

"The Zanzibar was where I definitely heard some blues. Homer Osborne, I saw him at the Zanzibar. That's also where I heard Mike Finnigan for the first time. Here was this soulful blues comin' out of this white boy's face. Jerry Hahn was a big influence in my life then. My daughter Earth's dad is Jerry. He was in San Francisco at that time. I called Jerry and told him that I heard the greatest organ player that I'd ever heard. And Jerry said, 'How did you know I was lookin' for an organ player?' And that was the forming of the [Jerry Hahn] Brotherhood.

"A lot of jazz was happening during the fifties, more jazz than blues here in Wichita because we had the Jazz Workshop down on Central and Indiana. It was truly a jazz club. Jerry played there a lot. Now if you wanted blues, there were blues players that were happening over on 9th and Grove, at the

Starlight. There was some blues that were happening down at the Smart's Palace. I didn't go there very often. Ninth Street was just a little rougher than what I had conditioned to grow up in."

Have you ever recorded?

"I was on a couple recordings with Rudy Love. I did a recording with Just Us. And that's about it. I've been close to a lot of recordings but I just haven't really done serious studio work, tell you the truth."

What is your definition of the blues?

"I think it's the music that expresses your feelings. If you can play music that expresses how you feel at that moment, regardless if it's love, down-heartedness, and someone else shares that moment with you, then you're playing and sharin' the blues."

What do you think the main style of blues is in Wichita?

"I think the mainstay of blues in Wichita is really the educated man's blues. Wichita's been divided so long. The blues players that played on 9th Street—the people that moved out to College Hill didn't want to hear that man's blues. I think that Wichita's real superficial about letting the world know who you really are and where you come from, and what you're made of."

So, you think that the city is divided over blues style?

"Yeah, I do. Because if you listen to working man's blues, then you might have to accept the fact that that's where you came from. If the person that put the shoes on your feet had to be a maid or whatever to allow that education for you, then don't turn your back on a person that had to scrub those floors to get you there. When we start accepting that, then we'll know who we are as a people a little better. When I was in school and it was just my dark face there, that never bothered me because I was very proud of who I was, because I wouldn't have been there otherwise."

How has the blues affected you, your playing career, and your life in general?

"I'm real happy that I'm playing it now, because it's opening up another new terrain for me. I might throw a little Bach fugue in there, because that's my blues, too."

What about the popularity of the blues? Is it as popular now as it was twenty years ago?

"Yeah, I think so. Look at the [Wichita] Blues Society. They had to really work to get Black people interested in the society. So, it's kind of interesting even though that's the way it has to be introduced. Maybe the Blacks that really know the blues won't be ashamed to come forward and say, 'Yeah, this is our music,' and it is. You've got your integration music, and you've got your blues. That's about all you've got in America. That's really our music. Jazz is educated music; blues and country are folk music."

Would you talk a little bit about the First National Black Historical Society of Kansas [now the Kansas African American Museum], a little of the history of why you started it and how it came about?

"My sisters and I, Doris Larkins and Ra'shualaamu Beruni who was Donna Marie Kirk at the time, growing up in Riverside, experiencing a lot of different things, we did have a lot of different kinds of influences and inputs. When they told us they were closing Calvary Church, the only church we'd ever known, we decided that it was just too great a church to go down."

What year was this?

"It was '74, I believe. We wanted to make it a historical museum and a culture retreat."

So you decided that you wanted to have a retreat?

"A historical society, a museum and culture retreat, that was the original idea. We felt like we could bring our culture back into the museum and put it back into the community, through all different kinds of ways—theater, skills, crafts, just sharing it all. I don't think any of the things we thought about in the first place are being realized right now. It's kind of just there. The society's not touching the community like our original dreams and plans were. The leaders of the people that are in there now, some of those people don't want to listen to the blues because unless it says 'dem, 'dat is de blues, like Stephen Foster wrote it."

[*Ra'shualaamu Beruni arrives.*]

"Here's one of the other founders of the Black Historical Society."

Would you like to sit down and talk a little bit with your sister?

Beruni: "I can't remember some of the things that we planned on."

Kerr: "It was a long struggle. We just grew up in Riverside in our own little world out there. And everybody kept tellin' us that we weren't proud of who we were. But every time our little Black faces was someplace where we were the only ones there, that to me was the biggest pride thing that you could possibly say. We just wanted, if somebody knew how to make a quilt, bring that knowledge back into the Historical Society, to the Museum.

"Take five kids from some other district or some other part of the world. Let 'em see how to make that blind stitch, because you don't have silk thread. Just really cultural, little ethnic things, that was our dream that we wanted to do with the Museum."

The County owned the property at that time, didn't they?

Beruni: "They had just bought it but Urban Renewal had it."

Kerr: "So we had to struggle to save the building."

Beruni: "They wanted to tear it down for an interloop. They would've torn it down. Well, we changed their mind. Just like the whole block. The whole district and one other building, the Masonic Lodge. That's the one they put on the Historical Register first. They didn't want to put the church on because they told us Frederick Douglass did not sleep there. It's like, well, Frederick Douglass doesn't matter in Wichita. We had one of the first Black females to graduate from Fairmont College. We had the first Black mayor, we had the first Black superintendent of schools.

"It was all the businesses, the hot area. And it was the only place where artists could come and stay at the Water Street Hotel. Joe Louis, people like that, they came to the Water Street Hotel."

So what was your fight like? Did you go to the press, or television?

Beruni: "We went to the news media and the 'Nightmare, red tape,' this was the first article. It upset everybody. Everybody told us it couldn't be done. So we was out there about three years, and it took almost sixteen years for people to realize what the whole concept was."

Did you mobilize the community? How many people were involved, just the three of you?

Kerr: "Yeah, in the beginning. Right, the whole city, the whole state. Doris, our oldest sister, wrote to the presidents. We got letters from presidents, congressmen; Shirley Chisholm, Dole, he was in there too. We didn't know, we just went in every direction."

Beruni: "Yeah, Bicentennial, that's where it all came about, 1975."

What was the first good news you had?

Kerr: "That they weren't going to tear it down."

Beruni: "Right. It was doomed to be torn down and I think Sis got a phone call before five o'clock."

Kerr: "So then we had to start fighting to get it on the National Register. We found out the only way we could save it was to get it on the Historical Register. And the hysteric Historians of Kansas, is what we had to fight. That's when they started tellin' us 'nobody important has ever gone to this church.'"

Beruni: "Even people from Washington, DC."

Kerr: "So we finally proved that everybody that was important to us was, or had been a member of that church."

Beruni: "Like, it's always been a community building. The Board of Education endorsed it with the church schools. It's always been a community building along with just being a church."

When did you finally incorporate or get a charter?

Beruni: "That was in '75. It was three years later we had it incorporated. It was like a dollar a year rent, but it really wasn't of any significance until it was on the Register. There was a massive leak from the roof and the building was about ready to cave in. We had to fight that."

They said it was unsafe?

Beruni: "Yeah, it was at that time, it was boarded up. It was not being used because Calvary had been moved to their new location. So it was no longer their lookout. The city or county wasn't doing anything."

Kerr: "They turned on us too real bad, the members of Calvary. They had gotten the money for it and then all of a sudden they saw that they really had made a mistake, and it really was something important to save. But they had already gotten the money, they'd already done their Uncle Tomness and gotten out of it."

Beruni: "They was irritated because three insignificant people here—we weren't Dr. so and so's daughters—could have so much power. So it was an irritation to them as well as the community. We had the fortitude to stand up."

But you were church members then, weren't you?

Kerr: "Oh yeah. In our little island there in Riverside we had learned how to deal with the establishment from a different side. Because they could not teach all the rest of their little kids in Riverside how to deal with the establishment and not teach us, too—all these little channels that they probably would not like to have given us. There was no choice."

Beruni: "We're ice breakers. We all had our own breaking period."

When did you achieve National Registry?

Kerr: "Oh man, what year was that?"

Beruni: "I have it on the historical video. I guess I should have it in mind [1993]. But seems like since, we been eliminated so badly and our voices haven't been heard."

When did you start working on the building?

Beruni: "That's been a transition in the last five or six years, but we had been working on it and trying to bring it up to the code and changing certain things by renovating. I wish I was better with dates."

You mentioned a video. Have you put together a video?

Beruni: "Yeah. Starting from the very beginning, when we started and talking about the city, the different letters, and we're talking about the inspiration."

What happened after you started to get the community interested?

Beruni: "Three things. The one thing that's really been a part of the beginning was the Martin Luther King tribute. That first started with us. And that's an ongoing thing. And then they had a Kwanzaa and the Juneteenth celebration. So basically all these three original ideas are from us, from the very beginning. And they have the socials and the different awards dinners. But basically I say the Martin Luther King tribute is from the beginning to now."

When did you have to step away from the museum?

Kerr: "I know what year it was. It was '76. It really happened when they decided that, because we didn't have a college degree, we weren't qualified to get grants."

They actually told you that?

Kerr: "My sister Doris was actually told that."

Beruni: "I asked to be on the board. I was never reelected as a board member or even as a consultant or anything. The heart of me tried and there's still the potential greater than what's going on now. I was hoping that it'd be kind of like we always have our own separate museum, which is important. But I was hoping the museum would be a museum of the human awareness that we have with each other—how we're all interrelated with our cultures. You can see the influence amongst all of us. And that would be something quite unique.

"That you can see the Indian, the Caucasian, all the different influences. That was always my future goal: to have how we all incorporate with each other in our history and our art. And that has a definite lap [shortcoming]. They kept the Indian Center and you have the Wichita Art Museum and it's all just focusing on one aspect of individuality, but it's not really that anymore."

What are you doing these days yourself?

Beruni: "I'm a single mom, and changing careers. Every time I go by the building, I still have this desire to be there."

Well they are talking about major changes there.

Kerr: "They want to cover it up, surround it with a jail expansion. I think that's not good. But we've always been snuffed in our own corners anyway. But it's so funny, the more they cover up with, the more it keeps sneakin' out. That ground that they're using to cover it up with is all Black Wichita originally. The courthouse sits on it."

Beruni: "Original migration point."

Kerr: "That was where we belonged. That was our little part of the world."

Any final thoughts? Any hopes for the future on the Historical Society?

Kerr: "I can't say for me."

Beruni: "I would like to maybe be more involved, and maybe be listened to. Because I have channels with the Smithsonian. The Smithsonian will come to the building, and help us establish a children's museum, but the mentality doesn't see the significance of the Smithsonian's being involved. I'm going, wow. I'm hoping they will be a little more open-minded and progressive. Because people have to accept the fact there are visionaries. This is part of life and we were visionaries and these visions I would like to see in the building and in the community. It's time for the community to not be so narrow-minded and tunnel vision, and under cover. I consider that building sacred. Like I said, it's not just African American, it's everybody's history. The energy is awesome."

Kerr: "I'm gettin' there by playing the blues. I'm going to be in their face in a different way, and all of a sudden, they will have to accept: well, she really is valid. When I look out and see my audience smilin' and sharin' my music, that's my stamp of approval. I know what the blues is, because I been there."

Chapter Nine

DISCUSSION OF RESULTS

Narrative Analysis; Wichita, Its Importance in Blues History

As displayed, the birth dates of each interviewee give an indication of age at time of interview—1996–97. The portrait photography is a big part of the story. "One picture is worth more than 10,000 words."[1] Fields of inquiry include:

Place and date of birth
Family information, size, tradition of music
Circumstances of being in Wichita
Education
Occupational experience
Church
Membership in organizations
Important events during life
Subject's definition of the blues
Folklore and traditional materials in informant's performance
Informant's commentary on performance
When, where and how often perform
Circumstances of learning the performance art
Use and meaning of poetics of the blues
Reason for current popularity
Future of the blues
Is the subject an agent of transferral to younger musicians?
Does subject's performance material or life experiences fit into any of the
    folklore genres: riddle, myth, legend, tale, proverb, or ballad?

Using the above as a starting point, the interview/conversation went the way the interviewee wanted to talk, as seen in chapters three through eight. Below is the narrative analysis, configured in representative episodes. Themes were taken from the above fields of inquiry and suggesting text.

AUDIENCE SATISFACTION

Perry Reed's recollections of touring with the Black Barons gives an indication of the climate in the region during the late 1930s. The band offered blues or jazz depending on audience response. He felt Wichita could be nothing more than an imitation of the larger urban centers, though its citizens could discern good blues when it was performed here.

Likewise, Harold Cary understood the dynamics between musician and audience, especially when he had begun playing for white Wichitans in the late 1940s. Performing such standards as "Don't Get Around Much Anymore," "Sometimes I'm Happy," "September in the Rain," and "Take the A Train," he added his flair in arrangements, putting "pepper" in it. In the symbolism of song selection, Cary's white audience appreciated boogie woogie but were responsive to the familiarity of majority-culture standards.

Remona Hicks's interaction with her audiences was straight-ahead blues. She did not sing rap, finding her own brand of blues could make the audience fight at times. And she did not interpret female singers. Her material was from Bobby Bland, B.B. King, and Johnnie Taylor. Her crowd knew what to expect: a change of gowns between servings of blues.

Berry Harris talks of dignity and respect, two intertwined concepts that are of immense importance to African Americans. Relations between whites and Blacks should always start out with this in mind. He believes Wichita's taste in blues to be that of Little Milton and Bobby Bland, both urban stylists who came through Wichita often. Albert Collins's lengthy stay in the city undoubtedly had an effect. All three reflect degrees of sophistication within the limited blues form. While Harris mentions jazz, it is obvious that blues was more popular. He accurately characterizes the distaste most Wichita Blacks have for the unadorned country blues. And he is correct in the charge that through this distaste, the young are ignoring a part of their heritage. However, in a people with memories of penury and utter misery, it is quite natural to diminish this period of existence.

INSTRUMENTS

Berry Harris told of the church-going, hard-working African Americans' attitudes toward guitars. His grandfather was a minister, and his father shared the same view that playing guitar indicated laziness and a proclivity for alcohol and women. Thus the symbolic negativity of the guitar as well as the content in many standard blues lyrics. This, of course, was balanced by blues audiences, where the interaction was one of positive reinforcement.

Gene Metcalf speaks of a yard trumpet, given him by Squench Davis, which he taught himself to play. He finally found his instrument in the trap set.

Shirley Green was exposed to the piano playing of his mother and sister as a youth. He chose to play a reed instrument and was given a chance to perform in the integrated East High School Band. This school sanctioned contribution must have been a welcome change from his earlier years of segregated classes.

Jesse Anderson's tale mirrors that of many young musicians. He asked his mother for a saxophone to learn on. Reluctant at first, she finally bought him a C-melody. He took it to Walton Morgan, who disparaged the instrument, hurting Jesse's feelings. Of course, Morgan began his own career with that instrument. Nonetheless, this type of saxophone is made for beginners since it is not necessary to transpose written notation. The symbolism here is one of professionalism in musical equipment.

The same criticism could be said of Albert Tucker's first guitar, a Harmony archtop he bought in 1943, when he was getting more interested in the blues. What better instrument for a legitimate representation of the blues? The guitar cost $3.50, and his father had to tune it with wire pliers, but it took him down the road.

If you take music seriously, you should have a serious instrument. That is the interactive outcome of these last two episodes. But blues performers often make very little money. Only the top players can afford good guitars, and in the rough and tumble of blues venues, a lot of them get damaged and have to be replaced.

AUTHENTICITY

Jerry Childers had a true love for the Hammond B-3 organ, finding that the electronic simulators and smaller keyboards could not match its sound. His B-3 had drawing power at jams, bringing a lot of musicians to the club to play it or play with it. This is authenticity of sound. No computer mimicry—he played a tube-preamplifier organ built between 1955 and 1975. Childers also had a Model A Hammond, built in the 1930s, that he played in his home. Authenticity is very important to the blues. Suffering is inherent in one form or another, in order to create blues composition or performance. If you are singing about human misery—or the sense of humor it takes to escape it—you have to experience it and to have an instrument that mimics the resonant moan in the voice.

Harmonica Chuck's authenticity is a strong selling point to those who hear him. It is obvious that he is playing the music that means life to him. And his years spent running the 904 Club gave him an education in the ways of the blues-buying public.

Albert Tucker was not a paid performer, but a true folk musician who played for enjoyment. The blues he heard in Oklahoma—either on record or listening outside of clubs—was worked into his repertoire through singing it as he labored in the fields before he came to Wichita.

SPONTANEITY

Blues jams are necessary to fulfill the need of musical expression in varying form. Franklin Mitchell talks of life in the stage show *Harlem in Havana*. When the show was over, they left to find a jam. These sessions were where he met a lot of talented musicians with new ideas. Later, when he was a session musician at Ace Recording Studios, he met several well-known musicians at parties and club jam sessions. There he was free to experiment musically and learn from others—something denied him in stage shows and recording sessions. As important as playing professionally was, Mitchell still needed to get out and meet other players. This echoes Shirley Green's experience in New York, as well as Henry Walker's in Wichita at the Esquire Club.

SUBJECT'S DEFINITION OF THE BLUES

Green is one of the interviewees who finds a distinction between jazz and blues difficult to make, other than number of measures. In his opinion, it is simply music that comes from the heart and soul, only later to be classified. In the 1930s, in his experience, the main style emulated in Wichita was that of Fats Waller, as well as the blues. On Green's return in the 1950s, standards along the order of "Moonglow" were popular. This could be a factor of where he played—the prestigious white clubs—or his musical predilections.

Gene Metcalf's account: blues is what you feel through experience represented in musical form. This is an eloquent assessment from a working musician. Erick Robinson, looking at Oklahoma blues, thought the lifestyle there different in that times were difficult and blues eased the burden. He reckons blues are played through sadness and happiness.

Jesse Anderson gives a stirring example of poetics, using imagery as a child to identify blues he wanted to hear, the key being the labels on seventy-eight recordings: bluebirds and the sun. Jesse also had a metadefinition of the blues. It was not a condition but an interpretation. He points out that the blues was sung before it was named. The name *the blues* came about because of those who performed it. It didn't really define the music—only the performers as a class.

Henry Walker has an eloquent take on the blues, calling it life, a feeling, an expression. This is truly a musician's representation of blues performance in language that is plain and compelling.

Albert Tucker does a splendid job of characterizing blues performance, assessing it as allowing your mind to wander as you extemporize on the guitar. In this manner, trouble in mind will be eased.

HUMOR

Gene Metcalf adds a bit of whimsy with his vignette. His tin can band with inner-tube bass, chitlins buckets, and errant cymbal that flew off into the audience was a familiar gambit in African American shows. The symbolism of rustic inhabitants at frolic comes through in this. It made the audience feel good about themselves, to feel sophisticated compared to the musicians. This rusticity is also touched on in Franklin Mitchell's experience in the carnival with his country show when the band was costumed in coveralls and straw hats.

Berry Harris speaks of a gig at the Elks Club for which he hired female impersonators to dance, and rented a casket. During the dance routine, the lights went off, a smoke bomb was set off, and a female impersonator came out of the casket and joined the dance. This is showmanship. The symbolism of celebrating in the face of death—listening to the devil's music—is a strong indicator to the African American of just where they were and what they were doing. Making light of it might have helped ease some of their misgivings of listening to the devil's music.

Jerry Childers's vignette is another of humor, rising above segregation or other woes besetting Black performers. It occurred when he was living in Los Angeles and a headline performer surprised him in the audience by calling for him to come up and play.

CHANCE

Chance plays a large part in the lives of the underprivileged. Arthur Bates relied on happenstance in the early part of his performance career. In high school, he had a dream of joining the orchestra. Doorman for a while, he thought that he could do a better job on bass than one of the students playing it, so before the teacher arrived, he took up the instrument. Nothing was said and this is how he joined the Booker T. Washington High School Band.

After graduation, a former girl student he knew came to town in the International Sweethearts of Rhythm out of the Piney Woods School in Mississippi. He asked if the school had a boys band and was given an address for the Don Clifton Collegians. After corresponding with them and telling them he didn't have a bass fiddle, he didn't hear back until they showed up at his home ready to take him on the road. He points out that he would not have gone to Mississippi under different circumstances.

VIOLENCE

Henry Walker's incident is one of fair frequency in the Wichita club stories. There was gunfire while he was performing, and Henry left the stage so fast that he left his guitar still ringing with a chord.

Charles Walker found violence to be mostly fistfights, during which the band kept playing. This was to keep attention away from the fight while the bouncer took care of it. On one occasion at Flagler Garden, a man was killed. He had been thrown out of the bar, came back and started shooting, and died when the bartender returned fire. Violence hangs heavy in the world of blues, oftentimes with some of the best early performers. The symbolism of violence and braggadocio is rife in the lyrics. Sometimes the anguish in the arrangement and composition is a foretaste to the actuality of fighting. Harmonica Chuck's music started a lot of fights, according to him.

Donald Dunn's description of the nights in Wichita on 9th Street and at the Sportsman are revealing of a Black community that was self-sufficient. The Sportsman, offering blues in the style of Bobby Bland, was a nice club, belying the notion that all 9th Street nightspots were dangerous. The Esquire, which encouraged sophisticated blues as well as standards, was described as a little nicer; but like the Sportsman's practice of allowing bootleg liquor, the Esquire had gaming tables in the back room. Both these clubs flaunted the laws their patrons found unnecessary.

During the 1960s, Joe Lotson's band wore suits and ties to achieve a "professional" look. He attributes less trouble in clubs to a more formal style of dress. The fights that he saw were of a lesser scale than the current gun battles "over basically nothing."

EMIGRATION

Donald Dunn tells of coming from Oklahoma to Wichita, being summoned by former bandmates. They showed up at his door, and it took him fifteen minutes to make up his mind to join Little Jesse Anderson and the Blues Toppers. Berry Harris had the same experience, driving a cab in Muskogee. Wichita held more opportunity. The pay for Berry was $35 per night plus room and board. Factory wages in Wichita were $75 a week. They must have really needed Berry in that band. The symbolism is ancient—leaving your present location for one of more promise. And in the African American community, there often were few material possessions to bring with you.

STAGE PRESENCE

Charles Walker talked about stage attire, acting as his own tailor, creating sparkly outfits to match the band name, Willie Wright and the Sparklers. At the Esquire, they wore matching sport jackets and pants. On 9th Street, the dress code was casual but striking.

Jesse Anderson and Harmonica Chuck both recall being unwilling to pick up money thrown on stage during their performance when they first started out. The carriage of an artist was already developing. The symbolism is a style and comportment that reassures the audience that they are truly being entertained by one who deserves the designation of showman.

Franklin Mitchell's credo, that there will always be a more capable musician than yourself, was likely developed through his extensive exposure to the professionals in Chicago and Detroit. His answer to this was to perform at his best.

OUTSIDE INFLUENCES

Harold Cary gives a participant's perspective in the effect President Roosevelt had on Black America with his story of cow kills. Attributing to the president a personal touch in the free distribution of beef, he says: "Roosevelt . . . put it in the paper."[2]

Ray Valentine brought a more cosmopolitan approach to Wichita. In the air force, he was stationed around the world and found good blues in Paris and Nashville. Paris had Club Sagele and Nashville had Jimi Hendrix. Ray was friends with Billy Cox in Nashville and this was his connection to playing with Hendrix. This is a symbolism of exotic climes and virtuoso performance.

After national touring, Franklin Mitchell and Jesse Anderson also brought in outside influences to the blues of Wichita, although Mitchell didn't stay long in Wichita after returning from the carnival, moving on to Illinois.

Berry Harris brings up the crossover influence of hillbilly music on his material. His grandfather was a fan of the *Grand Ole Opry*, which factored into Harris's influence gleaned from the old men who played guitar around the good-time houses in Oklahoma.

COMMUNITY SUPPORT

Walton Morgan's recollections are brief but telling. His uncle went to Jenkins Music and bought instruments: baritone sax, piano, and clarinet. This depicts a tradition of music in the family. His teacher was from the 9th Cavalry, Fort Riley. When Morgan formed the Syncopators, another member's parents offered their house for practicing. Their uniforms came from Sexton Cleaners on a low payment plan. Donald Dunn's sister bought him an expensive Rickenbacker electric guitar. There are many such examples of community support in the interviews. African Americans value their children and the outlet of music. The symbolism is one of benevolence that is repaid for years afterward.

Gene Metcalf also tells of the ineffable appeal of Wichita. He was drawn back to the city, ostensibly by ties to his grandmother. But within the affable community of Blacks, and the increasing acceptance by white Wichitans who were discovering Black music with vigor in the 1950s, outside influences also must have been a factor.

Donald Dunn's experience with his musicians' club shows the ambivalent arrangement the Wichita police had with the Black community. Occasionally he was raided for running a speakeasy, but for the most part he was allowed to operate his club, as it kept "the people off the streets." This is a pattern that was seen throughout the interviews. Law enforcement officials knew of the infractions going on in the Black clubs, but as long as they kept to themselves, African Americans were left in relative peace. The musicians failed to support Dunn—that is, they likely did not want to participate in performance for the little money he could pay—so he hired a DJ.

Charles Walker's group, Willie Wright and the Sparklers, had lengthy tenures at Wichita's premier Black clubs, indicating ability and the stylistic verve to keep abreast with the changing tastes in Black music. Their material was more popular—rhythm and blues, soul music, and later disco—with a blues and jazz set. He was a professional musician in Wichita for fifteen years, relying on a handshake of a club owner rather than a contract.

On the founding of the First National Black Historical Society of Kansas (later named Kansas African American Museum), Barbara Kerr (aided in recollection by her sister, Ra'shualaamu Beruni) gives insight into the difficulty they faced from majority-culture bureaucracy and minority-culture jealousy. According to her, because the three sisters, including the late Doris Kerr Larkins, did not have the credentials deemed necessary to pursue accreditation, control over the museum was wrested from them by other African Americans.

AGENTS OF TRANSFERRAL

Walton Morgan taught music to Wichita African American grade school children for thirty-one years, showing him to be a definite agent of transferral to younger musicians. Gene Metcalf's early experiences with the touring musicians who stayed at his grandmother's rooming house obviously had an effect on his musical career. These were members of the bands of Basie, Lunceford, and Ellington, unable to find rooms in Wichita hotels other than the Water Street Hotel.

Harold Cary first heard piano in the home, the hymns played by his mother. In addition, Cary's transmission of musical idiom through the minstrel pianist Jake adds years to the normal generational change. It is almost as if a century were encapsulated in his style. He is self-taught, unable to read music, and played only in the key of D-flat, just as his minstrel mentor. Just as performance skills were passed to him, Joe Lotson used the great out-of-doors in his transferral, hanging around the backyard to watch Chuck Rucker with the Smart Brothers as they rehearsed. Lotson in turn helped Charles Beans, who also listened to rehearsals in Lotson's backyard.

Franklin Mitchell learned the power of song from a blues troubadour, an "old Oklahoma boy" who played on his front porch. In addition, the

blues played at McKinley Park, located in the African American neighborhood, by acoustic musicians also influenced him. Both are instances of
a folk approach to the transferral of tradition, though Mitchell became a
thoroughly urban performer.

As a teen, Jerry Childers taxied older men to the Mambo Club to hear
the touring acts. Black policemen assigned to security limited his time
inside, but their willingness to let him in at all indicated the Black community's appreciation for music as an outlet for youth.

Wichita Blacks who heard Albert Tucker assessed his music as "a rarer
type of music," attesting to the uniqueness if not the appeal. No one has
asked to apprentice himself or herself to learn his style, though he sees
some interest from the younger members of his church.

Harmonica Chuck was a beneficiary of familial transferral, learning
harmonica from an older brother who picked it up from their father and
other relatives. Both Chuck and Albert Tucker, folk performers, depict
the transferral of culture from the folkways of rural Oklahoma to those
of the urban setting of a thriving 1950s Wichita. The simple haunts and
easily met fellows singing folk blues was replaced by the aircraft factories
and salvage yards of the largest city in Kansas. Thus, we see a dying out
of the folk influence, to be replaced by the urban blues style, mixed with
soul and funk in many later examples. All of this is, of course, a product
of changing musical tastes and living conditions. African Americans are
some of the most innovative musicians this country has to offer. It is little
surprise that folk blues has fallen into disuse. What is noteworthy is the
sustaining force of the blues, evolving with modernity yet easily recognizable from one decade to the next.

SHEET MUSIC VS. HEAD ARRANGEMENTS

Walton Morgan made use of written music for the majority of his performance, though he mentions Wichita jam sessions. He could appreciate
the extemporization of Charlie Parker and offered him a place to stay. This
genius, who performed in Wichita as a teen, influenced those he played
with and who heard him. This was both positive and negative influence.

The originality of arrangements Arthur Bates strived for when playing
with Homer Osborne should be noted. This takes the music to a level
above simply being a live jukebox. Unique arrangements tailor the songs
to the band's strengths and to the locale.

USE AND MEANING OF POETICS OF THE BLUES

Remona Hicks tells it from a woman's perspective, calling the blues a familiar entity since her beginning on the farm. She felt the blues had been good to her, allowing her to raise a family through singing. This describes the balancing act of a female performer. Throughout her interview, the poetry of blues and childcare are intertwined.

Berry Harris advances the notion that old ways should be respected and Black culture honored. The music he plays is his praise of his past. African Americans have been at the forefront of stylistic innovation in popular music for over 150 years. It is quite natural for Blacks to leave the fashion of yesterday for the new, given the lack of respect the majority society has offered them. Why honor your past if all you had was poverty and segregation? Harris sees beyond the hardships of his childhood in the Depression. He does not listen to Robert Johnson and Son House, considering their music old-fashioned, which of course, it is in a way. His music is a living entity with lyrics that are, as Sterling Brown wrote, poetry for the people.

Ray Valentine is another performer who felt the blues to be "an inner feeling." His remarks on the soothing power of the blues, for the performer and the audience, are testament to the power of good performance. He judged the city's blues to be "just as good as anywhere else." This might be a conciliatory gesture to some extent, but it can be taken as an assessment that Wichita blues performers create a challenging and rewarding atmosphere for musicians who come into the city.

Barbara Kerr's music is influenced by her integrated background. She is just as comfortable playing with a country and western band—anathema to Shirley Green—as she is with the blues. Walton Morgan gave her violin lessons, establishing a link between the pioneers in this study and its latter participants. Her views of working-class Blacks—their childhood games and the blues they listen to—echo the social strata that exist within the African American community, as reported by Jackie Lugrand Sr. The civil rights movement of the 1960s aided Kerr's integrative progress, through her ability as a folk singer in Wichita's beat coffee houses, and in the general (mostly young white) emigration to California. A meeting with Taj Mahal gave her the impetus to improvise, a largely unlearned skill in the academic musician.

Finally, on a distressing note, we hear Kerr's episode concerning her first hearing of the N-word. She was with another little girl, and thought the taunts were meant for her white friend who had freckles. Then she learned from her mother that the name was meant for her. I'm sure most African Americans recall times they were singled out in hurtful ways because of their race. How does a child deal with that? In Barbara's case, just as when she later encountered the KKK member, she used poetics to work it into her life and song.

HOW WICHITA WAS VIEWED NATIONALLY

When Shirley Green was readying his return to Wichita from New York, his fellow musicians assumed he was going to Kansas City. Green's fellows seemingly understood leaving New York for Kansas City, as the music scene there was well known. It would have been too hard to understand why anyone would leave New York for Wichita.

Indeed, Perry Reed's visual characterization of Kansas City, as pertains to jazz style, comes to mind. Kansas City was known for its style of jazz, and was the hub for neighboring towns and cities.

Jesse Anderson's first impression of Wichita, similar to Harmonica Chuck's, was unfavorable. He reports that Tulsa took care of her Black youth, offering many activities. And there was housing discrimination between Wichita Blacks and Blacks from Oklahoma and Arkansas. Of course, moving to a white neighborhood at that time was nearly impossible.

INTEGRATION

Perry Reed made a career in two branches of the Armed Forces because employment opportunities were limited. His comments on the segregation he experienced in World War II, with segregated albeit similar accommodation, disclose the fact that during the war it was not as noticeable as in peacetime.

Following World War II, Cary was one of the few African Americans attending Wichita University. He first started playing for fraternities and sororities, a function of his performances on campus. Through this, he found work in country clubs and better nightspots. University education was indeed an aid to his life chances. Also, his experience finishing high school in a larger Texas town points out one benefit of Black migration: segregated facilities in larger urban centers resembled majority amenities in the small towns. It was in Marshall that he became acquainted with more sophisticated blues. This urban style effectively dominated his Wichita repertoire.

Finding a job at Beech, Albert Tucker pursued his dream of equality in the work place—leaving the kitchen for skilled aircraft work. This is emblematic of Wichita's appeal for African Americans: high-paying jobs in a modern workforce. He noted few Blacks on the plant floor when he first arrived in Wichita in 1953.

Charles Walker's recollections of the cross-pollination between himself and Mike Finnigan exhibit the integrative pulse of the times.

Joe Lotson's story of the integration of a city golf course displays a wealth of information about Wichita's changing attitudes toward African Americans. One Black, who could pass as white, paid the green fees for a foursome. When his darker companions left their hiding spot behind trees and joined him, there were complaints from other players. The park commissioner told the park pro to let them play. And there you have it. Lotson was obviously put off by his fellow Black golfers having to use subterfuge to play on a public course—one their taxes had paid for. He mentions the adjustments he had to make when he came from Oklahoma to Wichita's integrated schools.

ENCOURAGEMENT

Jesse Anderson had a cheering vignette about being a young student in Tulsa. Self-conscious about a vision impairment, he was normally quiet, but when asked to sing, his talent stood out before the class. His teacher, Mrs. Hodges, encouraged him to keep singing, which he did, entering talent shows the rest of his time there.

Another instance involving Anderson: the Jenkins Music Company saleslady who arranged for him to try out a saxophone, to the rousing approval of the other customers. When she learned his family had no funds, she signed the finance papers for him. After his move to Chicago, he found recording success through performance and writing. His experience getting money from Chess is well substantiated by other Chess artists. Anderson's unique assessment of records being a vehicle for obtaining employment rather than a remunerative opportunity are reminiscent of the way musicians in the time of Charley Patton and Robert Johnson looked at them. He sheds some light on the recording process, pointing out that nightclub musicians were "not necessarily good studio musicians," and that the sales numbers determined the classification of blues or R&B, another singular observation from his time in the industry.

L'Ouverture School was another strong influence on the music of Black Wichita. Along with music teachers like Walton Morgan, the janitor Mr. Garrett performed in a manner that encouraged the young.

Franklin Mitchell's mother provides an appealing characterization of the African American family experience. She was at first reluctant to accept his desire to play, chasing him out of clubs and attempting to frighten him with the realities of what he would encounter in the harsh world of musical performance. But after she realized his determination, she offered him priceless advice: take care of yourself, respect people, and do not hesitate to call if in need.

RELIGION

Gene Metcalf's comments on the "sad sermons" and limited music in the Black churches of the 1930s and forties reveals just how far music has come in the African American worship process. Of course, there were always spirituals.

Jerry Childers credits the Catholic Church as an important influence in his youth. This structure was necessary to the vulnerable teenager playing drums in Wichita clubs.

Berry Harris, in speaking about fellow performer, Ira Morton "Bo" Jones, said he played both sides of the fence. In other words, Jones played clubs and in church. This was unique to the interviews. Of course, the old masters did a bit of both over the course of their careers—Son House, Skip James.

Harmonica Chuck, in his usual graceful way of telling a story, relates that churchgoers in Oklahoma did not welcome him. Likewise in Wichita, he found joining a congregation to be difficult. The reasons were unstated but likely were connected to his performing in clubs. Chuck reconciled the dichotomy by talking to his "Man" on a daily basis. He had his own way of worship, in his opinion just as devout.

Albert Tucker left the blues for church, finding that his wife "enticed" him through her "reputation" as a religious person. He was circumspect at his interview about performing the blues, yet he performed them.

IMPORTANCE AND APPEAL OF THE BLUES

Shirley Green recalls practicing many hours a day. This dedication and application is typical of a talented musician. The blues—and Green cites gutbucket blues as being most influential in his early playing—is an outlet for otherwise inaccessible feelings.

Arthur Bates felt that rock 'n' roll was "just a name," and that he had been performing rock "umpteen years." This observation details the difficulties in the shades of classification—complicated by race, since Black rhythm and blues when covered by whites was termed rock 'n' roll. As well, his opinions about excessive volume in the music today are well founded. It takes far more ability to play interesting music at a low volume. Blasting the audience may be one way to depict determination to surmount difficulties through the blues, but it is a stranger to accomplished performance. The hearing loss caused by noise from all types of live music will eventually become a factor in the nation's health care, if it isn't already.

Jerry Childers's remarks about first playing blues, "the beginning of Black culture," and graduating to jazz are representative of the aspirations of many musicians. Jazz is more complex and requires a different technical approach to perform. Nonetheless, it doesn't require more artistry or skill. The blues and other folk forms are best displayed in their limited context. Talent is appreciated within the strictures of the craft. He cites the mix of Texas, Chicago, and Oklahoma blues styles in Wichita, and comments on the high quality of out-of-town musicians who performed in the city, particularly Chicago bluesmen Kid Thomas and Tricky Marvin. Childers points out the geographical influence on music, allowing that his move to Los Angeles gave his organ playing that "West Coast sound" mixed with his Wichita heritage. And we have his view that music is an important tool in breaking down racial prejudice, and that Wichita had a true community of musicians. The last point no doubt had an effect on the first: a benign influence among blues performers on stage had to have an effect on audiences.

Upon his return to Kansas, Jesse Anderson attempted to play in the clubs but encountered musicians who were unaware of what it took to be a professional. As did Franklin Mitchell, he found Wichita artists "making the same mistakes" they were when he left town. This implies a stasis that has marked Wichita. Certainly, Charlie Parker felt the same way about this city, no doubt helped along by Jay McShann firing him on the bandstand of the Trocadero, as Gene Metcalf reported.

The rhythm and blues of the 1950s was replaced by the soul music of the 1960s, often performed by Donald Dunn in white clubs. This illustrates a departure from the segregation of the previous decade, a departure that was precipitated by the majority culture's increasing approval of the music of Black culture. Dunn still played the blues of B.B. King during the 1960s.

Albert Tucker recognized the longevity of the folk blues, cautioning his nephew Earl Starks, who later played with Harmonica Chuck, that rock 'n' roll was going to fade away. His recollections of learning guitar with Berry Harris reveal the two major approaches to blues performance, urban and rural, and how they can spring from the same soil.

Harmonica Chuck is an intuitive performer, relying on inspiration to determine his next song. This performance method was suggested by his mother. She was proud of his ability but reminded him that his talents could be displayed in the music of the church. He calls blues a relaxation, both through performance and listening. Its power takes your mind off troublesome intent, the guitar or dance floor taking the rough treatment you might have given to someone. This substitution of anger and violence through song is a very effective use of the art form. How many listeners do the same?

While with Harold Cary, Joe Lotson learned the inspirational ability of the bassist through association with Gilmar Walters. His comments on the solidity necessary in blues drumming are helpful in distinguishing the blues from jazz percussion. Lotson believed Black musicians play by feel and thus can give the technically proficient whites a lesson on realistic, believable performance. As has been noted, the latter qualities are paramount in winning audience approval. He assigns a color-blind quality to music, as do several other participants, and feels that all music "was derived from the blues." He characterizes Wichita audiences as preferring danceable rhythm and blues to jazz, and not demanding the highest quality. It is his opinion that there is only limited exchange of musical ideas between experienced and novice players, due to the fact of the semiprofessional status of most Wichita musicians. He did not find a distinct style of blues in the city.

FOLKLORE GENRES

Riddle, Myth, Legend, Tale, Proverb, or Ballad

Harmonica Chuck's rural blues is a wealth of folklore. Here are a few examples, the first two from when he was living on the farm in Oklahoma. As a teen, Chuck traded a pig for a Model A Ford, later using it to take his mother to town on the weekends for staples; also perhaps for him to go to dances. This has to qualify as the backbone of a myth—Chuck's hard work grants him a piglet which in turn grows large and valuable enough to be traded for a twentieth-century mode of conveyance that makes his mother's life easier. The second example comes from his attempts to try to get on stage in Wichita.

In what he called building up courage, Chuck went to various white clubs with his harmonica with the goal of performing. He wasn't always successful but, getting around the rejection, he took a lesson from his childhood in

Oklahoma. He wasn't supposed to go into white restaurants, but he did so under the guise of not knowing the rules.

This is, of course, a tale of the wiles of a child used against prejudice. Growing up in such an environment surely plays a heavy hand in maturity.

Chuck's big chance with the Hollywood talent scout is a familiar theme in many of the interviews. Nearly all the musicians had their near opportunity to establish themselves in the national market. In this case, numbering the times the agent asked him to go to California with him and the agent's observation that he would not ask again, resembles a folktale. Chuck later saw guys who looked like him but never saw the agent again, adding to the tale. He tried to point out to the scout that he was not of the same caliber as Little Walter and was answered with the fact of his uniqueness. The love and responsibilities of fatherhood kept him in Wichita. He recalled the financial details of the deal nearly forty years later.

And we have a legend: that of the naming of Harmonica Chuck. An older man in his hometown in Oklahoma asked his name and when told Charlie, he said he did not like it. The older man was known as Charlie, so he called him Chuck. Likewise in Wichita, Chuck's father-in-law, Tollie, objected to Charlie and began to call him Chuck. When Chuck began playing the harmonica, he added that to his name.

More than once in the interviews, we hear the story of going into a club when the band started playing and not exiting until daybreak, which resembles a tale of enchantment.

Then there are Aunt Kat and Uncle Bob, recurring characters in the interviews. When asked if the pair, who managed Chuck, paid him enough, his answer became a proverb. They never gave him enough money, and when he argued with them about it, Chuck was replaced by another harmonica player. As it turned out, the replacement was not a match for Chuck and the managers had to refund the money. There was also a fight at the gig. Here we have vindication of being dismissive of Chuck's talent and draw. In the retelling, he was not vengeful, more amused at the turn of events.

Albert Tucker, the other folk blues performer in this study, has a story of similar rural charm concerning meeting a fellow who carried something in a sack. This piqued his curiosity, and when the banjo was revealed and used to perform "West Texas Blues," Tucker was entranced. This story fits nicely into the riddle category. It is a rural episode from start to finish, and the finish had Tucker puzzling over the blues from that day forth. His method of learning blues songs was to ruminate on them in his farm chores after obtaining his own banjo and guitar.

Remona Hicks tells of country dinners hosted by several churches, and of winning a singing contest at age eleven. Her prize was a certificate and a gold Bible, the latter a visual indication of her spiritual worth, in the eyes of a child. Also in the winning was a trip to neighboring state Arkansas to sing in a much larger church. Gaining the legendary gold Bible through her vocal ability at a young age was a preamble to the rest of her life. Society rewarded her for her talent, and later, when she was put into a girls home, she sang her "way out." When Hicks came to Wichita, she was discovered again through her singing talent, this time reported as a tale. Franklin Mitchell saw her singing in a club on Murdock or 9th Street, likely for tips, and reported her talent to Aunt Kat. The agent recognized Hicks as her sister and retrieved her from that situation, setting her up in her home and with a backing group. This tale represents the up-and-down life of blues performance, especially difficult for a woman in those times. Hicks persevered of course, ending up successfully rearing four children by singing the blues.

Perry Reed joined the army just prior to World War II. He wanted to join the 9th Cavalry Band. When he approached the leader and told him he played drums, he was asked to try out. Reed could not decipher the sheet music, but he knew the Sousa march the band was playing from listening to recordings. He made it in, learning to read music a year later. This is on the dividing line between the beginnings of a myth and tale.

Joe Lotson's remarks concern the legendary blind drummer Homer Osborne. Already an accomplished percussionist (in his opinion) at seventeen, Lotson went to Osborne's house and was asked to show what he could do. Young Lotson showed a bit of his style and Osborne was not impressed. Lotson really got into playing some runs and turned to Osborne for his opinion. The blind drummer then floored him with his expertise, afterward telling him that he should always be ready to learn from others. Thus, another proverb.

Barbara Kerr tells a tragicomic folk tale concerning her time playing with a country band in Hattiesburg, Mississippi. She spotted a faithful fan always sitting in the back of the house. Finally, she went up and introduced herself, later learning that he was the grand wizard of the Hattiesburg, Mississippi Ku Klux Klan. The KKK member couldn't find it in himself to acknowledge her as being Black—he called her his "little Indian fiddle player." Kerr capitalized on his interest in her performance, encouraging him to obtain pastel sheets. She thought that her humor and his approval of her, however couched, would eventually lead to him becoming more tolerant.

Harmonica Chuck speaks of the mythic place of freedom, putting it as looking way, way north ever since childhood. In other words, he was not satisfied with the status quo in Oklahoma and leaving for Kansas fit his ideals. Surely this phrase has been used since the days of slavery as one of betterment and deliverance.

Harold Cary, who was at the forefront of breaking color lines in Wichita's clubs, found himself in foreign territory when he played a gig on South Broadway. During his performance, a woman, white, began doing her strip-tease to his music. This was not part of his show, as far as he knew. Cary was in a very touchy situation, watched by the audience almost as much as the female entertainer was, to see if he would turn around and take in her show. He kept playing. South Wichita is just that: South Wichita. He had a tricky situation and handled it with aplomb. It seems the clubgoers missed the real show watching him in an unfriendly fashion. His risqué vignette falls into the genre of a humorous tale.

Next, we look at current performers in the city.

MAJORITY CULTURE BLUES IN WICHITA

The songs of folk blues recording artists John Koerner, Dave Ray, and Tony Glover, as well as the Chicago blues of the Paul Butterfield Blues Band, influenced a lot of white musicians in the 1960s. Here were players of their culture who were recreating African American music. This rippled through Wichita. There is mention of the next generation of blues players in the interviews—nearly all majority culture. Berry Harris spoke of the right of white performers to sing the blues, mentioning Hank Williams and Bob Wills. Both performers were squarely in the category of authenticity. He also mentions some Wichita majority-culture performers who came to the Black clubs to learn: Jerry Hahn (primarily a jazz performer, but he did dip into blues rock in the Jerry Hahn Brotherhood with Mike Finnigan), Pat McJimsey, Jerry Wood, Rene Aaron, Rick Meyer, and, from previous decades, Dempsey Wright and Luther McDonald.

Gene Metcalf points out the cultural transference of King B's, a Black club that served as informal apprenticeship for the white blues players. At the time of her interview, Barbara Kerr was playing with a white blues band. A sampling of current Wichita blues performers and followers give their thoughts on majority culture blues and the inspiration for it.

DAVID GRAHAM, HARMONICA AND VOCALS

"I'm a big fan of Sonny Terry and Charlie McCoy. The Hohner Blues Harp is what I play. It's just a little bit heavier brass than the Marine Band, maybe a little bit more lifetime. I also like Sonny Boy Williamson, and Little Walter, Big Walter. Paul Butterfield is kind of like the middle between them.

"Homesick James came here with Walter Horton, at the Coyote Club. The next time he came, he was at the Spot. Pat McJimsey [lead guitar], Hank Elder on the trumpet, and Rick Meyer on saxophone. And that was a relatively good show, too. Now, in the meantime, I had been kind of hanging out, you know, shaking his hand and just being a fan. And so, the next time Homesick James came, he was down at the Spot again. He was driven up here by this lady named Pat. And she played bass. So, it was the two of them, and they needed a band. The way I remember it, Renee Aaron, another fellow harmonica player here in town, we were friends. He couldn't get off work or had to play another gig. Anyway, I got to step in. At that time, I had a group called the Generators. This is a Friday night show. It was really the first time I ever played with somebody of that caliber. He was just a great guy. Kind of tough, you know, just not knowing what to do exactly. No set list—he just called them out. But he's in open tunings like E or A or D. The bass player would tune me up. And so, everything was okay. That night, we went to his hotel room and partied and all this stuff, hanging out with James. And he was a wild man. At that time, probably in his seventies. [In] 1985, I was twenty-eight.

"So, the next day, it's like, what's going to happen? I went to his hotel room, knock on the door and wait and wait and wait, and knock on the door and he finally comes to the door. Woke him up. I said something about playing with him that night if he still needed a harmonica player. And he told me a few choice phrases, you know. And then he just looked me up and down. This is dead silence, not even a grin and nothing, and I was just standing there dying. And he goes, 'Yeah, nine o'clock.' So, I was completely humbled to a point where I was just even tentative. I had already been put in my place the night before. But the funny thing is, it was recorded on cassette. And he's great on it. He's fantastic. And on top of all that, I had borrowed Renee Aaron's amplifier, and the bass player plugged into it, too. And we blew the speaker, so I was in trouble all the way around. That was a good dose of the blues.

"I played with Clif Major in the Del Rays for quite a while. And then, as it would go along, that became the House Rockers and a few other names. But the reason why it was so steadfast, we just kind of hit it off. Clif is a hard guy to get to know. But given time, he ended up being a loyal friend. I had the David Graham Band and Clif joined that. There was Al Satterly,

Stephanie Decker, and Tommy Crabb on drums. That's good. Yeah. And when Stephanie moved away, and Alan dropped out, we had Jesse Major [Clif's son] on bass for quite some time."

Graham talks about African American influence on his performance style.

"Well, one of the first guys I saw was Jerry Childers. And I only saw him a couple of times. But that was my eye-opener. From there, my very favorite of course is Harmonica Chuck. I thought he was wonderful. I played with him at the Spot. 'Hey, this Black guy wants to play.' I backed him up and I was so glad I did. I played with Berry Harris a number of times—made him plenty mad, too. Too fast, too busy, too rock 'n' roll. There's a lot of ways to put it, but there's a certain style of playing that he did. It was kind of a funk thing, and you just had to bow down to it and take your place in line. And I know how to do that. But sometimes, he would just unplug and walk off the stage."

He describes a Wichita style of blues certainly not unique to the city.

"Lots of orchestration [arrangement]. That's how I would describe them. It usually has a lot of parts to it, at least three if not more. If you have an organ or piano, organ and guitar, and then horns. But now, for me, as a harmonica player, I tried to make that the focus. But not like I used to. Nowadays, less is more."

Other Wichita majority culture players:

"I played with Pat McJimsey out at the Roadhouse at those Harmonica Blowouts. He was real nice. I'd say he was an R&B player. Chico [John Marshall]. Yeah, yeah. We were doing the jams at the Roadhouse with Clif Major, Donn Lentz on bass, and Tommy Crabb on drums, and myself. Just about every time on Thursday night, Chico would come out to play the B-3 organ. He always had some young thing taking him around.

"Ray Valentine was great. Henry Walker is fantastic. Because they were the elders. And when you play in the old blues bands like that with those guys, there's a hierarchy. And, like the Homesick James story of being humbled to understand your place, you know, go for it when they say go for it. So yeah, they were all mentors. You didn't want them to unplug their guitar and walk off like Berry did. Oh, yeah. It was insane, because we'd all laugh it off. But really, it kind of hurt."

DUSTIN ARBUCKLE, HARMONICA AND VOCALS

"I always loved the Blues Brothers movie when I was younger, because it's hilarious and there is actually a lot of great music. Then there was the *House of Blues Radio Hour*, which of course, was hosted by Dan Ackroyd. My dad

David Graham Band (left to right): Clif Major, Al Satterly, Tommy Crabb, Graham, and Stephanie Decker, photo by Arthur Kenyon.

was very much in the blues, and just kind of traditional American music in general. I started to feel the interest in that music. He had been a gigging musician around town for at least a few years in the mid- to late sixties, before he went to Vietnam. He talked to me about playing with Mike Finnigan, Jerry Wood, Clif Major, and I think that's how he and Bill Garrison became connected. I decided that I wanted to try harmonica and so, dad wanted me to meet Bill, because Bill being a great harmonica player. We took the drive out to Kingman, where Bill was living, hung out there all day. Bill played guitar and harmonica for us, and he had a great vinyl collection. And he had these bootleg VHS recordings, that I think had come to him via Wes Race, of all those German TV broadcasts of the American Folk Blues Festival from back in the 1960s. Sonny Boy Williamson II, Mississippi Fred McDowell, John Lee Hooker, Buddy Guy, Howlin' Wolf, Hubert Sumlin, Willie Dixon, Big Mama Thornton, and Big Walter Horton. Between getting to hear someone like Bill play right in front of me, and then seeing these old live videos of some of the greatest of all time like that, it inspired me.

"Next weekend, my folks bought me a harmonica, and I just started playing all the time. If I was driving in my car, listening to blues CDs, I was trying to play along with it. I didn't realize until a while later that it was really essential to have more than one harmonica. Bill explained all that to me, but I didn't really grasp it at the time. And I played a lot of things out of tune for about a year. Bill was huge, and David Graham, as harmonica players. While

(Left to right) Ray Valentine, Henry Walker, and Berry Harris at the Kansas African American Museum, 2008. Photo by author.

Bill was kind of that guy who explained some basics of the instrument, David taught me more actively about playing the instrument. David's a wonderful human being and a really enthusiastic guy and extremely genuine. I met him because he was playing one of the open jams at the Roadhouse.

"Berry Harris was always very kind to me in a somewhat curmudgeonly way. He was pretty cool and pretty encouraging. I remember being around Jesse Anderson a little bit, but I never got to know Jesse very much. Blues is Black music, born out of the Black experience. I think all American music to some point is a melting pot. I came along at a time when a lot of the older Black performers in town were dying out or weren't really playing around much anymore. Berry was probably the one I was the closest to, and the one that I jammed with the most. And maybe you'd go to see him play and he'd say, 'Come on up.'

"Being central here, we are subjected to a lot of different regional influences. And so, if there is a Wichita blues style, I feel it's something that's sort of in the middle of Texas style. I feel like Berry seemed to gravitate toward a Texas influence with maybe a little bit of Memphis vibe. And I felt like most of the older guys around Wichita had more of that Texas influence, especially in a guy like Chico as a B-3 guy. He was really into more swing and almost kind of jump blues. You get a little more of that Kansas City influence from guys like Basie and Big Joe Turner. I think, you know, if there is a style for

Wichita, I feel like it's sort of a cross-pollination between those styles. As you go forward in time, with the proliferation of recorded music, more influences come in a way that's maybe a little less organic. I've always felt like the blues that was most influential on me was Chicago blues. As a harmonica player, it's hard to ignore Little Walter, and Big Walter Horton and Junior Wells, James Cotton, Paul Butterfield.

"But also more country blues, and that's everything from Delta Blues, like Charlie Patton and Son House to Sonny Terry and Brownie McGhee. Sonny Terry and Brownie McGhee were one of my dad's absolute favorites, and I feel Bill Garrison was oriented toward a lot of that kind of stuff. Sonny Terry's rhythmic approach was huge for me as I was learning to play. But, you know, as far as the direct influence of a particular artist around here, I don't know how much that affected me, from a stylistic standpoint, as much as it did just from an encouragement standpoint.

"Moreland and Arbuckle [Alligator Records]—we started playing together in 2002. Aaron was interested in the real heavy Mississippi blues. Early on, that's what we were doing. And then, we started to move toward doing electric stuff as well. Then we really focused more heavily on kind of electrified Mississippi blues and early real gritty Chicago blues."

Arbuckle now plays in several groups, folk to blues, in order to perform regularly.

LEWIS COWDREY, HARMONICA, GUITAR, VOCALS

Lewis Cowdrey [Fan Club, Antone's], born 1945 in Albuquerque, NM, is one of the original founders of the Austin blues scene. His band, Storm, featured a who's who of the Austin legends. Lewis is a world-class harpman, vocalist, guitarist, and bandleader. He has been living in Wichita, Kansas, for several years and playing locally. Lewis was based in L.A. in 1968 leading a Black blues band featuring Pee Wee Crayton. He also worked with Johnny Otis on a belated recording project before returning to Lubbock, where he met a young woman who admired his record collection (Angela Strehli). Strehli and Lewis Cowdrey formed the Fabulous Rockets. Lewis also was co-founder of Storm, a legendary Austin, Texas Blues band that boasted Denny Freeman, Jimmie Vaughan, Keith Ferguson, and W.C. Clark.[3]

"A Wichita style of blues comes from classic rock mainly. And this is for white folks. This is the Air Capital. Those people [African Americans] came here. There were educated people with jobs. I assume it was similar to that in Little Rock, OK City. And I've always been interested in how so much super international talent ended up here. And you know, Berry gave lessons to Tony Mathews, the guy that played for Ray Charles.[4] *Hit Parader* was where I first read about Bob Koester [Delmark Records owner, born in Wichita]. Now, Bob thinks very little of Wichita. He asked me one time, 'What are you going back to Wichita for?'

"But anyway, on all of these people who I came close to but I hadn't met before: Jesse Anderson told me a story that I had read in the Earl Hooker book. He said that when Otis Rush came and played one of those Boeing Blues shows [Wichita Blues Society sponsored], first thing he said when got off the plane 'Where's Jesse?' Which is what any bandleader, singer, whoever, would say. You know that song with Duane Allman on it, 'Loan me a dime?' Jesse wrote that. You know the story? Jesse booked the studio the day it was recorded. He arranged it, he called up Fenton Robinson, who's the guy that sang it, and who gets credit for having written it. And Jesse cowrote "Come on Sock It to Me," one of the biggest solo blues records of all time, with Syl Johnson [and J. Amstead, according to the label]. There's plenty of really good players here. Henry Walker is one of my favorite all-time musicians because he doesn't sing. And he's a hard-working guy.

"Why did Blacks quit playing the blues? Well, there were two reasons. And I can only speculate. For one thing, it mostly fell off the charts. Totally. It was gone. And you couldn't have your little band together that you'd had for twenty years. And when you'd started playing "Down the Road a Piece," that Nat King Cole–type R&B and jazz. And then you saw everybody playing rock 'n' roll. Muddy Waters himself wasn't really playing much. You know, it just changed. And of course, what changed it after that? Stevie [Ray Vaughan]. I can't see anything else in this capitalist plot, you know, to take the music of Africa, and have white folks play it and make it anything better than, you know, Eric Clapton or something.

"The money is in the pocket of the guy that tells you what to do. People always say you could make a million doing that, man. It's like Clif [Major]. I've played with eight or ten or twenty boy wonder guitarists, and everybody would come in to see my band. And then they would say, "Oh, that guitar player's great; he can make a million." But he wouldn't know what songs to play if I wasn't on stage."

Lewis Cowdrey Band (left to right): Cowdrey, George Grabill, Don Stewart, Scott Riggs, and Al Satterly, photo by Arthur Kenyon.

WES RACE

Wichitan Wesley Race III, blues poet, recording artist, and entrepreneur, moved to Chicago in the late 1960s to be closer to the source. He is now living in Texas, another blues regional center, and writes in a personal correspondence:

"I'd say that the Southwest Blues/Jazz Centers like Kansas City and Dallas certainly played a role in shaping the Wichita blues scene. From what I've read, Wichita was sort of a sleepy musical town until the 1940s when the aircraft factories started revving up—and a lot of Blacks from Oklahoma, Arkansas and Texas moved to Wichita to start working on the aircraft assembly lines. Having musical places like the Mambo Club which featured a lot of touring blues and R&B acts certainly helped too. . . .

"I actually don't see Wichita as having its own blues style—but there were different schools like Finnigan & Wood learning from Bobby Blue Bland and Freddie King, and then Clif Major paving the way to absorbing blues and rockabilly roots. But Harmonica Chuck must certainly have been listening to Little Walter and both of the Sonny Boy Williamsons.

"I got Harmonica Chuck a gig at the Coyote Club. One of the most inspirational nights was a Christmas Eve when Rick Meyers and I went up on Ninth Street and caught a Jerry Childers gig. I got Jerry Childers a matinee gig at the Spot on a Saturday afternoon along with a Black sax player from Wichita [possibly Morris Atchison] along with Phil Campbell on drums and Bnois King from Dallas (they were members of the Smokin' Joe Kubek band). It'd be interesting to know what Berry Harris's influences were. You and Bill Garrison were also an integral part of the Wichita blues scene for many years."[5]

BILL GARRISON (1948–2020)

The following is from a piece written by Bill's older brother Tom.

"When he showed up in San Francisco in 1969, I took him to Berkeley for his twenty-first birthday. After some pretty strange 'performance art' the main act began. It was a pair of Black musicians and storytellers who had ridden the rails and played together for years: Sonny Terry and Brownie McGhee. . . . I don't think Bill was ever the same after that.

"I also won't forget our great nights as fans of some of the great musicians and venues in Wichita. Dancing to Mike Finnigan and the Serfs at the Stagedoor Inn. Late nights at the Early Bird Café (after boot camp prior to Nam). One of Bill's favorite nights was listening to Jerry Hahn and Mickey Sheaks play the Coyote with Mose Allison. . . . Music always made our life experience richer and more memorable. Thanks to all the musicians who are here today. You make our world a better place."

Here is a word from Wichitan Craig Steward:

"Bill and I met in the winter of 1967 at A Blackout, the only bar/tavern in Wichita that embraced integration . . . a genuine piece of Greenwich Village and Haight-Ashbury. It had the greatest jukebox in town. Bill and I fell in love with the harmonica at exactly the same time. Our first major influence was Canned Heat with Alan Wilson. Bill and I went and bought identical mics and small amps. From that day on we nurtured and pushed one another musically. As the years went by Bill was a very accomplished electrified harp player along with his acoustic style."

Their original idea was to perform as a harmonica duo, but both ended up playing with others. In 1972, Frank Zappa did a Petit Wazoo performance in Wichita and went out later to hear some live music. He saw Steward sitting in with the band Bliss at a westside bar, Caesar's Palace. Wowed by Steward's ability, Zappa offered to fly him out to LA to audition. He did so, but it took a few more years of practice before he was used as a session man on *Joe's*

Garage Act I. Craig went on to play harmonica on more Zappa recordings, moving out to California and working as an arborist.

PAT MCJIMSEY (1950–2004)

Pat McJimsey was an accomplished lead guitarist, fronting many Wichita bands: Bear Valley Blues Band, the Entire British Navy, 4 Brothers and the Pat McJimsey Band. His vocals were effective and heartfelt, driving his various groups through soul and blues renditions. His death in his early fifties was the impetus for the PAT Fund. This fund, sponsored by the Wichita Blues Society, is a repository for helping sick or injured musicians.

CLIF MAJOR (1948–2014)

"A fixture in the local blues, bluegrass, rock, and gospel scene, started performing with his high school band, the Outcasts, in the 1960s. Other bands Major performed with were the Del Reys, Southwind, the Jukes, and the Prairie Grass. In 1978, Major opened C Major Guitars . . . where he sold vintage guitars and other instruments and equipment, as well as giving guitar lessons."[6]

Clif opened Rockin' Daddy's, a place for music performance in 2004. In 2014, he was elected to the Kansas Music Hall of Fame. Clif played with the Smart Brothers on 9th Street for a time, getting a feel for African American performance.

BAT SHUNATONA (1949?–2005)

Bat was a Native American lead guitarist. His sister Sue writes: "Bands he was in, Soul Survivors, Red Neck. He sat in with people. Mike Finnigan (and Wood), Red Neck, Sawdust Charlie. He also worked as a salesman on car lots. Well, he worked a lot of lots. He sold a car filled with water!"

RUBY WHITE, PIANO AND VOCALS

Connie "Ruby" White began her career playing clarinet in the South High School band. She joined her first rock group, Gold Plush Blues, as lead singer while still a teenager. After several years fronting hard rock groups, she found inspiration listening to a KMUW public radio program *Strictly Blues*, broadcast on Sunday nights in the 1980s. She was growing tired of "being left out of band meetings and decisions about songs to do" and decided to form her own blues group, Ruby White and the Blues. This patriotic nominative has served her for thirty-plus years. She got her material from the blues played on that radio program, as well as from musicians she played with in her group. Sporadic piano lessons as a ten-year-old helped her put out some blues on the electric piano, following a heritage of ladies at the keyboard. She writes:

> I started singing some Janis Joplin stuff in 1971 in last year of High school. Joined Hard Road in 1971 thru 1974. . . . 1978 to 1982 was in Headstone band . . . Both local house bands in Wichita. After a stint in a Rock band called Medusa for 3 years, I decided to form Ruby White and the Blues in 1990 with George Graybill on Bass, Kenny Brown on guitar, Steve Swaim on Drums. Brenda Castleberry sang Janis Joplin and blues songs with Pat McJimsey in a band called Bear Valley Blues band in 1970 and '71. At that time, she and I were the only girl singers in town for the sixteen- to twenty-five-year-old crowd.

LYNN AVANTS

Lynn is a working guitarist and vocalist. He got into blues when the 1990s rolled around, one of the periods of high interest in the music. The other two were the 1920s to early 1930s and mid-1950s through the 1960s. It could be that we are due for another period of renewed interest and research. Through correspondence, he provides the following:

> I started playing out in 1986 (rock) but decided to pursue and focus solely on blues music in late 1991. Rick Lane, Johnny Mack (McWilliams), and Berry Harris took me under their wings within the first

Current Wichita blues performers (left to right): Clayton Crawford, Ed Macy Jr., Bill Garrison, George Graybill, and Connie White, photo by author.

year. I could probably name a hundred or so musicians that dabbled in the blues locally and I believe that you are familiar with a significant portion of them already. I would consider many to be rock musicians that dabbled in blues. Bill Garrison, yourself, Rick Lane, George Graybill, Tommy Crabb, and Johnny Mack were a few dedicated blues musicians locally. The Macy Brothers definitely followed the Finnigan blueprint with blue-eyed soul, as McJimsey did!

I was influenced by most that you interviewed back in the '90s. After playing in Berry's band, I joined Gene Metcalf's band that had Jesse Anderson, Donald Dunn, myself, and Dewell on bass. I don't recall the name of the drummer. This was the last lineup at King B's club on 9th Street and we frequently played at Panama Red's [Old Town] as well. I spent a lot of time with Harmonica Chuck, who probably taught me more about Blues and prepared me for my move to Texas at the end of 1995. I played with Berry, Ray Valentine, Jerry Jackson, and Erroll Patton frequently about the time that the Spot Recreation closed down.

In Texas, I was with Johnny Mack initially until he joined forces with James Hinkle after leaving Marcia Ball's band. I spent a lot of time following Sam Meyers, Hashbrown (Brian Calaway), and Holland Smith while doing a bit of third-tier road gigs as a sideman. I got married and stopped playing in 1998 and enjoyed my kids while they were young. My playing improved a great deal after moving to Texas and it has taken me about a decade to get back in shape. Wes Race was instrumental in providing some much needed guidance in Texas. I was very fortunate!

Sam Meyers, Hashbrown, and Holland Smith hosted/participated in jams when they weren't touring and were mentoring younger generations such as myself, so we saw each other frequently and became friends. Nick Curran, Paul Size (Red Devils) and the Moeller brothers (Fabulous Thunderbirds) are a few that they mentored before I moved there. Generally, I worked as a sideman opening for bigger acts at the time like Doyle Bramhall and Robert Ealey. The scene was almost entirely focused on pre-60s blues at the time. I jammed with Kenny Wayne Shepherd right after I moved there because everyone else there refused to. Johnny Mack sang and played washboard, which brought a Big Joe Turner vibe that they were into. He had an album put together with James Hinkle that was nominated for a Grammy in 2007.

Avants provides a list of some white blues musicians in the Wichita area:

Primarily blues: Fred James, Lewis Cowdrey, Clif Major, Tommy Crabb, Rick Lane, Bill Garrison, Pat O'Connor, Connie [Ruby] White, Tom Szambecki, Johnny Mack, George Graybill, Kevin May, David Keller, David Graham, Donn Lentz, Dustin Arbuckle.

Blues-influenced genres: Mike Finnigan, Jerry Wood, Ed Macy Sr., Fred James Sr. (and brothers/children), Pat McJimsey, Drake Macy, Ed Macy Jr., Winston Blair, Mike West, John Salem, John Collison, Bob Hartley, Dawayne Bailey, Craig Steward, Shawn Lee, Scotty Lee, Randy Fields, Kenny Brown, Karen Kirby, Jim Keefer, Dee Starkey, Scott Zackula, Richard Clemons, Dennis McDermott, David Casmaer, Eddie Z. Scott, Jay Paul Bland, Terry Quiett, Donnie Baker, Jeff Corbett, Michael Peltzer, Justin Murray, Aaron Underwood, Mitch King, Colby Aiken, Caleb John Drummond, Rod Baker, Michael Horton, Rachelle Coba, Dan Monnat, Doug Webb, Kent Overaker, and Bill Kraske.

It can be seen that blues-influenced genres outpaced blues. Avants discusses blues cultural transmission:

It may well be a generational trend which has resulted in the blues-rock genre eclipsing most "blues" performances today. It is happening unilaterally across the country currently and is causing a great deal of unrest as well as some semi-public lashing out. A number of older generation players discussed this at length earlier this year when I was in Texas. The problem becomes: how does one pass on the old traditions to a generation that doesn't value them?

So the old ghost of disappearing blues is seen in terms of today: blues rock eclipsing steady rolling blues. But that is the history of the form: classic blues, country blues, urban blues, jump blues, R&B, rock 'n' roll. Tastes change; the blues remain.

SUMMATION

The original nineteen interviews reveal a strong African American community, with neighbors who helped look after the children, and business owners and members of professions who provided support for the musical endeavors of youth. This same African American community, whether it was in the original North Main and Water Street district or in the later-developed East 9th Street area, offered a self-sufficiency not unlike that of the Black colonies that formed in Kansas in the 1870s. There was help from the majority culture; especially from Jenkins Music Store, who extended credit to African Americans and offered lower-priced used instruments. Just as they were helped when young, many of those interviewed wanted to leave something for the youth of today: Perry Reed's big band for high school students, Shirley Green's work with the Children's Home, and Walton Morgan's lifelong calling to teach music (for many years in segregated schools), which showed his influence in more than one of the musicians interviewed.

The breakdown of that self-sufficient African American community came in large part through two phenomena: urban renewal and integration. The initial Wichita African American settlement close to city center gradually was replaced by majority-culture urban structures, a process that greatly increased during the urban renewal movement of the 1960s. The 9th Street restaurants and clubs, including the Dunbar Theatre, closed in large part due to integration, which allowed African Americans to go to white clubs and major movie houses. It should be noted that the Dunbar is currently under extensive renovation as a performing arts center.

A marked aspect of African American life is the lure of migration as a solution for economic deprivation. During the twentieth century, Wichita drew African Americans from Oklahoma and Arkansas just as Chicago and Detroit drew them from the Deep South. Migration definitely brought a more developed musical heritage to Kansas. Another major consideration is the evidence that music contributed to breaking down color lines, a process begun in the nineteenth century.

As to the central question of this study, the answer is no; Wichita does not have a recognizable blues style. Though some of the participants thought there was a potential for a Wichita sound, this might have been a reflection of their self-opinion—that is, local musicians would be talented enough to create a recognizable style of blues. Other participants disparaged Wichita in favor of Kansas City or other urban centers. A majority of the African Americans interviewed in the original study, nine, were from Oklahoma; six from Kansas; and four from other states. Most of the Oklahomans transplanted this Territory style—electric guitar as lead instrument, accompanied by saxophone (which could also play lead), organ, and sophisticated vocal stylist—to Wichita. Following World Wars I and II, Chicago welcomed or at least tolerated Mississippians who influenced the city's blues and eventually created the 1950s Chicago style. During the 1950s, the sizable diffusion from Oklahoma to Wichita made local innovation unnecessary. But the transplanted Oklahomans did not create a new style, either due to lack of playing opportunities or insufficient collective verve.

Another factor to consider is the evolution of the blues, currently to what is called blues rock: a Wichita tradition could be in process of creation. As in Kansas City, which had a corrupt, wide-open town during the twenties and thirties,[7] a strong market allows the music to flourish. If employment in Wichita holds up, the general economic well-being (as well as encouragement from city officials for live music venues) will foster performance. Composition as a welcome addition must also be encouraged. This is somewhat at variance with the current switch to blues rock, though a unique regional interpretation would help begin a style. While most young Black Wichita musicians do not play blues, favoring the latest genres, like rap, R&B, and hip-hop, and whatever is next, Lynn Avants lists African American musicians who were full-time members of a blues/R&B/soul group in Wichita at one time, 1990–2023:

Jerry Jackson, Bill Lynch, Eugene "Beaver" Howard, Larry Sanders, Ray Drew, Big Clyde Sheely, Ray Murray, Bill Landrum, Vince Clendenon, Victor Kinchion, B. Alan Garrett, David Shaw, Fred Agee, Byford Landry, Reggie Littleton, Erroll Patton, Rickey Brothers, Marvin White,

Don Level, Mr. Lee, Carl Stovall, Johnny Neal, Brian Powell, Troy Tolbert, Deanna "Lady D" Custard, Val Williams, Jeff Stidham, Storm Herrington, Josh Rutledge.

Avants also lists Wichita-area Hispanic and Native American blues musicians with the same criteria:

Hector Chavez, Eddie Jaso, Arnold Jaso, Mac Orsbon, Andy Abasolo, Tony Jasso, Vincent Jaso, Mike Reece, Jessie Medina, Gil Ponte, Daniel "Bubba" Martinez, Jaime Linares, Dennis Balderes, A. J. Harvey.

It must be noted that these three lists from Avants, while extremely helpful, are not exhaustive.

Then we have Winfield's Clayton Crawford, an African American lead guitarist and vocalist that can tear up any stage in rock or blues.

I am known for being a blues Rock player, but I just say I'm a guitarist/musician. I enjoy most forms of music and have played many including New Latino music. My main influence was my grandfather who was a minister and a gospel guitar slinger. I met Berry Harris as an adult and treasure those memories.[8]

Crawford has often played in Wichita, as well as in Hawaii, California, and Spain. Fronting the Wichita rock band Built For Comfort for a number of years, he also has been a member of the Buffalo Blues Band in Redlands, California. Crawford, and others named by Avants, may be the spark for a new regional rock blues style.

As observed in the *Negro Star*, the *Wichita Eagle*, and the *Beacon*, the blues has been popular in Wichita at least since the 1920s. It is a geographically isolated city with big-city pretensions, and in this resembles the evolution of the blues. And the loneliness in modernity, with the particular search for "something to do" to relieve the boredom, is adequately represented in the city's blues. There is not the centuries-old Southern culture to encourage music, but there is a developing heritage of the blues.

Most of the original interviewees were semiprofessional musicians. This was a condition of the paucity of nightly entertainment opportunities and regular employment possibilities in Wichita, and not an indication of ability. Jesse Anderson, Franklin Mitchell, and Shirley Green recorded; Jerry Childers, Arthur Bates, and Donald Dunn performed with national acts; Barbara Kerr and Charles Walker toured the country. But when they returned to Wichita, many had to settle for weekend engagements.

Berry Harris spoke with affability about his early musical experiences in Oklahoma, and with animation about the poor treatment he received during his stage career, from both club owners and other musicians. Oklahoma had a community spirit among African Americans, possibly due to segregation. The elders took time to encourage sports and music in the young. In Wichita, still with de facto segregation but without the acceptance of one another that was seen in the South, the African American neighborhoods exhibited a self-serving attitude that Jesse Anderson found distressing. According to a 2021 interview with Gerald Norwood, who grew up in northeast Wichita on Wabash St. in the 1950s, the African American neighborhoods did not expand geographically to accommodate the large influx of Blacks during that time. Many small "backyard houses" were built to ease crowding.[9]

What makes the Wichita blues performance narratives of interest? The folk art involved in the process of playing in a small city. Many other locales across America can be similarly categorized: a town or city where blues is popular and played in mimicry of the major styles. Either several new styles are developing, or the different regional centers are being supplanted by one grand national form of blues, as performed on recordings. The latter explanation is far from likely. Just as dialects and colloquialisms have failed to be obliterated by the mobile and electronic culture, so too will regionalism in music performance remain.

The blues has a simple message: I am here, doing the best I can. The import is a resilience that depicts the African American spirit, and that can be utilized to show civilization's current stance. White performers may have to carry on the blues tradition, due to the lack of emerging young African Americans interested in this type of music. There is no negative connotation of tradition among whites—rather an interest in a less sophisticated style that better serves the blues. But whoever in Wichita carries forth this music must acknowledge the nineteen pioneering African American musicians in this work, as well as the many others who weren't around to tell their stories—for African Americans are the founders of the blues and are gracious in spreading their knowledge and influence.

APPENDIX: JAZZ PERFORMERS WHO PLAYED PREWAR WICHITA

The following table is included as an aid to understanding live performance in Wichita during part of the time studied. A lot of work went into this by the late Joshua Yearout.

PERFORMER	DATE(S)	VENUE(S) PLAYED	RACE	NOTES
Gus Arnheim Orchestra	Circa 1940–41	Blue Moon Ballroom	White	
Karl Barber and His Famous Band	June 3–10, 1934	Club Evergreens	Unknown	Came to Wichita direct from the Plantation Cotton Club in St. Louis. Former house band of the Hotel Peabody.
Dick Barrie	Circa 1940–41	Blue Moon Ballroom	White	
Dad Barrett ———— Also performed as: Dad Barrett's Five Piece Band; "Dad" and His Versatile Band; "Dad" Barrett's Dance Orchestra	1930s	Riverside Club; Hidden Acres Dine and Dance Club; Paramount Buffet	White	
Blue Barron	Circa 1940–41	Blue Moon Ballroom	Unknown	
Gene Beecher	January 1941	Blue Moon Ballroom	Unknown	
Gage Brewer ———— Also performed as: Gage Brewer's Versatile Orchestra; Gage Brewer's Hawaiian Entertainers; Gage Brewer's Radio Orchestra; Gage Brewer's Versatile Seven Piece Band	1930s–1940s	Wichita Gun Club; Shadowland Dance Pavilion; York Rite Temple; Arcadia	White	Local performers

241

PERFORMER	DATE(S)	VENUE(S) PLAYED	RACE	NOTES
Bugs House and His Collegiates	1934	Wintergarden Ballroom	Unknown	
Sunshine Butler and His Broad-way Stompers	July 9, 1939	Hollow Inn	Unknown	
Cab Calloway and the Cotton Club Orchestra	May 31, 1936; June 14, 1936; July 4, 1942	Forum; Trocadero	African American	
Whitey Clinton's Eleven Piece Orchestra	1930s	La Casa Grande; Riverside Supper Club	Unknown	
Shorty Coburn Band ——————— Also performed as: Shorty Coburn Orchestra	1930s	Pastime Gardens; Club Evergreens; Club Urban; Hotel Lassen Ballroom	Unknown	Local musicians
Del Courtney	Circa 1940–41	Blue Moon Ballroom	White	
Loren Cox	1930	Wishbone Villa	Unknown	
Gene Coy and His Black Aces	1927	Unknown	African American	
Johnny "Scat" Davis Orchestra	June 16, 1940	Blue Moon Ballroom	White	
"Squeaky" Davis and His Fox Trot Boys	1930s	Four Leaf Clover	Unknown	
Clettus Driskell and His Orchestra	1937	Silver Moon	Unknown	
Ernie Fields ——————— Also performed as Ernie Fields Band; Ernie Fields and His Famous Twelve Piece Band	May 1934	Arkota Dancehall; Club Evergreens	African American	Fields was known as the colored Guy Lombardo
Ted Fio Rito	Circa 1940–41	Blue Moon Ballroom	White	
Howard Fordham and His Band ——————— Also performed as Howard Fordham's Ten Harmony Boys	1930s	Rock Castle; Shadow-land; Hidden Acres Dine and Dance Club; La Casa Grande	White	Local musicians
Phil Harris	1940s	Blue Moon Ballroom	White	
Vic Harris	1930s	Riverside Supper Club	Unknown	

PERFORMER	DATE(S)	VENUE(S) PLAYED	RACE	NOTES
Tommy (Gabe) Hunt's Orchestra ———————— Also performed as Gabe Hunt's NBC Band	1930s	Freshfield	Unknown	
Art Jarret and his Orchestra	Circa 1942	Blue Moon Ballroom	White	
Junior Johnson ———————— Also performed as: Wichita's Foremost Colored Entertainers (when paired with Tiny Taylor); Junior Johnson and His Hot Swing Band	1930s	Rustic Inn; Rex Black's Wonder Lunch; Ritz Inn	African American	Local performer often paired with local musician Tiny Taylor
Isham Jones Orchestra	1938	Blue Moon Ballroom	White	
Doc Koepper and His Tavern Band	1930s	Freshfield	Unknown	
Larry Lane's Band	1930s	Rustic Inn	Unknown	
Clarence Love and His Colored Orchestra ———————— Also performed as Nationally Famous Clarence Love and His Eleven Colored Artists	1930s	Wintergarden Ballroom; Club Evergreens	African American	
Ted Lewis and His World Famous Orchestra	1940s	Blue Moon Ballroom; Orpheum Theatre	White	
Freddie Martin	Circa 1940–41	Blue Moon Ballroom	White	
Morris Martin's Ten Piece Collegiate Band	1930s	Freshfield	Unknown	
Clyde McCoy and His Sugar Blues Orchestra	August 9, 1940	Blue Moon Ballroom	White	

PERFORMER	DATE(S)	VENUE(S) PLAYED	RACE	NOTES
Jay McShann Orchestra —————— Also performed as: Jay McShann His Piano and Orchestra	August 1940	Trocadero	African American	The orchestra included a young Charlie Parker on saxophone. An amateur recording was made of their performance at the Trocadero. The orchestra also recorded at radio station KFBI while in Wichita.
Benny Meroff with America' Greatest Entertaining Band	1938	400 Club	White	
Carlos Molina	Circa 1940–41	Blue Moon Ballroom	Unknown	
Bennie Moten and His Thirteen Piece Victor Recording Orchestra	January 19, 1930	Ritz	African American	
Mutt —————— Also performed as: Mutt's Eight Ball Band; Mutts Cotton Club Band; Mutt's Five Piece Rhythm Band; Mutt's Cotton Club Orchestra; King Mutt's Cotton Club Band	1930s	Freshfield; Wishbone Villa; Cotton Club	African American	
Verne Nydegger and His Great Orchestra —————— Also performed as: Verne Nydegger and Orchestra; Verne Nydegger Orchestra	1930s	400 Club; Maplewood Supper Club; Palms	White	Orchestra composed of local musicians
Homer Osborne —————— Also performed as Home Osborne and His Cotton Club Boys	Primarily active 1920s–1940s, but continued to perform well into the 1970s	Arkota Dancehall; Lassen Hotel Ballroom; Idlewise; Meadows Club	African American	A onetime member of the King Oliver Band before coming to Wichita
Paul Pendervais	Summer 1940	Blue Moon Ballroom	Unknown	

PERFORMER	DATE(S)	VENUE(S) PLAYED	RACE	NOTES
Red Perkins and His Fourteen Musicians	March 22, 1936	Palms	African American	Perkins was billed as one of the country's greatest colored musicians
Ben Rothstein and His Orchestra	1930s	La Casa Grande	Unknown	
Rustic Revellers	1930s	Rustic Inn	Unknown	
Rolle Sense and His Ten Wintergarden Artists	1930s	Wintergarden Ballroom	Unknown	
Arlie Simmonds and His Featured Radio Orchestra	1930s	Club Urban	Unknown	
Ernest Storey and His Rhythmaires	1930s	Hidden Acres Dine and Dance Club	Unknown	
S. K. S. L. Orchestra	August 6–12, 1933	Danceland	Unknown	
Syncopators	1930s–1940s	Area high school dances; Ark Valley Lodge	African American	Composed of local musicians
Tiny Taylor ——————— Also performed as: Tiny Taylor and His Chocolate Drops; Tiny Taylor and Junior Johnson; Tiny Taylor's Orchestra; Tiny Taylor & His Music; Tiny Taylor & The Boys; Wichita's Foremost Colored Entertainers (when paired with Junior Johnson)	1930s	Rustic Inn; Ritz Inn; Rex Black's Wonder Lunch; Freshfield	African American	Local performer
Orrin Tucker	Circa 1940–41	Blue Moon Ballroom	White	
Marshall Van Pool and His Famous Orchestra	1930s	400 Club	White	
Sugar Walker and his Brown Buddies	1930s	Hidden Acres Dine and Dance Club	Unknown	

PERFORMER	DATE(S)	VENUE(S) PLAYED	RACE	NOTES
Frank Waterhouse and His Orchestra ————— Also performed as Frank Waterhouse and His Seven Piece Band	1930s	La Casa Grande; Kaliko Kat	White	
Chet Wiley and His 12 RKO Artists	1934	Wintergarden Ballroom	Unknown	
Jack Winters	1936	400 Club	Unknown	
Paul Whiteman and His Orchestra	1927; October 8, 1937	Forum and Miller Theater	White	
Fred Wolcott and His Famous Collegians	1930s	400 Club	Unknown	

Sources: *Wichita Eagle*, 1919–45; *Wichita Beacon*, 1919–45; *Negro Star*, 1920–45; *Wichita This Week*, 1933; *Downtown Wichita*, 1933–45; Gage Brewer newsletters; Gage Brewer Papers; Reed and Morgan interviews: Wichita Blues Project. Table compiled by Joshua Yearout, MA, for his book *Wichita Jazz and Vice Between the World Wars*, Rowfant Press, Department of History, Wichita State University.

NOTES

INTRODUCTION

1. Joshua Yearout, *Wichita Jazz and Vice Between the World Wars* (Wichita, KS: Rowfant Press, 2010), 40.

2. Kerry Kudlacek, "The Oklahoma Blues Tradition," *Blues Gazette* (Summer 1996): 4.

CHAPTER ONE: EARLY AFRICAN AMERICANS IN KANSAS: COWBOYS, SOLDIERS, SETTLERS, AND MINSTRELS

1. Eugene H. Berwanger, *The Frontier Against Slavery* (Urbana: University of Illinois Press, 1967), 110.

2. Berwanger, 116.

3. Huddie Ledbetter, "When I Was a Cowboy," Ludlow Music, 1959.

4. Colonel Bailey C. Hanes, *Bill Pickett, Bulldogger* (Norman: University of Oklahoma Press, 1977), 31.

5. Hanes, 5.

6. William Loren Katz, *The Black West* (Garden City, NY: Anchor Press/Doubleday, 1971), 146.

7. Duram, Philip, and Everett L. Jones, reported in *The Negro Cowboys* (Lincoln and London: University of Nebraska Press, 1965), 45.

8. Duram and Jones, 65–66.

9. Duram and Jones, 68.

10. Duram and Jones, 69.

11. Duram and Jones, 194.

12. Duram and Jones, 199.

13. Duram and Jones, 62.

14. Duram and Jones, 58.

15. *Leon Press*, April 19, 1888.

16. Charles Wolfe and Kip Lornell, *The Life and Legend of Leadbelly* (New York: HarperCollins, 1992), 109.

17. Alan Lomax, *The Folk Songs of North America* (Garden City, NY: Doubleday, 1960), 299.

18. Austin and Alta Fife, *Ballads of the Great West* (Palo Alto, CA: American West Publishing, 1970), 26.

19. Correspondence from Dr. Evans, August 26, 2015.

20. Austin E. and Alta S. Fife, Introduction, in *Songs of the Cowboys by N. Howard ("Jack") Thorpe*, Variants, Commentary, Notes and Lexicon by Austin E. and Alta S. Fife (New York: Clarkson N. Potter, 1966), 5.

21. W. C. Handy first heard the blues in St. Louis in 1892.

22. B. A. Botkin, *A Treasury of American Folklore* (Kingsport, TN: Kingsport Press, 1944), 852.

23. Kenneth Wiggins Porter, *The Negro on the American Frontier* (New York: Arno Press and the New York Times, 1971), 467.

24. Porter Forward, xii.

25. Dudley Taylor Cornish, *Kansas Negro Regiments in the Civil War* (Topeka: State of Kansas Commission on Civil Rights, 1969), 7.

26. Major George E. Knapp, "Buffalo Soldiers, 1866 Through 1890," *Military Review* (July 1992): 66.

27. Knapp, 66.

28. Schubert, Frank N., *Voices of the Buffalo Soldier* (Albuquerque: University of New Mexico Press, 2008), 127–28.

29. Schubert, 23–28.

30. Zornow, William Frank, *Kansas: A History of the Jayhawk State* (Norman: University of Oklahoma Press,1957), 233.

31. Kenneth Wiggins Porter, *The Negro on the American Frontier* (New York: Arno Press and the New York Times, 1971), 1.

32. Painter, 114.

33. Hinger, Charlotte, *Nicodemus* (Norman: University of Oklahoma Press, 2016), 12.

34. Hinger, 32.

35. Hinger, 16.

36. Hinger, 20.

37. Hinger, 34.

38. Hinger, 37.

39. Hinger, 37.

40. Hinger, 38.

41. Hinger, 46.

42. Painter, 159.

43. Painter, 154.

44. *Cincinnati Enquirer*, April 28, 1879, 4.

45. Athearn, 70.

46. *Weekly Clarion* (Jackson, Mississippi), July 30, 1889, 2.

47. Hinger, 68.

48. Hinger, 112.

49. Hinger, 115, 116.

50. Robert C. Toll, *Blacking Up: The Minstrel Show in Nineteenth-Century America* (New York: Oxford University Press, 1974), 51.

51. Toll, 26.

52. Carl Wittke, *Tambo and Bones* (Westport, CT: Greenwood Press, 1930), 54.

53. Eileen Southern, *The Music of Black Americans: A History* (New York: W. W. Norton, 1971), 269.

54. Alan Lomax, 202.

55. Toll, 216.

56. Toll, 228.

57. The play *The Shoo-Fly Regiment* and the Black Patti Troubadours tour have been included in the listing because they were important Black productions a step above minstrelsy.

58. *Emporia Gazette*, September 14, 1898.

59. Bernard L. Peterson Jr., *A Century of Musicals in Black and White* (Westport, CT: Greenwood Press, 1993), 44.

60. Peterson, 309.

61. Sampson, 195.

CHAPTER TWO: EARLY URBAN CENTERS IN KANSAS:
TOPEKA AND WICHITA

1. Thomas C. Cox, *Blacks in Topeka Kansas 1865–1915* (Baton Rouge and London: Louisiana State University Press, YEAR), 35.

2. Cox, 6.

3. Cox, 7.

4. Cox, 10.

5. Cox, 16.

6. Cox, 17.

7. Cox, 17.

8. Cox, 18.

9. Cox, 19.

10. Cox, 24–25.

11. Cox, 31.

12. Cox, 49.

13. Cox, 63.

14. Cox, 107.

15. Cox, 139.

16. Cox, 146.

17. Cox, 149.

18. Cox, 150.

19. Cox, 152–56.

20. Cox, 197.

21. Kansas African American Museum, *African Americans of Wichita* (Charleston, SC: Arcadia Publishing, 2015), 9.

22. *People's Friend* (Wichita), May 24, 1894, 1.

23. *People's Friend*, June 14, 1894, 1.

24. *Abstract of the 14th Census of the United States.*

25. Presentation given by Lemuel Sheppard at the Wichita Genealogical Society meeting, February 18, 2023.

26. Kansas African American Museum, 29.

27. Kansas African American Museum, 48.

28. Kansas African American Museum, 51.

29. Michael Knepler, "June 21, 1925: Black Baseball Team Beats Klan Players," Zinn Education Project, https://www.zinnedproject.org/news/tdih/black-team-beats-klan.

30. Kansas African American Museum, 58.

31. Kansas African American Museum, 40.

32. Kansas African American Museum, 61.

33. Kansas African American Museum, 44.

34. *Wichita Community Voice*, Black History, 2006.

35. *Wichita Community Voice*, Black History Section, 2006.

36. Gretchen Eick documented the sit-in, as well as other protests, in *Dissent in Wichita* (Urbana: University of Illinois Press, 2001).

37. Kansas African American Museum, 61.

38. Kansas African American Museum, 68.

39. Chester I. Lewis papers, Spencer Research Library, University of Kansas, Lawrence, KS, https://archives.lib.ku.edu/repositories/3/resources/2691.

40. Eick, *Dissent in Wichita*, 24.

41. Kansas African American Museum, 89.

42. *Weekly Eagle*, April 1872, 3.

43. *Weekly Beacon*, May 7, 1873, 5.

44. *Weekly Beacon*, June 24, 1874, 5.

45. *Weekly Beacon*, September 19, 1877, 3.

46. *Weekly Beacon*, January 2, 1878, 5.

47. *Wichita Herald*, March 9, 1878, 2.

48. *Eagle*, August 14, 1885, 4.

49. *Wichita Beacon*, February 14, 1893, 4.

50. *Wichita Beacon*, February 22, 1919, 6.

51. *Negro Star*, April 7, 1922, 3.

52. *Negro Star*, April 7, 1922, 3.

53. *Negro Star*, September 17, 1920, 4.

54. *Negro Star*, October 15, 1920, 4.

55. *Negro Star*, January 14, 1921, 4.

56. *Negro Star*, February 4, 1921, 4.

57. *Negro Star*, November 11, 1921, 5.

58. *Negro Star*, May 21, 1926, 1.

59. *Negro Star*, March 23, 1923, 3.

60. *Negro Star*, December 21, 1923, 6.

61. *Wichita Eagle*, September 16, 1923, 6.

62. *Negro Star*, February 15, 1924, 1.

63. *Negro Star*, September 26, 1924, 3.

64. *Wichita Eagle*, February 21, 1928, 6.

65. *Negro Star*, February 18, 1921, 2.

66. Wichita State University Library Special Collections, Wichita, Kansas.

CHAPTER THREE: THE 1930s:
WALTON MORGAN, SHIRLEY GREEN, PERRY REED

1. *Negroes in the United States 1920–1932*, Bureau of the Census.

2. *Negroes in the United States 1920–1932*, Bureau of the Census.

3. Local 297, American Federation of Musicians, chartered May 14, 1903. Barring African Americans hasn't occurred for many years.

4. Jacqui Malone, in *Steppin' on the Blues* (Urbana: University of Illinois Press, 1996), 100, reports that the Savoy opened in 1926 in a block-long building that accommodated five thousand.

5. This venture resulted in the formation of the Air Capitol Jazz Band, a big band composed of adult volunteers who rehearse and play these same Count Basie arrangements.

CHAPTER FOUR: THE 1940s:
GENE METCALF, HAROLD CARY, ARTHUR BATES

1. Planeview was a hastily built neighborhood designed to house aircraft workers streaming into the city during World War II. It is still in existence, but many of the structures have deteriorated.

2. In a March 1997 interview, Brown recalled the group to be the Bronze Mannequins.

3. Max Cohen was reputedly head of Wichita's gambling and bootleg operations in the 1940s. Bob Brunch owned the Swingland Club and had a loose association with Cohen.

4. The African American holiday Juneteenth originated in Texas, commemorating the belated arrival (June 19, 1865) of enforcement of the Emancipation Proclamation.

5. Joshua Yearout, *Wichita Jazz and Vice Between the World Wars* (Wichita, KS: Rowfant Press, 2010), 26.

6. Yearout, 27.

CHAPTER FIVE: THE 1950s:
FRANKLIN MITCHELL, JERRY CHILDERS, HENRY WALKER

1. Donald O. Cowgill and F. Samuel Osterlay Jr., *The People of Wichita (A Report of the Center for Urban Studies, Prepared for Wichita-Sedgwick County Metropolitan Area Planning Commission, January 1962)*, 26.

2. Jacqui Malone reports that *Harlem in Havana* had a thirty-year connection with the Royal American Shows. Leon Claxton was the producer. Jacqui Malone, *Steppin' on the Blues* (Urbana and Chicago: University of Illinois Press, 1996), 68.

3. At the time of the interview, Mitchell was pastor of Wichita's Trueword Baptist Church.

4. The spinet has less keys and pedals than a console organ.

5. *Shindig!* was a primetime television show featuring rock hits of the day.

CHAPTER SIX: FOLK ARTISTS IN THE 1950s:
HARMONICA CHUCK, ALBERT TUCKER

1. Jeff Husson came to Wichita because his good friend, DJ Pete Drummond, had come there and found opportunity for an announcer speaking the Queen's English during the British Invasion. The author knew both of them. Husson had played in skiffle groups and had a wide repertoire.

2. Mike Finnigan was an influential white organist and vocalist who played in Wichita through the late 1960s. He went on to become a recognized session musician with an extensive list of album credits.

CHAPTER SEVEN: THE 1950s OKLAHOMA INFLUENCE:
JESSE ANDERSON, DONALD DUNN, BERRY HARRIS, CHARLES WALKER, REMONA
HICKS

1. McVey later became a promoter for Al Green and Delbert McClinton.

2. Blazmo (Donn Lentz), *Wichita Blues Society Newsletter*, 1999.

3. Berry Harris maintained that he wrote this song and that Jesse Anderson stole it.

4. Oklahoma State Training School for Incorrigible Negro Girls.

CHAPTER EIGHT: THE 1960s:
JOE LOTSON, RAY VALENTINE, BARBARA KERR

1. In a front-page story, the August 7, 1967, *Wichita Eagle*, announced that the curfew hours, originally from 10:00 p.m. to 5:00 a.m., were shortened to 10:00 p.m. to 4:00 a.m. This was to enable factory workers to reach their early morning jobs. There was a ban on the sale of firearms and ammunition. The Wichita riots, which followed the major incendiarism in Detroit in July, resulted in fifteen fires that caused $90,000 damage, primarily in the northeast quadrant. Business owners in other parts of the city complained that the restricted hours hurt their trade some $250,000 worth.

2. Clarence King is the son of the late Maurice King, musical director of artist development at Motown Records.

3. John Malachi performed in Billy Eckstine's band during the 1940s, a showcase for the new jazz that became bebop.

CHAPTER NINE: DISCUSSION OF RESULTS:
NARRATIVE ANALYSIS; WICHITA, ITS IMPORTANCE IN BLUES HISTORY

1. Chinese proverb.

2. Guido Van Rijn's *Roosevelt's Blues* (University Press of Mississippi, 1997) goes into great detail on Blacks' feelings for Franklin Roosevelt.

3. Illinois Central Blues Club, March 2016.

4. Mathews was born in Checotah, Oklahoma 1941, and began playing in clubs in Wichita at age sixteen. He played in Muskogee with Willie Wright and the Aces. "Tony Mathews," Sentir El Blues Time! Notebook of Blues Music, https://sentirelblues.blogspot .com/2020/08/tony-mathews.html.

5. Wes Race, written correspondence to author, 2021.

6. Clif Major biography, Clif Major and Kathy Rouse Collection, Special Collections and University Archives, Wichita State University Libraries. http://specialcollections. wichita.edu/collections/ms/2014-04/2014-4-a.html.

7. Nathan W. Pearson Jr., *Going to Kansas City* (Urbana and Chicago: University of Illinois Press, 1994), 92.

8. Correspondence from Clayton Crawford, 2022.

9. Gerald Norwood interview for the Wichita Old Neighborhoods Project, September 23, 2021.

BIBLIOGRAPHY

Athearn, G. *In Search of Canaan*. Lawrence: Regents Press of Kansas, 1978.

Barlow, William. *Looking Up at Down*. Philadelphia: Temple University Press, 1989.

Bastin, Bruce. *Red River Blues*. Urbana and Chicago: University of Illinois Press, 1995.

Benko, Georges B., and Ulf Strohmayer, editors. *Geography, History and Social Sciences*. Dordrecht, Boston, London: Kluwer Academic Publishers, 1995.

Berry, Chuck. *Chuck Berry: The Autobiography*. New York: Harmony Books, 1987.

Blakey, D. N. *Revelation: Blind Willie Johnson, the Biography*. Lulu.com Publishing, 2007.

Blazmo. *Wichita Blues Society Newsletter*. Wichita, KS: Wichita Blues Society, November 1999.

Broonzy, William. *Big Bill Blues*. New York: Oak Publications, 1964.

Castree, Noel, Rob Kitchin, and Alisdair Rogers. *Oxford Dictionary of Human Geography*. Oxford: Oxford University Press, 2013.

Charters, Samuel. *The Country Blues*. New York: Rinehart, 1959.

Charters, Samuel. *The Blues Makers*. New York: Da Capo Press, 1991.

Cowgill, Donald O., and F. Samuel Osterlay Jr. *The People of Wichita*. A Report of the Center for Urban Studies, Prepared for Wichita-Sedgwick County Metropolitan Area Planning Commission, January 1962.

Deffaa, Chip. *Blue Rhythms*. Urbana and Chicago: University of Illinois Press, 1996.

Denzin, Norman K., ed. *Studies in Symbolic Interaction*. Ningley, UK: Emerald Group Publishing, 2010.

Dixon, Willie, with Don Snowden. *I Am the Blues*. New York: Da Capo Press, 1989.

Dorson, Richard M. *American Folklore*. Chicago: University of Chicago Press, 1959.

Eagle, Bob, and Eric S. LeBlanc. *Blues: A Regional Experience*. Santa Barbara, CA: Praeger, an Imprint of ABC-CLIO, 2013.

Eick, Gretchen Cassel. *Dissent in Wichita*. Urbana and Chicago: University of Illinois Press, 2001.

Evans, David. *Big Road Blues*. Berkeley: University of California Press, 1982.

Ferris, William. *Blues from the Delta*. Garden City, NY: Anchor Books, 1979.

Fife, Austin, and Alta Fife. *Ballads of the Great West*. Palo Alto, CA: American West Publishing, 1970.

Fife, Austin, and Alta Fife. Introduction to N. Howard ("Jack") Thorp, *Songs of the Cowboys*, Variants, Commentary, Notes and Lexicon by Austin E. and Alta S. Fife. New York: Clarkson N. Potter, 1966.

Finkelman, Paul, ed. *Encyclopedia of African American History 1896 to the Present*. New York: Oxford University Press, 2009.

Ford, Robert. *A Blues Bibliography*, 2nd ed. New York and London: Routledge, 2007.

Ford, Robert. *A Blues Bibliography, Update to the Second Edition*. New York, London: Routledge, 2020.

Friedman, Albert B., ed. *The Viking Book of Folk Ballads*. New York: Viking Press, 1956.

Garon, Paul. *Blues and the Poetic Spirit*. London: Eddison Press, 1975.

Gioia, Ted. *Delta Blues*. New York: W. W. Norton, 2008.

Hanes, Colonel Bailey C. *Bill Pickett, Bulldogger*. Norman: University of Oklahoma Press, 1977.

Haymes, Max. *Railroadin' Some*. York, UK: Music Mentor Books, 2006.

Haywood, C. Robert. "The Hodgeman County Colony." *Kansas History, a Journal of the Central Plains* 12, no. 4 (1989): 210–21.

Herzhaft, Gerard. *Encyclopedia of the Blues*. Fayetteville: University of Arkansas Press, 1997.

Holiday, Billie, and William Dufty. *Lady Sings the Blues*. New York: Lancer Books, 1956.

Hughes, Langston, and Milton Meltzer. *Black Magic*. Englewood Cliffs, NJ: Prentice-Hall, 1967.

Jackson, Peter, and Susan L. Smith. *Exploring Social Geography*. New York: Routledge, 2014.

Jasen, David A., and Gene Jones. *Spreadin' Rhythm Around*. New York: Schirmer Books, 1998.

Katz, William Loren. *The Black West*. Garden City, NY: Anchor Press/Doubleday, 1971.

King, B.B., with David Ritz. *Blues All Around Me*. New York: Avon Books, 1996.

Kemmerling, James D. *A History of the Whitley Opera House in Emporia, Kansas: 1881–1913*. Emporia: Kansas State Teachers College, 1970.

Lomax, John. *Cow Camps and Cattle Herds*. Austin: Encino Press, 1967.

Lomax, Alan. *The Folk Songs of North America*. New York: Doubleday, 1960.

Lomax, Alan. *The Land Where Blues Began*. New York: Pantheon, 1993.

Malone, Evelyn L. "Swamp Blues: Race and Vinyl from Southwest Louisiana." Diss., University of Pennsylvania, 2016.

Malone, Jacqui. *Steppin' on the Blues*. Urbana and Chicago: University of Illinois Press, 1996.

McKee, Margaret, and Fred Chisenhall. *Beale Black and Blue*. Baton Rouge: Louisiana State University Press, 1981.

McNamara, Brooks. *Step Right Up*. Garden City, NY: Doubleday, 1976.

Murray, Albert. *Stomping the Blues*. New York: McGraw-Hill, 1976.

Oakley, Giles. *The Devil's Music*. New York: Taplinger, 1976.

Oliver, Paul. *Aspects of the Blues Tradition*. New York: Oak Publications, 1968.

Oliver, Paul. *Blues Fell This Morning*. New York: Cambridge University Press, 1990.

Oliver, Paul. *The Meaning of the Blues*. New York: Collier Books, 1960.

Oliver, Paul. *The Story of the Blues*. Philadelphia: Chilton Book Company, 1969.

Oster, Harry. *Living Country Blues*. Detroit: Folklore Associates, 1969.

Ottenheimer, Harriet. "The Blues Tradition in St. Louis," *Black Music Research Journal* 9, no. 2 (1989): 135–51.

Ottenheimer, Harriet. "Prewar Blues in St. Louis." *Popular Music & Society* 14, no. 2 (1990).

Pearson, Nathan W. Jr. *Going to Kansas City*. Urbana and Chicago: University of Illinois Press, 1994.

Peretti, Burton W. *The Creation of Jazz*. Urbana and Chicago: University of Illinois Press, 1994.

Porterfield, Nolan. *Last Cavalier: The Life and Times of John A. Lomax*. Urbana and Chicago: University of Illinois Press, 1996.

Reynolds, Larry T., and Nancy J. Herman-Kinney, eds. *Handbook of Symbolic Interactionism*. Walnut Creek, CA: AltaMira Press, 2003.

Rowe, Mike. *Chicago Breakdown*. London: Eddison Press, 1973.

Sackheim, Eric, ed. *The Blues Line*. New York: Thunder's Mouth Press, 1969.

Sampson, Henry T. *The Ghost Walks*. Metuchen, NJ: Scarecrow Press, 1988.

Schubert, Frank N. *Voices of the Buffalo Soldier*. Albuquerque: University of New Mexico Press, 2003.

Seale, Clive, ed. *Researching Society and Culture*, 4th ed. London: Sage Publications, 2018.

Shaw, Arnold. *Honkers and Shouters*. New York: Macmillan, 1978.

Silber, Irwin. *Songs of the Great American West*. New York: Macmillan, 1967.

Simon, George T. *The Big Bands*. New York: Shirmer Books, 1981.

Simon, Larry, and John Broven. *New York City Blues*. Jackson: University Press of Mississippi, 2021.

Southern, Eileen. *The Music of Black Americans*. New York: W. W. Norton, 1997.

Szymanski, Rachel A. "Beyond the Crossroads: Blues Scenes in Detroit and Lansing." Diss., Michigan State University, 2009.

Tracy, Steven C. *Going to Cincinnati*. Urbana and Chicago: University of Illinois Press, 1993.

Van Rijn, Guido. *Roosevelt's Blues*. Jackson: University Press of Mississippi, 1997.

White, Newnan I. *American Negro Folk-Songs*. Cambridge: Harvard University Press, 1928.

Wichita Rock Music Project Team. *Wichita Rock & Roll 1950s–1980s*. Wichita, KS: Wichita State University, 2017.

Wolfe, Charles, and Kip Lornell. *The Life and Legend of Leadbelly*. New York: HarperCollins, 1992.

Woods, Randall Bennett. *A Black Odyssey*. Lawrence: Regents Press of Kansas, 1981.

Yearout, Joshua. *Wichita Jazz and Vice Between the World Wars*. Wichita, KS: Rowfant Press, 2010.

INDEX